I0084408

Mora L. McLean

Editor

West African Youth Challenges and Opportunity Pathways

Editor
Mora L. McLean
Rutgers University-Newark
Newark, NJ, USA

https://doi.org/10.1007/978-3-030-21092-2

PREFACE

This book is a result of a transatlantic, transnational collaboration that brought together researchers and practitioners who focus on youth in and from West Africa. The collaboration, dubbed the *Forum on Expanding Youth Learning and Opportunity Pathways in, and Linked to, West Africa* (the Forum), facilitated the sharing of research and practical approaches with potential applicability across the multiple and varied geographic spaces that African and African-descendant youth occupy. The Association for Research on Civil Society in Africa (AROCSA) and Rutgers University-Newark issued a joint call for proposals in the winter of 2016, which was followed up in April of 2017 with a small convening at the University of Ghana Business School (UGBS) in Legon. The event was co-sponsored by the University of Ghana Business School (UGBS) Department of Public Administration and Health Services Management, the Rutgers University-Newark Graduate School, and Joseph C. Cornwall Center for Metropolitan Studies. A second gathering, designed as a workshop for this book's contributing authors, took place in Accra in October of 2018.

The Forum explicitly aspired toward transcending the boundaries of academic disciplines, theory and practice, and geography—an impossibly demanding set of goals, given impetus by a sense of urgency to advance two overarching concerns: First, the Forum organizers perceived a need to bring theory and practice to bear on the topic simultaneously, by bringing academic researchers and scholars in closer dialogue with practitioners affiliated with youth-focused nongovernmental nonprofit organizations. Second, the organizers also envisioned the Forum as a vehicle for spurring new research on youthhood experiences and exploration of practical approaches, with potential applicability in and outside the West Africa region, especially in the United States.

The Forum fell short of its ambitious agenda in several key respects. The call for proposals did not account sufficiently for language barriers, so that the Forum did not draw participants from Francophone and Lusophone West Africa. Also missing were scholars, activists, and practitioners whose work centered on youth with disabilities and youth with LGBTQ identities. The organizers also grossly underestimated the complexity and difficulty of bridging the gap between praxis and theory.

However, three intended features of the Forum endured and reflected in this collection. First, it sheds light on data, analyses, and insights provided by researchers, activists, and practitioners spanning multiple academic disciplines and both the nonprofit nongovernmental organization (NGO) and for-profit business sectors. Second, while there are hints of the enduring developmentalist framework that tends to serve as the dominant justification for examining issues pertaining to African youth (most notably in multilateral institution studies and reports), on the whole, the collection avoids approaching its subject from a development vantage point. The third feature is the purposeful examination of comparisons with, and linkages to, youth in continental and "New World" diasporas, within and outside West Africa—specifically the Central African region, South Africa, and the postindustrial City of Newark, New Jersey in the northeastern United States. The book aims to reach a wide audience, including policymakers, while increasing the scholarly appetite for more research-praxis exchange and comparative research on youth in Africa and in the African diaspora.

The contributing authors come from a variety of backgrounds, including academia and research and public policy, social justice activism, and business entrepreneurship. When the Forum was launched, most of the researchers and scholars in the group were at early stages in their academic and professional careers. This was another distinctive feature of the Forum, which aimed to provide a platform for lesser-known and new voices. The majority of the contributors originate from, or are based in, West Africa. The authors share an abiding interest in understanding the factors that impede the social mobility and well-being of youth and finding ways to address and remove those barriers.

Newark, NJ   Mora L. McLean

ACKNOWLEDGMENTS

This edited collection, and the convening of practitioners and scholars that inspired it (the Forum), were made possible by a grant from the Ford Foundation. I am grateful not only for the foundation's financial support, but also for the encouragement and insightful feedback provided throughout the project journey by Innocent Chukwuma and Dabesaki Mac-Ikemenjima of the foundation's West Africa office in Lagos.

I am especially grateful to the Rutgers University-Newark community, which enabled both the book and activities surrounding it, in the first instance. Enormous thanks are due to Irene O'Brien, who appreciated my calling and intellectual commitment to work in the borderlands between local and global inequality, and thanks also to Kyle Farmbry and Oliver Quinn, who entrusted me to lead the project that yielded this book. The transatlantic discussions and essential hands-on collaboration involved along the way simply would not have happened without Kimaada Sills, Mahako Etta, and Michael Simmons, my fellow project team members. They embraced the project vision from the outset, helped to fine tune it, and undertook the organizational tasks, big and small, to realize its transition from a mere idea to a concrete initiative.

Kimaada Sills is in a league of her own: she maintained deft oversight of the project administration from inception to completion. I owe her and Irene Welch a special debt of gratitude for skillfully managing the intricate travel arrangements and other logistics that, on two separate occasions, brought together participants from four countries and two continents. The project benefited tremendously from input from Rutgers University-Newark graduate students: Alice Benishyaka contributed yeowoman service at the inaugural project gathering in Accra, Lauren Kaplan and Mi Hyun Yoon helped to research the literature, and Yvan Yenda weighed in insightfully on the project design.

Three other key members of the broader Rutgers University network gave me confidence that the idea for the Forum was feasible and worth pursuing. Kevin Lyons, Rutgers Business School Professor, introduced me to the innovative work of young, largely unsung, African social entrepreneurs. Carolyn Brown, Professor of History and a member of the Center for African Studies (CAS) at Rutgers University-New Brunswick, inspired me with her work on Global Timbuktu, a multidimensional project that brought together high school students and teachers and academic scholars from Mali, New York, and New Jersey to examine the place of Timbuktu, Mali in the history, culture, and imagination of Africa and its global diaspora. I was also both inspired guided by Cati Coe, Professor of Anthropology at Rutgers University-Camden. Author of a groundbreaking study of the transnational parenting strategies of Ghanaian parents based in the United States, Professor Coe could not have been more gracious and generous in responding to my many requests for help with identifying emergent scholars interested in exploring new angles on topics related to West African youth. Her intellectual commitment to analyzing how inequality manifests in people's lives is at least equaled by her generosity and insight. I am honored as well as deeply grateful to have benefited from her advice on this project.

The Association for Research on Civil Society in Africa (AROCSA) and the University of Ghana Business School (UGBS) were indispensable partners in the true sense of the word. AROCSA's network afforded a robust response to the Forum's 2016 call for proposals. The Forum's success in sustaining the avid engagement of researchers and practitioners from different disciplines and sectors in deep discussion over several days is due in no small part to Esi Ansah's insightful guidance on the agenda and format. She, along with Sabina Akwei Yaboah, facilitated contacts with key individuals and contributed to our warm welcome in Accra. That welcome was made complete by Justice Bawole and Betty Brew at UGBS, our other institutional partner and co-host of the first convening in Accra. The UGBS campus-based conference facilities at Legon provided a collegial setting for the discussion and debate.

Shara Davis, Kusum Mundra, Adrienne Petty, Robin Semple, and two anonymous readers contributed immeasurably with their careful reading of portions of the book manuscript and helpful comments at various stages. The process of editing this book gave new meaning to the phrase, "The devil is in the detail." At different stages, I had the great fortune of being helped by Natasha Gordon Chipbembere and Courtney Kelsch Ward, two superb copy editors who caught every glitch, while never failing to keep our work to complete the book on track.

Last but far from least, my heartfelt appreciation goes to the contributing authors—for the chapters that comprise this book, and especially their ongoing efforts to both illuminate and address the concerns of West African and African-descendant youth. This book is dedicated to every young person on the African continent and in its diasporas, especially Oluwatimileyin and Oluwatomiwa Adeyemi, Kora and Kyle Koker, and my beloved, Atinuke McLean Lardner.

CONTENTS

Notes on Contributors

Alh. Muhammad Salisu Abdullahi is the Founder and Chief Executive Officer of Haleematus Sa'adiyya Enterprises in Nigeria. A recipient of the 2016 Mandela Washington Fellowship and an Associate Fellow of the Nigeria Leadership Initiative, he unveiled eTrash2Cash (www.eTrash-2Cash.com) as a platform to reach the most economically disadvantaged young people, the Almajiri people, aged 12 to 26 in the northern part of Nigeria.

Adedeji Adeniran, PhD is a senior research fellow at the Centre for the Study of Economies of Africa (CSEA), an economics think tank based in Abuja, Nigeria, responsible for leading the research team on Program Evaluation and Poverty Analysis. His research interests include public choice economics, poverty, vulnerability analysis, and Education Economics.

Mahako Etta is a doctoral candidate at the Rutgers University-Newark School of Public Affairs and Administration and former Program Manager of the Newark City of Learning Collaborative, a postsecondary attainment initiative under the auspices of Rutgers University-Newark, Joseph C. Cornwall Center for Metropolitan Studies in Newark, New Jersey, USA.

Cecilia Fiaka is the Founder and Director of the Nneka Youth Foundation, an NGO in Ghana. She holds an MBA in Project Management and a BSc in Human Resource Management, both from the University of Ghana Business School, Legon. Nneka Youth Foundation offers life changing opportunities to youth, especially girls and young women, in rural, less privileged areas, through summer camps, educational and social orientation seminars, and other activities designed to tap into the creativity of young people. She published her memoir, *Tideless Sea*, in 2012 to raise seed money for her foundation.

Lanre Olusegun Ikuteyijo, PhD is a senior lecturer and researcher in the Department of Sociology and Anthropology, Obafemi Awolowo University, Nigeria. His research interests include migration, urbanization, and community policing. He was a visiting researcher to the Department of History, McMaster University, Canada under the auspices of the Center for International Governance Innovation (CIGI), Waterloo, Canada. Ikuteyijo has received a number of academic grants, including research grants from the Qualitative Research Network Africa and the Council for Development of Social Research in Africa (CODESRIA).

Joseph Ishaku is a research associate at the Centre for the Study of the Economies of Africa (CSEA), an economics think tank based in Abuja, Nigeria. His research interests include economics of education and sustainable development.

Chimaraoke O. Izugbara, PhD is Director of the International Center for Research on Women (ICRW), and a professor-at-large at the School of Public Health, University of the Witwatersrand, South Africa. He previously directed the Population Dynamics and Reproductive Health Research Program at the African Population and Health Research Center (APHRC) in Nairobi, Kenya. His research focuses on youth development, sexuality, and sexual and reproductive health.

Kenneth Juma is an epidemiologist, a research officer at the African Population and Health Research Center (APHRC) in Nairobi, Kenya, and a doctoral candidate at the School of Medicine, Makerere University, Uganda. Kenneth's research interests are in non-communicable diseases including mental health, young people's health and wellbeing (including sexual and reproductive health), as well as maternal health issues in low resourced settings.

Caroline W. Kabiru, PhD is an associate with the Population Council, Kenya, and currently serves as the Senior Technical Advisor for the Evidence to End FGM/C Research Consortium. Prior to joining the Council, Caroline worked as a research scientist with the African Population and Health Research Center (APHRC). Her research interests center on issues related to young people's health and wellbeing.

Daniel Owusu Kyereko is a doctoral student with the Bayreuth International Graduate School of African Studies (BIGSAS), University of Bayreuth, Germany. His research interests center on migration within the global south, inclusion, and issues of education and marginalization. His current research project is on the inclusion of international migrants and education in Ghana.

Dabesaki Mac-Ikemenjima, PhD is a program officer at the Ford Foundation office for West Africa in Lagos where he leads the Foundation's Youth Transitions program. His work includes supporting efforts aimed at developing successful models for the path from education to employment for youth.

Mora L. McLean is principal investigator for the 2017–2018 Forum on Expanding Youth Learning and Opportunity Pathways in, and Linked to, West Africa, designed, with support from the Ford Foundation, to facilitate collaboration between practitioners and researchers concerned about the well-being of West African and African descendant youth. Between 2015 and 2018 she was a senior fellow with the Joseph C. Cornwall Center for Metropolitan Studies at Rutgers University-Newark. She is president emerita of the Africa-America Institute (AAI), the oldest US-based nonprofit devoted to expanding educational opportunities for Africans.

Carsten Mildner holds a Master of Science degree in Anthropology from Copenhagen University and is a doctoral candidate at the Bayreuth International Graduate School of African Studies (BIGSAS) in Bayreuth, Germany. Having done applied work in the fields of inclusion and accessibility in arts, theater, and higher education, his research interests include deafness, disability, dynamics of identity, and the anthropology of the body. He has conducted field research in Mali, Uganda, Germany, and Benin.

Sally A. Nuamah, PhD is a professor in the School of Education and Social Policy at Northwestern University. She is the author of *How Girls Achieve* (Harvard University Press, 2019).

Michael Simmons, PhD is Senior Program Manager with the Rutgers University-Newark, Joseph C. Cornwall Center for Metropolitan Studies in Newark, New Jersey, USA, responsible for youth crime and delinquency programs aimed at strengthening supportive services to young adults disconnected from educational and employment opportunities, addressing place-based crime and safety issues, and improving the life chances of males of color.

Frederick Murunga Wekesah is an epidemiologist, a Research Officer at APHRC, and a doctoral candidate at the Julius Global Health, Julius Center for Health Sciences and Primary Care, University Medical Center of Utrecht University, the Netherlands. Frederick carries out research in non-communicable diseases, specifically on cardiovascular diseases, and on child and adolescent mental health.

Adekunle Yusuf is a research associate at the Centre for the Study of Economies of Africa (CSEA), an economics think tank based in Abuja, Nigeria.

LIST OF FIGURES

List of Tables

CHAPTER 1

Introduction

Mora L. McLean

The West African youth presence in the American postindustrial port City of Newark, New Jersey, is significant, varied, and intricately woven into the social fabric, in both present-day and historic terms. The outwardly seamless integration of these young Black immigrants into Newark's residential, social, and commercial life belies the distinctive circumstances under which they have arrived, kinds and levels of resources upon which they can draw, and pathways available to them as they endeavor to thrive. For instance, in 2010, under the headline "Held as slaves, now free," CNN reported the crackdown of a highly profitable child trafficking operation in the Newark Metropolitan Area. Some 20 girls, most in their early teens, from various West African countries, testified to being held captive by a Togolese couple, who tricked them into traveling to the United States on the promise of an education, then forced them to work 14- to 16-hour days in hair braiding salons, boasting a largely African American clientele (Bronstein, Lyon, & Poolos, 2010; Salomon, 2010). Speaking before the thousands who attended Rutgers University-Newark's, 2018 commencement, the then undergraduate student body president reflected on the travails and triumphs of transitioning from her birthplace in Nigeria to life in New

M. L. McLean (✉)
Rutgers University-Newark, Newark, NJ, USA
e-mail: m.mclean@rutgers.edu

© The Author(s) 2020
M. L. McLean (ed.), *West African Youth Challenges and Opportunity Pathways*, Gender and Cultural Studies in Africa and the Diaspora, https://doi.org/10.1007/978-3-030-21092-2_1

Jersey, and how the iconic image of Queen Latifah—the rapper, songwriter, actor, producer, and Newark native—inspired her to persevere. Offering words of encouragement to many in the audience, she pronounced: "To every black girl who has ever felt undeserving, underestimated, unworthy, this is for you!" (Rutgers University-Newark, 2018). In 2019, the New Jersey Historical Commission awarded support for the work of a young Ghanaian-born researcher who is using archived "fugitive slave" advertisements to document the enslavement of African people throughout the state of New Jersey in the period between 1783, the official end of the American Revolution, and 1808, when the US government officially banned American participation in the transatlantic slave trade (Amemasor, 2002). The seeds of his passion for probing this history took root after he earned his bachelor's degree from the University of Cape Coast, and took on a first job educating visitors to Ghana's Cape Coast Castle Museum—established at the infamous seventeenth-century fortress and slave trading post. After going on to earn a doctoral degree from Rutgers University-Newark, he shifted the focus of his passion for probing this history to the US side of the Atlantic.

In the spring of 2016, the Joseph C. Cornwall Center for Metropolitan Studies (Cornwall Center) at Rutgers University-Newark announced the results of research showing an exceptional increase in the African-born immigrant portion of the Newark's majority Black population. The findings confirmed that Newark's majority Black (48.7%) and Hispanic (34.4%) population is complexly diverse. Members include descendants of families who were part of the Great Migration—the twentieth-century exodus of millions of Black southerners seeking escape from the routinized humiliation and violence of Jim Crow segregation—and subsequent waves of new immigrant families from Brazil, the Caribbean, and the African continent, following the elimination of racially biased US immigration quotas in 1965. Today, West Africans—largely from Ghana, Nigeria, and Liberia—are among the fastest-growing segments of the city's immigrant population, arriving in numbers exceeding foreign-born residents from every other world region, except Central America.

The release of these findings came on the heels of Rutgers University-Newark's announcement of a comprehensive plan for realizing its commitments as an anchor institution, serving the needs of residents of the Greater Newark Area, New Jersey's largest—and second poorest—metropolis, just minutes west of New York City (Rutgers University-Newark, 2014). The plan, which remains in effect, accords high priority to community–university partnerships aimed at addressing acute, long-standing educational and other poverty-related challenges, stemming from decades of systematic exclusion, the decimation of manufacturing, chronic joblessness, and increasing income and wealth inequality.

Emerging from this context, this book collection offers a transatlantic, transnational exploration of barriers that undermine conditions of life for African and African-descendant youth, and limit their horizons. Beyond providing data and analysis, it also describes practical approaches to overcoming barriers and strengthening young people's ability to transition from youthhood to satisfying adult lives. Moreover, departing from the prevalent tendency to privilege US frameworks and perspectives, the dominant focus of this collection is on learning more about the African context in which increasing numbers of Newark youth spend significant portions of their young lives and, after emigrating, often maintain active family connections. In addition, by focusing on African youth, and mainly from African researcher and practitioner perspectives, the collection makes groundbreaking contributions to the field of youth studies.

The Need for Comparative Research

The methodological and theoretical challenges posed by any attempt to analyze conditions associated with youthhood, let alone devise ameliorative interventions, and transcontinentally, are formidable. But as scholar-activist Joschka Philipps (2014) argues, it is possible to surmount such challenges, and taking them on holds the potential to yield important breakthroughs in our understanding of "how different contexts, be they geographical, economic, political or professional, impact young people" (p. 1363). Philipps proffers an analytical and methodological approach to overcoming academic disciplinary silos that are part of the colonial legacy. He argues for transgressing the conventional divide in academia whereby "youth studies" and the "core disciplines," such as sociology, focus mainly on the so-called developed world, while the so-called developing world draws the attention of anthropology and area studies (Philipps, 2018, p. 2). Philipps (2018) makes the case for transforming youth studies so that it encompasses the majority of the world's youth. Drawing on the literature (e.g., Comaroff & Comaroff, 2005), he argues that research on Africa—the world region with the largest concentration of youth, one-fifth of the world's youth population, and rapidly increasing (Yahya, 2017)—is a fruitful source of methodological and theoretical insights from which sociological and other studies of "global youth" stand to benefit. This collection is congruent with the premise that the field of youth studies (which largely ignores African youth) and the field of African Studies (which focuses on African youth, but mainly in ways that are self-referential) would be mutually enriched by more encompassing approaches to studying "youth" (Philipps, 2014).

Adopting a case-based, comparative analysis approach to investigating the range of attitudes, behaviors, and experiences of African youth and youth in the African diaspora in the United States makes sense for historical as well as heuristic reasons. It is no accident that, regardless of geographical context—and whether measured at the local, national, or global level—health, education, employment, and other indicators of well-being for Black youth are poor relative to White youth and, except in rare instances, youth in other ethnic and racialized categories. Nor is it coincidental that—whether analyzed from a youth studies or African studies perspective—scholarly investigations of youth-associated characteristics that are perceived to be threatening or dysfunctional (e.g., urban crime, violent protest, and irregular migration) focus disproportionately on young Black men (Philipps, 2018, pp. 6–7).

From the perspective of social and political philosophy, Charles Mills' (1997) analysis of the core centrality, and unstated assumptions, of white supremacy in structuring the modern world provides a useful framework for understanding the shared predicaments of African and African diaspora youth, and similarities in the ways in which they are viewed and characterized, in contrast to non-Black youth. He articulates the centuries-long process of "norming space" and "spacing individuals" by imprinting them with certain characteristics. The racialized identity and spaces with which contemporary Black youth (and other subaltern persons) are associated worldwide function together as a circular indictment: "You are what you are in part because you originate from a certain kind of space, and that space has those properties in part because it is inhabited by creatures like yourself" (Mills, 1997, p. 42). The circular indictment functions equally whether applied to the African continent in the global context or "inner cities" of the United States.

Observing a similar construct, historical analyses of the intellectual foundations of policy prescriptions for understanding the causes of US domestic and global poverty note a tendency to draw linkages between explanations of juvenile delinquency, criminology, and social unrest and understandings of poverty as ultimately a problem of individual or group failings, rather than imbedded structures. These patterns prevailed during the overlapping era of Cold War "development," and the US domestic War on Poverty, in the 1960s (Katz, 2013, pp. 10–12, 148–155; O'Connor, 2001, pp. 113–125) and have since reemerged. Regardless of particular explanations of cause and effect, whether they reside in the Global North or the Global South, young people who live in poverty and are African-born or of African descent are disproportionately burdened by the global phenomena of increasing income and structural inequality. Thwarted by systemic barriers and discrimination based on gender, ethnicity, race, and other forms of identity, they face daunting obstacles in meeting basic needs, accessing education, transitioning to meaningful and decent work, engaging in civic participation, improving their conditions of life, and achieving their full potential. As Alcinda Honwana (2014) observes, "waithood" best captures the reality that for many, if not most, of these youth, conventional paths to adulthood are perceived to be, and are in fact, out of reach.

The changing demographics of majority Black urban populations in the United States and the historical bases of structural inequality are among the factors spurring contemporary transatlantic Black youth movements—yet another potentially fruitful area for more transatlantic collaboration among researchers and practitioners and comparative research. For instance, the Black Lives Matter movement was initially sparked by the 2013 murder of Trayvon Martin, but has since purposefully transformed itself into a global network (Black Lives Matter, n.d.). Opal Tometi, one of the movement's cofounders, also previously led the New York-based Black Alliance for Just Immigration (BAJI), which advocates on behalf of Black immigrant communities from Africa, the Caribbean, and Latin America (BAJI, n.d.). She attributes much of her worldview and activism to her Nigerian immigrant family origins combined with her experience growing up Black and female in the United States. The Black Lives Matter movement's transnational commitment reflects a recognition of connected existential, socioeconomic, and political challenges that impact Black people, and especially Black youth, around the world, demanding strategies and solutions which extend beyond borders (BBC News Africa, 2018; Flanders, 2015; Tometi, 2015). Historian Barbara Ransby (2018) and sociologist Alondra Nelson (2016) situate the Black Lives Matter movement within a long lineage of transcontinental youth movements. Along these same lines, Krystal Strong (2018) observes:

> A generation or more removed from the struggles that achieved political independence in African nations and the attainment of certain legal rights

for Black people in the United States, Black youth across continental boundaries are calling into question deeply held ideas about intergenerational progress. (p. 276)

In her essay, provocatively titled "Do African Lives Matter to Black Lives Matter? Youth Uprisings and the Borders of Solidarity," Strong advocates in favor of "more meaningful engagement with contemporary scholarship and struggles in Africa and other global contexts, in the interest of research and solidarity practices that have as their aim the full valuation of Black lives everywhere" (p. 266).

More widespread and purposeful exploration of these connections would illuminate how and why the life experiences and challenges of Black youth in Africa and in the United States (as well as other parts of the world) are both similar and different, and how proposed interventions on either side of the Atlantic might be mutually informed and better conceived.

"YOUTH" AND "DEVELOPMENT"

Consistent with the social science literature, the collection as a whole treats youth as a constructed, contingent, and shifting category, dependent not merely upon biological age and psychological processes, but also shaped by specific historical, socioeconomic contexts and cultural understandings and meanings (Durham, 2000; Honwana & De Boeck, 2005). Taken together, the chapters draw on multiple approaches to analyzing challenges and opportunities as youth navigate various life transitions. The life course framework—especially the movement into, through, and out of school—figures prominently, but the salience of youth agency and worldviews as well as social forces is also recognized (Hardgrove, Pells, Boyden, & Dornan, 2014).

Collectively, the book contributors recognize that the material challenges to well-being among African youth are real. With roughly 40% of the population under age 15 and a youth population aged 15 to 24 estimated at 226 million (or 40% of the world's total), Africa has the world's fastest growing and youngest population. Western and Eastern Africa account for more than half of the continent's births and are projected to account for two-thirds by the end of the twenty-first century. For instance, by 2050, one-fifth of children under 18 in Africa will live in Nigeria (United Nations International Children's Emergency Fund [UNICEF], 2014). With its expanding megacities, high proportion of youth, and insufficient educational resources and opportunities for gainful employment to meet demand, Nigeria epitomizes the Western Africa trajectory.

This collection acknowledges the significance of statistical evidence pointing to Africa's so-called youth bulge, but the "development imperative" is not a central or otherwise explicit concern of any of the chapter contributions in this book. Where educational access and attainment and employment are discussed in these chapters, the concern is with how these variables undermine or strengthen the capacity of marginalized youth to improve their material conditions and secure basic needs, to escape long-term poverty, and to achieve well-being. In the literature, poverty is firmly established as a variable associated with trauma, harmful stress, and a sense of hopelessness—the psychological and other burdens that can compromise the cognitive resources, mental health, and noncognitive skills human beings need to pursue a satisfying life.

The collection is organized into three parts, emphasizing the themes of (1) migration; (2) agency and aspirations; and (3) vulnerability and well-being, respectively. These three dimensions figure prominently in the lives of West African youth in and beyond the continent, shaping the obstacles they face and the pathways by which they seek to surmount them. The chapters clustered within each section foreground the theme under which they are organized in contrasting ways. But just as in lived experience, to varying degrees, the themes surface throughout the book.

MIGRATION

Contrary to the news headlines emanating from mainstream European and US media, the volume of migration within West Africa and to other regions of the continent is at least ten times greater than toward European countries (Charrière & Frésia, 2008). The pervasiveness of migration within and to West Africa is such that the number of immigrants residing in the region exceeds that of any other region of the continent.

Youth are at the forefront of spurring ongoing changes in the configurations of migration in and from West Africa. They are also the segment of the population most vulnerable to any associated negative consequences. In 2008, the United Nations High Commissioner for Refugees (UNHCR) observed that "West Africa ... has the distinguishing feature of many urban refugees, most of them citizens of ECOWAS [Economic Community of West African States] countries" (Charrière & Frésia, 2008 p. 16), and that the majority are under 40, including significant numbers of adolescents and children under 18. The UN agency further concluded:

> The demographic explosion, urbanization and the economic slowdown have resulted in a growing individualization of life and family styles, redefining the place of young people, who now are handed the responsibility of making a living for their parents. Today more than ever the majority of young people see mobility as the best—if not the only option to secure their family's situation. (Charrière & Frésia, 2008, p. 11)

West African youth classified as internal migrants (at times perceived as foreigners, even in their own country), or undocumented immigrants abroad, are in a situation where their safety and security is compromised (Mberu & Pongou, 2010). They are among the world's most vulnerable "stateless" populations—excluded from enjoying the benefits of citizenship, including access to educational resources that are critical to improving their life chances.

The dynamic of internal youth migration in West Africa is the focus of Daniel Kyereko's chapter. His study of out-of-school migrants in Ghana makes a contribution to both research and practice focused on increasing access to education in Africa, and especially West Africa. It highlights the prevalence of south-south migration overall, and intra-West African migration in particular. The study goes beyond the conventional focus on sterile, quantitative data by providing qualitative analysis and insights into the thinking and motivations of migrant parents and children, as well as teachers and school personnel in Ghana, the host country. Kyereko's research reveals that, in contrast to findings of existing research focusing mainly on dropouts, migrant children in Ghana are, for varying reasons, more likely to never have enrolled in school in the first place. Among these reasons, migrants' distrust of the local school system looms large. The question of whether education is an efficacious poverty intervention, especially where there is deep-seated distrust of the educational system, is one that also emerges in Muhammad Salisu Abdullahi's chapter on the Almajiri system for educating young males in Nigeria's predominately Hausa-Muslim northern region.

Regardless of the route they take, or where they end up, West African youth who migrate (or emigrate) often find themselves in a double bind: on the one hand, increasingly clandestine and perilous passages expose them to life-threatening risk and exploitation; on the other, restrictive visa and immigration policies, anti-Black racism in Global North countries, and xenophobia in South Africa, further curtail their upward mobility. Despite this, as Lanre Ikuteyijo's chapter on youth migration as a survival strategy shows, for certain young Africans, the allure of emigration, especially to Europe and North America, is strong. The responses of the young women and men interviewed in Ikuteyijo's study are in stark contrast to those of the university students interviewed by Dabesaki Mac-Ikemenjima in his chapter on youth aspirations. In his study, which appears in Part II of this book, Mac-Ikemenjima found that across gender university students had minimal interest in migrating away from Nigeria.

Ikuteyijo's research on Nigerian youth who engage in extralegal, "irregular," migration responds to the challenge posed by Canadian-Nigerian scholars Charles Adeyanju and Temitope Oriola in their 2011 essay on the phenomenology of voluntary African migration to Western countries. Their analysis of "African desideratum for the West" led them to exhort scholars to "pay more theoretical and empirical attention to prospective African immigrants' and migrants' percepts of self and society and their implications for international and transnational migration" (Adeyanju & Oriola, 2011, p. 945).

Accordingly, using in-depth interviews and focus group discussions with youths in selected Nigerian urban centers who expressed a predisposition toward, or had actual experience with, migration, Ikuteyijo produced qualitative research revealing these youths' own perceptions and understandings of irregular migration, the kinds of survival strategies they adopted in destination countries, and their experiences as returnee migrants. His research shows that many of the youths who migrated irregularly were ignorant of migration law basics (such as the need to hold a passport), and most were not motivated solely by economic reasons. The majority of young people in his sample expressed a desire for social status or, as one of the young men put it, "integrity" at home in Nigeria. Ikuteyijo's findings support Adeyanju's and Oriola's (2011) nuanced tentative conclusion that: "In addition to scarcity of material opportunities, Africans' interests in the West are rooted in three interrelated extraeconomic factors: colonial discourse, migrants' accounts of presentation of self, and the contemporary mass media" (p. 961).

Ikuteyijo's chapter also highlights the disconnect between the "garnished front stage" and "concealed back stage" of migrants' lives, that is, between their representations of life abroad to family and peers within their social networks and the actual hardships, including racism, that they face in Europe and North America. Adeyanju and Oriola (2011) suggested that "one of the reasons why non-White migrants traverse their ancestral or former and current or host societies to 'show off' is to compensate for their experience of racialization in the latter" (p. 958).

Research questions pertaining to migration and race are also surfaced in the chapter on Black immigrant youth in Newark, New Jersey, coauthored by Mahako Etta and Michael Simmons. Etta and Simmons highlight the need for greater awareness and more in-depth study of emergent educational challenges and opportunities presented by the increasing presence of West African immigrant youth within Newark's school population. The City of Newark is the largest city in the state of New Jersey, and one of the poorest cities in the United States, with a highly diverse, majority Black and Hispanic, population. The city is often seen as an exemplar of a US nationwide trend of lagging educational attainment and increasing economic vulnerability: the rate at which Newark residents obtain any type of postsecondary degree or credential is among the lowest for comparable postindustrial US cities. As Etta and Simmons allude, removing barriers to post secondary attainment is among the key challenges that local youth-serving organizations have set out to tackle (Burd, 2015; Backstrand & Donaldson, 2018).

The starting point for the study conducted by Etta and Simmons is evidence showing a significant increase in Newark's foreign-born population since 2000. They trace this increase to changes in US immigration laws dating back to the 1960s, and find that immigrants mainly from Ghana and Nigeria account for it. They probe perceptions of Newark schoolteachers, principals, and other adults who are beginning to observe the newly unfolding demographics at one of Newark's largest local public high schools. Their findings reveal that the same youth categorized as "vulnerable" in the West African employment context are also viewed as youth at risk (school dropouts or juvenile delinquents) or "model minorities" (i.e., vis-à-vis native-born Black youth) in the United States.

Etta and Simmons' call for both disaggregated, school-level data, on Newark students' immigrant status to enable a more fine-grained understanding of the city's "Black" student population, and qualitative research examining the social interactions and academic achievement levels of students who are West African-born, also signals a drawback of this book collection's main focus on Anglophone West Africa. Adult volunteers who work with African immigrant youth in the Newark and New York Metropolitan Area report that youth whose families originate from Francophone West African countries are forced to grapple with "intersecting inequalities" compounded by language barriers, as well as other factors, such as low educational levels and underemployment of parents (see also Suárez-Orozco, Yoshikawa, & Tseng, 2015). They observe that, contrary to the "model minority" stereotype, many Newark Area immigrant youth of Francophone (as well as similarly situated youth of Anglophone) West African origin are at least as vulnerable and "at risk" as many Newark Area Black youth who are native-born Americans (Z. Yamba, A. K. Khalfani, and D. Kassimou, personal communication, March 25, 2017; D. Kassimou, personal communication, July 2, 2019). Together with Etta and Simmons' findings, this observation about the complexities of immigrant-native differences, and constraints on the socioeconomic mobility of Black immigrants in cities like Newark (Bennet & Lutz, 2009), points further to the range of issues that could be the focus of transatlantic research-practice collaborations.

AGENCY AND ASPIRATIONS

Departing from the developmentalist literature that focuses on at-risk and delinquent behaviors of African youth, the chapters in this section explore how youth in West Africa exert agency and aspire toward the future, often with high expectations, even when facing harsh circumstances. They are resourceful and enterprising in identifying and accessing tools at their disposal (Kabiru, Mojola, Beguy, & Okigbo, 2013). Additionally, contrary to the global mass media images that portray African youth, especially young African men, as desperate, reckless, and readily inclined to risk life and limb to leave the continent, the youth portrayed in these chapters adjust their expectations to circumstances. All three chapters respond to the call for more research on African youth agency and aspirations and expectations.

Sociologist Charles Payne (2012) observes that the "intellectual development for Black children [in the United States] is ordinarily development under hostile conditions" (p. 6). Despite major gains in recent years, the same assessment applies with respect to the vast majority of children living in Africa. A research study conducted by the Center for Universal Education at Brookings found that, despite increasing access to education in sub-Saharan African countries, rates of extreme education poverty and inequalities between the rich and poor within countries persist (van Fleet, 2012). The researchers concluded that of "Africa's nearly 128 million school-aged children, [some] 37 million African children will learn so little while they are in school that they will not be much better off than [the estimated 17 million] kids who never attend school" (van Fleet, 2012). The authors of the study point to "a deeper learning crisis that needs to be addressed" (van Fleet, 2012). These hostile conditions necessarily weigh on the attitudes and aspirations of marginalized Black youth in the multiple (educational, livelihood and employment, family formation, civic participation, etc.) dimensions of their transitions from youth to adulthood.

Yet, as Cecilia Fiaka's first-person testimony attests, even for children and youth living in difficult circumstances, cultural and familial bonds and individual character traits such as tenacity can shield individuals from the harshest consequences of poverty. These kinship, familial, and individual resources provide the basis for meaningful hope and real positive improvement in youths' lives and prospects for satisfying conditions of life in adulthood. Fiaka's experience evokes Afua Twum-Danso Imoh's (2016) critique of the conventional literature and its "overwhelming focus on childhoods [in Africa] defined by what they lack" (p. 456), a tendency which, she argues, has led to "the creation of a false dichotomy between Northern childhoods and the multitude of childhoods that are located in the diverse contexts that exist in the South" (p. 457). Fiaka recounts her personal testimony of growing up in an economically depressed region of rural Ghana in the 1960s. Hers is the compelling story of how she went from being a "house help" to a banker to an activist on behalf of rural youth. Her journey led her to become the founder and director of the award-winning Nneka Foundation, which works in rural communities across Ghana.

Dabesaki Mac-Ikemenjima's chapter on youth aspirations contributes to filling the gap in the literature on the content of youths' goals in sub-Saharan Africa—a gap in understanding that especially pertains to subgroups of youth like undergraduate students. Mac-Ikemenjima's analysis is based on data from interviews, focus group discussions, and the administration of a questionnaire to undergraduate students in the Niger Delta city of Port Harcourt, Nigeria. Through a grounded theory analysis of the data collected, he identifies an array of youth goals that he ascribes to four categories: material, achievement, generativity, and relationship. Except in one area, both the qualitative and quantitative analyses show consistency across gender, with all respondents showing minimal interest in migrating away from Nigeria. This is in stark contrast to the results of Lanre Ikuteyijo's qualitative study of how (largely unemployed and less educated) youth in five cities in western Nigeria view the prospect of emigration favorably. Additionally, as compared to their male peers, the female undergraduates in Mac-Ikemenjima's study were far more likely to aspire to the goal of marriage, as a path toward economic stability. Other research shows that while, increasingly, marriage does not provide the economic refuge that young women might seek, it does spare them the stigma of single womanhood, and sanction their having children, in Nigeria (Ntoimo & Isiugo-Abanihe, 2014). The research on women suggests that there may be more to the gender disparity in undergraduates' views on marriage than meets the eye. These findings provide nuanced insights, and raise questions for further investigation, pertaining to the disparate perspectives of young people in West Africa facing different challenges and, as Mac-Ikemenjima urges, should prompt more in-depth and comparative research on youth aspirations.

In West Africa, as elsewhere, the process of "being" as well as "becoming" is all the more complex for young people who live with some form of disability. In his chapter, Carsten Mildner examines how three young people who are deaf navigate obstacles as they transition to adulthood. As these three life sketches illustrate, being deaf is not just a medical condition but a social role within both a community of peers and the broader society. Mildner's study portrays the multiple layers of relationship within various settings (family and caregivers, school, within and beyond communities of other deaf people, etc.) and the hurdles that these young people must navigate. Despite, and perhaps because of, their disability, the young people in his study exhibit a high degree of determination and resilience as they at once strive to determine themselves and are being determined.

This chapter provides a compelling glimpse into the largely unexplored frontier of youths living with disabilities in West Africa. It highlights how little is known, and how much there is to learn, about the dynamics—positive as well as negative—of experiencing life, nurturing aspirations, and moving toward adulthood as young persons whose disabilities are part of a multifaceted, intersecting, and shifting set of identities. What are the intricacies of present-day challenges facing young people with disabilities who function in settings where colonization, enslavement, and legalized racial segregation and discrimination are part of the historical legacy? Do such legacies call for further questioning of assumptions about identity, belonging, cultural influence, and definitions of community? What viable educational policy alternatives exist for the majority of Beninese deaf youth who do not know the Francophone West African variant of American Sign Language, whose grasp of French grammar is limited, or who live in rural communities where the predominantly spoken languages are indigenous rather than European? These are some of the questions that lend themselves to comparative investigation. For instance, based upon empirical and qualitative research conducted in South Africa and the United States, respectively, South African Sign Language and Black American Sign Language (Black ASL) have both been recognized as coexisting (rather than derivational) forms of signing, each with its own distinctive structure, grammar, and culturally embedded sociality (Reagan, 2008; Sellers, 2012) Researchers formally regard Black ASL as "a rich signing system that reflects both a history of segregation and the ongoing influence of spoken [Black] English" (Sellers, 2012).

Despite the numerous multilayered, day-to-day, and broader challenges they face, each of the young people whom Mildner profiles displays creativity, ingenuity, and grit in envisioning and striving toward possibilities. Together the profiles further challenge the globally applicable, dominant paradigm according to which deafness is essentially a condition of deficiency to be "measured against the hearing norm" (Reagan, 2008 pp. 166–167, 172). Related to this, the profiles also expose the fallacies and pitfalls of the pervasive tendency to view African (and African-descendant) youth from a deficit rather than asset perspective (see, e.g., Boyd, 2010). The profiles provide evidence of the interplay of individual characteristics, family, school, culture, community, and worldview in contributing to the resilience of youth whose physiology and identity qualities somehow set them apart from a particular mainstream (see, e.g., Boyd, 2010; Williamson, 2007). Youth resilience in the face of disability is another topic area worthy of exploration from a transnational and comparative perspective.

Sally A. Nuamah's chapter on girls' achievement contributes to the body of research showing that achievement-oriented identities, and individual characteristics such as grit, resilience, and confidence, though important, are not sufficient to assure viable pathways to youth success and well-being. Nuamah is a Ghanaian-born scholar-activist based in the United States whose research on the significance of confidence as a variable in girls' achievement challenges conventional views that prevail among researchers concerned about youth outcomes. Nuamah proffers analysis and insights that researchers, practitioners, and others in a variety of national settings—outside as well as within Africa—will find critical for understanding and devising strategies to eliminate gendered barriers to girls' achievement. The choice to compare conditions in Ghana and South Africa, a "lower middle income" and a "middle income country," respectively, is purposeful and illuminating. In Ghana, facially neutral policies (for instance, deferred university enrollment after secondary school completion as a mechanism to manage the acute shortage of capacity to meet demand for tertiary education) have a disproportionately negative impact on girls, given the prevalence of forces, e.g. family pressure to marry, inclined to divert girls from educational pathways. In a similar vein, despite its higher national income and distinctively progressive national constitution and progressive laws, South Africa ranks poorly on global indices of gender equality and math and science performance and achievement. Nuamah's analysis shows that a singular focus on increasing confidence—that is, on girls' character traits—is insufficient for closing the girls' achievement gap. Her call for more research that probes the impact of entrenched structural barriers, and measures that bolster individual-level factors, e.g. deeply committed teachers, positive broad community engagement, and other supports, should command the attention of researchers and practitioners concerned with girls' achievement, whether in Ghana, South Africa—or the United States.

Vulnerability and Well-Being

The chapters in Part III explore issues of youth vulnerability on multiple levels, beginning with obstacles that stand in the way of securing a modicum of economic security. For the vast majority of youth in Western Africa, working poverty is the norm (International Labour Organization [ILO], 2016). Studies show that these young people lack educational access and credentials and need multiple income-generating activities in order to survive. Over time, even for those who have the advantage of relatively higher levels of educational attainment, the pervasive lack of access to supported pathways for personal growth and development yields progressively worsening employment prospects and a permanent wage gap in lifetime earnings (ILO, 2015, 2016; UNICEF, 2014). This scarring effect is felt worldwide by youth from low-income families around the world, including Black youth in the diaspora.

In their regression analysis of youth vulnerability in Ghana's labor markets, researchers Adedeji Adeniran, Joseph Ishaku, and Adekunle Yusuf highlight the prospect of long-term scarring that looms large in the work lives of the vast majority of youth in West Africa. Here again the variability of how youth is defined is underscored: life expectancy in Ghana is pegged at age 64, and, therefore, in this study, the time spans between "youth" (people between the ages of 15 and 24), "middle age," and "old age" are relatively small. The study undertaken by Adeniran et al. probes well-established research findings and theory that conclude that gender, education, and location are major determinants of labor market vulnerability. They show that the probability of vulnerability increases for youth who are female, who lack formal education, and who reside in rural areas. But the main contribution of the study is the evidence it provides of how vulnerability appears to taper off during "middle age," the age range from 25 to 54, but then resumes at age 55. This evidence of the connection between vulnerability during youth and prospects for later life will help to inform and shape policy interventions that target youth but not in isolation from other age cohorts.

The vulnerability of the young people that Muhammad Salisu Abdullahi writes about takes the form of joblessness and material insecurity, created and compounded by historical and cultural forces. The *Almajiri* system of traditional Qur'anic "boarding schools" that exists throughout northern Nigeria is used mainly by poor rural families who lack other educational alternatives. Abdullahi, who is an entrepreneur trained in biochemistry, cites social anthropologist Hanna Hoechner, who traces the history of the Almajiri system's decline beginning during the era of British colonial rule. As the introduction of "modern education" by the British undermined the control of literacy by northern Nigerian religious scholars, the system went from being a reliable and prestigious avenue for enrolled children and youth (known as *Almajirai* or *Almajiranci*) to transition to successful adulthood, to an entrenched coping strategy for the extreme poor. Unable to afford the modern Islamic education available to members of the middle class, and distrustful of the poor quality of the secular schools that are accessible to them—and with good reason—poor peasant households persist in demanding Almajiri.

Like the parents of out-of-school immigrants who are the focus of Daniel Kyereko's study in Part I, the parents of Almajirai are distrustful of the modern model of formal schooling, which has become "firmly established within development discourse and practice as the development intervention *par excellence* [and] one of the defining features of modern childhood" (Hoechner, 2011, p. 712). An estimated 9.5 million-plus children and youth are enrolled in Almajiri Qur'anic schools across Nigeria, most in the northern part of the country where Abdullahi's enterprise is based (Creative Associates International, 2015; Hoechner, 2011).

Abdullahi contrasts his experience of growing up in a middle-class Hausa-Muslim family with the struggles he witnessed of Almajirai friends in his neighborhood, which inspired him to direct his training and entrepreneurial talent toward devising a positive intervention. Whereas much, if not most, of the policy literature focuses on these youth as a security challenge, if at all, this chapter sheds light on the religious and historical roots of the practice—including its positive elements, such as its contribution to community cohesion and role in introducing literacy. It also shows how young West Africans like Abdullahi are not oblivious to the impact of structural inequality and, although seldom credited in press reports emanating from of the West (Europe and the United States), are in the vanguard of social entrepreneurial efforts to improve poor peoples' lives in West Africa. Among many, including influential business leaders and philanthropists and politicians in the United States, there is a growing realization that education access is not a panacea, and school reform is not an adequate substitute for inadequate household incomes (Hanauer, 2019; Strauss, 2019). Viewed in this wider context, Abdullahi's chapter suggests the possibility of transnational comparative investigation of not only the efficacy of social entrepreneur-led interventions, but also policies to provide guaranteed basic incomes, efforts to promote distributive justice, and other approaches to easing financial pressures on families and expanding meaningful educational opportunities for children and youth—in the United States and in African countries.

In the final chapter, Kenneth Juma, Frederick Murunga Wekesah, Caroline W. Kabiru, and Chimaraoke O. Izugbara, a Pan-African group of public health specialists based in Kenya and the United States, take up the issue of poor mental health among youth in West and Central Africa, from a public health services perspective. They begin by contextualizing the many challenges that cut across these regions—for instance, the acute lack of data and documentation, and the large numbers of diagnosed youth who go untreated—by observing that the prevalence of youth mental and substance use disorders as well as the treatment gap are global issues.

This observation is borne out by research focused on the United States. A 2016 study found that more than a third of children across the United States had experienced childhood trauma "such as the death or incarceration of a parent, witnessing or being a victim of violence, or living with someone who has been suicidal or had a drug or alcohol problem," which increased the likelihood of "[derailed] healthy physical, social, emotional, and cognitive development" (Robert Wood Johnson Foundation, 2017). In the state of New Jersey alone, the rate of exposure to adverse childhood experiences was reportedly 41% for children under the age of 17 (NJ Partnership for Healthy Kids, 2018). Moreover, in the United States "evidence consistently suggests that, across the life course, mental disorder prevalence varies significantly according to race and ethnicity" (Alegría, Green, McLaughlin, & Loder, 2015, p. 15), with issues such as lack of treatment impacting Black and other youth of color disproportionately. Indeed research shows that even high economic status does not inoculate Black American youth from the debilitating mental health effects of long-term exposure to systemic racism (Assari, Gibbons, & Simons, 2018).

Notwithstanding enormous regional differences in the availability of data, documentation, and analysis, resources of all kinds, and levels of awareness, this chapter suggests topics for collaborative and comparative research. In their review of the literature, the coauthors "found gendered differences in the epidemiology of poor mental health, with adolescent girls in West and Central Africa being more vulnerable to depression than boys." This contrasts with research in the United States possibly showing a greater susceptibility to depression among Black boys of color who suffer exposure to trauma and violence (Rich, 2016). Suggesting a possible area of congruence, also worth examining, the chapter cites research suggesting the efficacy of school, community, and culture-based mental health interventions, for instance in Nigeria, Liberia, and Sierra Leone. In his historical overview of the introduction of Western psychiatry in the colonial era, and its practice in the postcolonial period, in Africa, historian Emmanuel Akyeampong notes that "in Africa a precedent was set for community care in mental health before this direction became evident in the West" (Akyeampong, 2015, p. 27). Given shared concerns about the impact of exposure to trauma, lack of information compounded by stigma and cultural beliefs, and the ubiquitous lack of capacity to meet the demand for treatment, researchers and practitioners concerned about gaining a handle on mental and substance abuse disorders among young people in Africa and Black diaspora communities could usefully examine and compare and contrast the efficacy of community- and culture-based mental health care approaches across national and continental borders.

*   *   *

Unfolding national, local, and global permutations of inequality are prompting practitioners, activists, and scholars—including those among the contributing authors to this collection—to hold the challenges facing youth in Africa and in the diaspora "in simultaneous view." These more unconventional ways of framing and approaching youth-related challenges depart from thinking solely about "places of poverty" (Roy, 2015). They move toward border-transcending analytical frameworks and problem-solving approaches that are more likely to increase understanding of the nature of African and African diaspora youth challenges and better suited to designing opportunity pathways for them. This book aspires toward the vision of both focusing in on and transcending space as a way of gaining a more fine-grained understanding of the challenges of African and African-descendant youth, exploring opportunity pathways, and providing additional rungs for moving further in that direction.

References

Adeyanju, C. T., & Oriola, T. B. (2011). Colonialism and contemporary African migration: A phenomenological approach. *Journal of Black Studies, 42*(6), 943–967.

Akyeampong, E. (2015). A historical overview of psychiatry in Africa. In E. Kyeampong, A. G. Hil, & A. M. Kleinman (Eds.), *The culture of mental illness and psychiatric practice in Africa* (pp. 24–49). Bloomington: Indiana University Press.

Alegría, M., Green, J. G., McLaughlin, K. A., & Loder, S. (2015). *Disparities in child and adolescent mental health and mental health services in the U.S.* Retrieved June 12, 2019, from https://wtgrantfoundation.org/library/uploads/2015/09/Disparities-in-Child-and-Adolescent-Mental-Health.pdf

Amemasor, J. A. (2002). Opening the door of return. *The International Journal of Narrative Therapy and Community Work: African American Perspectives, Healing Past & Present* (2), 60–63.

Assari, S., Gibbons, F. X., & Simons, R. (2018). Depression among black youth; Interaction of class and place. *Brain Sciences, 8*(6), 108. https://doi.org/10.3390/brainsci8060108. Retrieved June 3, 2019, from https://www.ncbi.nlm.nih.gov/pmc/articles/PMC6025590/

Backstrand, J. R., & Donaldson, K. (2018). Post-secondary outcomes of Newark High School Graduates (2011–2016). Newark, NJ: Newark City of Learning Collaborative, Rutgers University-Newark Joseph C. Cornwall Center for Metropolitan Studies. Retrieved September 12, 2018, from https://nclc2025.org/wp-content/uploads/2018/09/UPDATE-2018-Post-Secondary-Outcomes-Report.pdf

BBC News Africa. (2018, December 15). *Opal Tometi: How Nigeria helped inspire #BlackLivesMatter* [video]. Retrieved March 29, 2019, from https://www.youtube.com/watch?v=PrcGMozDdSY

Bennet, P. R., & Lutz, A. (2009). How African American is the net black advantage? Differences in college attendance among immigrant blacks, native blacks, and whites. *Sociology of Education, 82*(1), 70–100.

Black Alliance for Just Immigration (BAJI). (n.d.). Who we are. Retrieved March 29, 2019, from https://baji.org/who-we-are/

Black Lives Matter. (n.d.). *Herstory*. Retrieved March 29, 2019, from https://blacklivesmatter.com/about/herstory/

Boyd, A. C. (2010). The trials and triumphs of Black deaf students. *The Journal of Deaf Studies and Deaf Education, 15*(2), 204.

Bronstein, S., Lyon, A., & Poolos, A. (2010, December 3). Held as slaves, now free. *CNN*. Retrieved May 10, 2019, from http://www.cnn.com/2010/CRIME/12/02/slave.labor.ring.busted/index.html

Burd, S. (2015, July 1). One struggling city's bold effort to increase its number of college graduates. *The Hechinger Report*. Retrieved December 5, 2018, from https://hechingerreport.org/one-struggling-citys-bold-effort-to-increase-its-number-of-college-graduates/

Charrière, F., & Frésia, M. (2008). *West Africa as a migration and protection area*. New York, NY: United Nations High Commissioner for Refugees. Retrieved May 3, 2016, from http://www.unhcr.org/49e479c311.pdf

Comaroff, J., & Comaroff, J. (2005). Reflections on youth from the past to the postcolony. In A. M. Honwana & F. De Boeck (Eds.), *Makers & breakers: Children & youth in postcolonial Africa* (pp. 19–30). Oxford, UK: James Currey.

Creative Associates International. (2015). *Integrated Qur'anic education: Nigeria case study*. Washington, DC: Author. Retrieved March 29, 2019, from https://www.creativeassociatesinternational.com/wp-content/uploads/2003/01/Integrated_Ed-Nigeria.pdf

Durham, D. (2000). Youth and the social imagination in Africa: Introduction to parts 1 and 2. *Anthropological Quarterly, 73*(3), 113–120.

Flanders, L. (2015, August 5). Opal Tometi on building a transnational movement for Black lives. *Truthout*. Retrieved March 29, 2019, from https://truthout.org/articles/opal-tometi-on-building-a-transnational-movement-for-black-lives/

Hanauer, N. (2019, July). Better schools won't fix America. *The Atlantic*. Retrieved June 20, 2019, from https://www.theatlantic.com/magazine/archive/2019/07/education-isnt-enough/590611/

Hardgrove, A., Pells, K., Boyden, J., & Dornan, P. (2014). *Youth vulnerabilities in life course transitions*. New York, NY: United Nations Development Programme, Human Development Report Office. Retrieved December 5, 2018, from http://hdr.undp.org/sites/default/files/hardgrove_boyden_hdr_2014.pdf

Hoechner, H. (2011). Striving for knowledge and dignity: How Qur'anic students in Kano, Nigeria, learn to live with rejection and educational disadvantage. *European Journal of Development Research, 23*(5), 712–728.

Honwana, A. (2014). 'Waithood.' Youth transitions and social change. In D. Foeken, T. Dietz, L. De Haan, & L. Johnson (Eds.), *Development and equity. An interdisciplinary exploration by ten scholars from Africa, Asia and Latin America* (pp. 28–40). Leiden, Netherlands: Brill.

Honwana, A., & De Boeck, F. (2005). Children & youth in Africa, agency, identity, & place. In A. M. Honwana & F. De Boeck (Eds.), *Makers & breakers: Children & youth in postcolonial Africa* (pp. 1–18). Oxford, UK: James Currey.

International Labour Organization. (2015). *Global employment trends for youth 2015: Scaling up investments in decent jobs for youth.* Geneva, Switzerland: International Labour Office.

International Labour Organization. (2016). *World employment social outlook: Trends for youth 2016.* Geneva, Switzerland: International Labour Office. Retrieved May 31, 2016, from https://www.ilo.org/wcmsp5/groups/public/%2D%2D-dgreports/%2D%2D-dcomm/%2D%2D-publ/documents/publication/wcms_513739.pdf

Kabiru, C. W., Mojola, S. A., Beguy, D., & Okigbo, C. (2013). Growing up at the 'margins': Concerns, aspirations, and expectations of young people living in Nairobi's slums. *Journal of Research on Adolescence, 23*(1), 81–94.

Katz, M. B. (2013). *The undeserving poor: America's enduring confrontation with poverty.* New York: Oxford University Press.

Mberu, B. U., & Pongou, R. (2010). Nigeria: Multiple forms of mobility in Africa's demographic giant. *Migration Information Source.* Retrieved March 29, 2019, from https://www.migrationpolicy.org/article/nigeria-multiple-forms-mobility-africas-demographic-giant

Mills, C. W. (1997). *The racial contract.* Ithaca, NY: Cornell University Press.

Nelson, A. (2016). The longue durée of Black Lives Matter. *American Journal of Public Health, 106*(10), 1734–1737.

New Jersey Historical Commission. (2019). *New Jersey Historical Commission, fiscal year 2019 grant awards.* Retrieved July 3, 2019, from https://www.nj.gov/state/historical/assets/pdf/fy2019-grants-all.pdf

NJ Partnership for Healthy Kids. (2018, January 16). Adverse childhood experiences among biggest issue facing children. Retrieved June 12, 2019, from https://www.njhealthykids.org/adverse-childhood-experiences-among-biggest-issue-facing-children/

Ntoimo, L. F. C., & Isiugo-Abanihe, U. (2014). Patriarchy and singlehood among women in Lagos, Nigeria. *Journal of Family Issues, 35*(14), 1980–2008. https://doi.org/10.1177/0192513X13511249

O'Connor, A. (2001). *Poverty knowledge: Social science, social policy, and the poor in twentieth-century U.S. history.* Princeton, NJ: Princeton University Press.

Payne, C. (2012). Countering the master narratives: The 'why?' of education for liberation. *Voices in Urban Education, 34*(Summer), 6–14. Retrieved May, 22, 2017, from http://www.annenberginstitute.org/sites/default/files/VUE34.pdf

Philipps, J. (2014). Dealing with diversity: African youth research and the potential of comparative approaches. *Journal of Youth Studies, 17*(10), 1362–1377.

Philipps, P. (2018). A global generation? Youth studies in a postcolonial world. *Societies, 8*(1), 1–18.

Ransby, B. (2018). *Making all Black lives matter: Reimagining freedom in the twenty-first century.* Oakland: University of California Press.

Reagan, T. (2008). South African Sign Language and language-in-education policy in South Africa. *Stellenbosch Papers in Linguistics, 38*, 165–190.

Rich, J. (2016). *Moving toward healing: Trauma and violence and boys and young men of color.* Retrieved July 9, 2019, from https://media.wix.com/ugd/fb2077_b4d750a1479a4072972e774db167db5f.pdf

Robert Wood Johnson Foundation. (2017, October 19). *Traumatic experiences widespread among U.S. youth, New data show.* Retrieved June 12, 2019, from https://www.rwjf.org/en/library/articles-and-news/2017/10/traumatic-experiences-widespread-among-u-s%2D%2Dyouth%2D%2Dnew-data-show.html

Roy, A. (2015). Introduction: The aporias of poverty. In A. Roy & E. S. Crane (Eds.), *Territories of poverty: Rethinking north and south* (pp. 1–35). Athens: University of Georgia Press.

Rutgers University-Newark. (2014). *Where opportunity meets excellence. Strategic plan 2014.* Retrieved May 25, 2016, from http://www.newark.rutgers.edu/sites/default/files/run_strategic_plan_-final.pdf

Rutgers University-Newark. (2018, May 14). *Queen Latifah receives honorary doctorate at commencement 2018.* Retrieved May 14, 2018, from https://www.newark.rutgers.edu/news/rutgers-university-newark-announces-queen-latifah-commencement-speaker-and-honorary-degree

Salomon, S. H. (2010, December 5). African girls held as slaves in New Jersey. *The Root.* Retrieved May 10, 2019, from https://www.theroot.com/african-girls-held-as-slaves-in-new-jersey-1790881860

Sellers, F. S. (2012, September 17). Sign language that African Americans use is different from that of whites. *The Washington Post.* Retrieved July 7, 2019, from https://www.washingtonpost.com/lifestyle/style/sign-language-that-african-americans-use-is-different-from-that-of-whites/2012/09/17/2e897628-bbc2-11e1-8867-ecf6cb7935ef_story.html?noredirect=on&utm_term=.ed448a0ad35b

Strauss, V. (2019, June 19). A mega-wealthy philanthropist changes his mind about school reform and what kids really need—and Barack Obama has a surprising reaction. *The Washington Post.* Retrieved June 20, 2019, from https://www.washingtonpost.com/education/2019/06/19/billionaire-changes-his-mind-about-school-reform-what-kids-really-need-barack-obama-has-surprising-reaction/?utm_term=.75db8bb34c25

Strong, K. (2018). Do African lives matter to Black Lives Matter? Youth uprisings and the borders of solidarity. *Urban Education, 53*(2), 265–285.

Suárez-Orozco, C., Yoshikawa, H. & Tseng, V. (2015). *Intersecting inequalities: Research to reduce inequality for immigrant-origin children and youth*. Retrieved July 24, 2018, from http://wtgrantfoundation.org/library/uploads/2015/09/Intersecting-Inequalities-Research-to-Reduce-Inequality-for-Immigrant-Origin-Children-and-Youth.pdf

Tometi, O. (2015, April 30). What Pew's new report didn't tell you about Black immigrants. *Huffington Post*. Retrieved March 29, 2019, from https://www.huffingtonpost.com/opal-tometi/what-the-pews-new-report-didnt-tell-you-about-black-immigrants_b_7174070.html

Twum-Danso Imoh, A. (2016). From the singular to the plural: Exploring diversities in contemporary childhoods in sub-Saharan Africa. *Childhood, 23*(3), 455–468.

United Nations International Children's Emergency Fund (UNICEF) (2014). *Generation 2030 Africa 2.0. Prioritizing investments in children to reap the demographic dividend*. Retrieved March 29, 2019, from https://data.unicef.org/wp-content/uploads/2017/11/Generation_2030_Africa_2.0.pdf

van Fleet, J. (2012, September 17). Africa's education crisis: In school but not learning. *Brookings*. Retrieved June 12, 2019, from https://www.brookings.edu/blog/up-front/2012/09/17/africas-education-crisis-in-school-but-not-learning/

Williamson, C. (2007). *Black deaf students: A model for educational success.* Washington, DC: Gallaudet University Press.

Yahya, M. (2017, August 7). Africa's defining challenge [Blog post]. *United Nations Development Programme*. Retrieved August 11, 2017, from http://www.africa.undp.org/content/rba/en/home/blog/2017/8/7/africa_defining_challenge.html

PART I

Migration

CHAPTER 2

Education for All: The Case of Out-of-School Migrants in Ghana

Daniel Owusu Kyereko

INTRODUCTION

The world has witnessed significant progress toward increasing access to education for children of school-going age since the 1990 World Conference on Education in Jomtein. But for many in countries in sub-Saharan Africa, the goal of achieving universal access to education remains elusive. Children in sub-Saharan Africa comprise a major portion of the out-of-school population, with children of migrants identified as being among the most vulnerable and most at risk of dropping out of school (Majgaard & Mingat, 2013; United Nations Educational, Scientific and Cultural Organization [UNESCO], 2010; UNESCO Institute for Statistics [UIS], 2017; UIS and Global Education Monitoring Report [GEMR], 2016).

In 2017, South-South migration accounted for 38% of 258 million international migrants documented worldwide. Over a third of all international migrants moving from the South settled in another country in the global South (United Nations Conference on Trade and Development

D. O. Kyereko (✉)
Bayreuth International Graduate School of African Studies, Bayreuth, Germany
e-mail: Daniel.Kyereko@uni-bayreuth.de

© The Author(s) 2020
M. L. McLean (ed.), *West African Youth Challenges and Opportunity Pathways*, Gender and Cultural Studies in Africa and the Diaspora, https://doi.org/10.1007/978-3-030-21092-2_2

[UNCTAD], 2017). Motivations for contemporary South-South migration can be partly attributed to the increasingly restrictive immigration policies being introduced in countries of the Global North and the growth in the economies of countries within the Global South. Migration between neighboring countries accounts for about 84% of all migration in West Africa (Awumbila, 2017; Bartlett, 2015; Ratha & Shaw, 2007). According to the 2010 Population and Housing Census in Ghana, migrants account for about 2.5% of the country's population. Migrants from within West Africa account for 68.3% of Ghana's migrant population (Ghana Statistical Service, 2013). This immense increase in South-South migration not only impacts schooling in host countries but also global efforts to achieve the Sustainable Development Goals (SDGS). Thus, studying out-of-school migrants and the motivations underpinning their choice to stay out of school has broad national and global policy implications.

This study delves into the experiences of migrants in Ghana with the aim of uncovering the factors that prevent them from enrolling in schools. The major question the research seeks to answer is: What are the obstacles keeping migrant children and youth out of school in Ghana? In answering the question, the work tries to distinguish which obstacles are migration related and which ones are not migration related. It also seeks to ascertain whether some groups of migrant children are more prone to being out of school than others. The analysis is based primarily on interviews with migrant children, migrant parents, and school authorities (head teachers and teachers).

LITERATURE REVIEW

Research shows that migrant children and youth across the world face challenges in exercising their rights to education due to their lack of adequate documentation. The requirement that migrants provide documents to prove their age, immunization history, and residency before being admitted into schools often serves as a barrier that limits their access into educational systems (Buckland, 2011; Crush & Tawodzera, 2011; Greenberg, Adams, & Michie, 2016; Heckmann, 2008; Nusche, 2009). In a study of a third of migrants sampled from countries in the Global North, the United Nations Development Programme (UNDP) (2009) found migrants without proper documentation stayed out of school. The research showed that in countries such as Belgium, where education is free and compulsory for citizens, education is not compulsory for children of migrants without the required legal documentation. Further, in Poland the lack of documentation also impacted public funding for education, as children of migrants without proper documentation are not counted by the schools and thus are not included in school population statistics reported to the state. The lack of funding coverage by the state limited the migrants' access to schools. Even in countries that guarantee the right to education for all regardless of legal status, fear of being reported to authorities made migrants without the required authorization reluctant to place their children into the educational system. In countries where education is not entirely free, the inability to pay school fees and other associated costs also served as a barrier that prevented migrants from attending schools (UNDP, 2009).

Schapiro (2009) maintained that children migrating alone are the most disadvantaged when it comes to education. She asserted that such children face barriers to school enrollment that are difficult to overcome. Migrants without the requisite documentation, as well as documented migrants, face challenges to accessing school systems. Crush and Tawodzera (2011) and Buckland (2011) shed more light on the barriers migrant children face, regardless of legal status, when accessing education in host countries. Their research centering on migrants and schooling in South Africa demonstrated how the absence of proper documentation often forced migrant children to stay out of school. The status of migrants had a telling effect on the way they even accessed support within the school system, with undocumented migrants often missing out. These barriers often encourage migrants to stay out of school. In addition to barriers stemming from their migrant status (whether they are unaccompanied by adults, documented, or undocumented) child migrants also face traditional access barriers that impede school access for native-born children in the host country as well, such as the lack of funds to cover fees and other school-related costs (uniforms, books, transportation, feeding). Crush and Tawodzera (2011) and Buckland (2011) point out that, regardless of legal status, migrants face additional challenges in accessing education in their host country. Xenophobic attacks, barriers associated with language, and lack of access to information are some challenges keeping migrants out of school. Additional problems faced by out-of-school migrants can be attributed to policies that are not explicit on how migrants' education should be managed within host states (Buckland, 2011; Crush & Tawodzera, 2011).

Schapiro (2009) further posited, based on evidence from case studies, that many of these challenges are encountered when migrants move to the level of education that is not compulsory and free. She cites the case of migrants without required legal documentation in the United States, who have difficulty accessing college funding from public universities.

For Sabates-Wheeler (2009), the line between migrants without the right documentation and migrants with the required documentation is blurred. For example, issues of language, which many countries fail to address, affect migrants whether they have the necessary documentation or not (Sabates-Wheeler, 2009). Citing research in South Africa, Sabates-Wheeler (2009) posited that even legal migrants are sometimes denied school access as school authorities deem their documents insufficient to meet admission requirements. Although in such cases migrants have a right to seek legal action, their lack of awareness and the inaccessibility of the legal system prevents them from doing so (Sabates-Wheeler, 2009).

Research suggests school access for migrants also depends upon the economic standing of the country of destination. Migrants who move to the richer countries in the Global North are more likely to have better entry into schools than those migrating to countries in the Global South. Furthermore, migrants from the Global South who migrate to the Global North on temporary visas have problems gaining access to schools. Other factors that account for the high rate of out-of-school migrants include the nature of work their parents or other adult caregivers are engaged in, usually poor and hazardous working conditions, as well as the segregation within the sociocultural environment (Green, 2003; Schapiro, 2009; Stevenson & Beck, 2017). According to Stevenson and Beck (2017), educational disadvantage among children of migrant farm workers in the United States remains pronounced. They cite dropout rates among children of the migrant farmworkers as the highest among any group in the country. In their research focused on a summer literacy program for intermediate and middle-level children of migrant farmworkers, Stevenson and Beck (2017) noted that, despite the dangerous nature of the agriculture jobs that migrant parents and children are involved in, these jobs are poor paying. The need to make ends meet forced migrant children to join parents on the farm fields as a financial necessity to augment family resources, distracting their time and attention from schoolwork.

According to Christianakis (2010), despite concerted efforts aimed at getting Roma migrants into schools in many European countries, the problem persists. Many Roma parents decide against sending their children to schools because they deem the school curricula to be unimportant and irrelevant to problems in their everyday life. In her work on Roma children in Greece, Christianakis (2010) points out the role of cultural assimilation in serving as a barrier that keeps many Roma migrants from enrolling in school. By distancing themselves from people outside the Roma ethnic group, they avoid all institutions that might create avenues for integration, including schools.

The circular, temporary, and repetitive nature of migration for some migrant workers serves as another distinctive barrier to the education of their children. This is most visible in the case of children who are passive movers accompanying seasonal working parents on their migration journeys. The lack of economic opportunities may push parents to migrate into areas where they can be engaged in meaningful economic activity. This may affect their desire to enroll their children in schools. Rigid school admission policies may also serve as disincentives for these children, as frequent relocation with parents may not be in alignment with formal school rules. Migrants without the requisite documentation in South Africa, according to Sabates-Wheeler (2009), were denied access because they were unable to produce the required residency permits and had no right to appeal such treatment. This may in some cases prevent them from enrolling in the first place or, for those who are already enrolled, force them to drop out (Burra, 1995).

The limited literature on South-South migration compared to North-South migration points to the need for more research on migration and education among Global South nations. This research gap is especially acute with respect to intra-African migration, as most of the work on migration and education focuses on South Africa. Additionally, the existing literature employs a limited definition of access to education. For instance, most of the research focuses on migrants who drop out of school. There is little research that examines the factors preventing them from enrolling in the first place.

DEFINITION OF TERMS

The definition of out-of-school children differs across research. The various definitions broadly include children who are not enrolled in school, children who are in school but are not learning, and children who have dropped out of school. This study defines out-of-school migrants as children and youth between the ages of 6 and 21 who are either not enrolled in, or have dropped out before completing, basic education. Although education is compulsory in Ghana from ages 4 to 14, this study focused on migrant children from age 6 to 21, as it considered children of age 6 and above old enough to articulate their views and thus be active voices in the research. The extension above 14 years allowed for the experiences of older children outside of the official age group to be captured. Adjusting the definition allows for the many migrants who fall out of the age limitation of UNESCO to be included. This research focuses on basic education in Ghana, which encompasses kindergarten, primary school, and junior high school.

METHODOLOGY

The study that is the subject of this chapter adopted a qualitative research approach aimed at collecting rich data. The researcher employed an interpretive approach to arrive at the research conclusions. Interpretivism involves arriving at an understanding of the social space by analyzing the worldview of the target group. It assumes that the interpretation social actors give to events is important in constructing their reality (Guba & Lincoln, 1994). Accordingly, this research constructed knowledge by focusing on the perceptions of migrant children, migrant parents, and school authorities, as well as the underlying motivation for migrant children and youth to stay out of school.

A purposive sampling technique was complemented by snowballing with the target population usually belonging to networks relevant to the work. This was important in helping facilitate access to the target group. The study utilized semi-structured interviews. This afforded the participants the flexibility to express their views while being guided by the overarching aim of the research. Interviews were conducted with migrant children and parents. Migrant children and parents interviewed did not constitute households; the migrant children and parents interviewed were not from matching families. In total, the researcher interviewed 40 migrant children and youth (30 males and 10 females) and 20 parents (12 males and 8 females). The researcher also interviewed 40 school heads and teachers (20 males and 20 females). The number of interviews was determined when each sample population reached its point of saturation.

To ensure anonymity and confidentiality, all names used in this chapter to represent participants are pseudonyms. Migrants interviewed, whether children or parents, were either unemployed or employed within low-level paying jobs. All participants interviewed had migrated to Ghana for at least three months. All interviews were conducted by the author as the primary researcher. Interviews took place during three field trips to Accra, Ghana: from May to July 2015, September to November 2016, and July to October 2017. All migrants interviewed lived within Accra, the capital of Ghana. Accra is in a region that hosts the largest number of non-Ghanaian population (58.4%) (Ghana Statistical Service, 2013).

Thematic analysis was adopted in the analysis of the data through the identification of common themes that emerged during the interviews. All interviews were transcribed; codes were generated from these transcripts and subsequently drawn into thematic categories. Thematic analysis provided the research with the flexibility that was needed by drawing patterns from interviews regardless of how complex or simple they were. Adopting thematic analysis served as a foundation for this qualitative work. The thematic analysis of the data was guided by Braun and Clarke's (2006) guide regarding the utilization of the approach; thus, themes that did not occur often and those that were not salient to the work were discarded (Tables 2.1 and 2.2).

FINDINGS

Lack of Awareness of Fee-Free Education at the Basic Level

Existing research shows that parental decisions not to enroll migrant children into schools often stem from lack of information about the workings of educational systems in host countries. The limited information available

Table 2.1   Country of origin of out-of-school migrants

Country	Frequency	Percent (%)
Benin	1	2.5
Burkina Faso	2	5.0
Ivory Coast	3	7.5
Mali	4	10.0
Niger	21	52.5
Nigeria	7	17.5
Togo	2	5.0
Total	40	100.0

Compiled from the fieldwork

Table 2.2 Country of origin of parents with out-of-school children

Country	Frequency	Percent (%)
Guinea	1	5.0
Mali	3	15.0
Niger	12	60.0
Nigeria	3	15.0
Togo	1	5.0
Total	20	100.0

Compiled from the fieldwork

to migrant parents undermines their ability to maximize educational opportunities that exist outside their countries of origin (Platform for International Cooperation on Undocumented Migrants [PICUM], 2012; Organization for Economic Co-operation Development [OECD], 2016; United Nations International Children's Emergency Fund [UNICEF], 2017). Nusche (2009) thus emphasized the importance of providing migrant parents with information on the educational system that will aid them in making good choices.

This research on Ghana confirms that ignorance on the part of migrant parents and children is a factor contributing to their failure to enroll in schools. Most migrant parents whose children were not in school knew nothing about the educational system and the support available at the basic level of education in Ghana, which is made up of two years of kindergarten, six years of primary education, and three years of junior high school. For instance, these migrants were not aware of the fee-free public school education offered at the basic level in Ghana. They also did not understand the repercussions of not sending their children to school in Ghana, where schooling is compulsory for all children. The shorter the duration of stay in the country, the more likely the migrant was to cite lack of information on the educational system as a cause for not sending their children to school.

Sadat, a migrant parent from Mali stated:

We have been in this country for close to a year. I have a wife and two children. I don't think about education in this country. I am not aware of any of the laws that govern education in Ghana. I am not aware that education is free at the basic level. This is new to me. I will try and verify what you said and take my children to school provided it is true that education at the basic level is free.

Another participant, Dassa, said, "No one has told us anything about education since we came to Ghana. We came here to make a living. We are unaware education is free at the basic level."

Although the lack of information was the most common reason migrant parents and migrant children gave for not enrolling in school, probing further showed deeper and unexplored stories behind their present circumstances. This was confirmed by the many migrants who had never tried enrolling in schools. One Nigerian parent, Abu, said, "I have not even made the attempt of sending him to school. I have never been approached by any official about going to school."

Temporary Migration as a Barrier to Education Access

Another common reason cited by migrant parents whose children were out of school was their intention not to stay permanently in Ghana. Although in some cases such migrants had stayed for more than five years, they insisted that their stay was temporary and that, therefore, they could not send their children to school.

Beyond the expressed intention to stay in Ghana for a short period lay other factors that kept the children of these migrants out of school. A Nigerian migrant parent, Randa, explained:

We are here primarily to seek economic advancement. We did not migrate with all our children as those left at home are older and live on their own. We arrived two years ago. That explains how come the children are not in school. We didn't come here to stay so our children will not go to school. That's not part of our plans of coming to Ghana. We came here because of poverty.

The interview with Mustapha Ibrahim echoed this point:

I am fourteen years. I come from Niger. I have been in Ghana for only four months. I do not go to school. I am out of school because my father said we are not going to stay here for the whole schooling period. He therefore cannot take me to school. He said we have our own system of schooling back home, i.e. our own style of writing and learning, so he will send me to school when we go back home.

The research revealed that most people who cited their short stay as a reason for their plight had other underlying reasons. The likelihood of a migrant child staying out of school also depended on factors such as the values and beliefs of parents, the age of children at the time of immigration, the nature of migration, the economic position of the family, and the social support received. The reasons enumerated for migrants' nonattendance of school often did not act in isolation but were inextricably intertwined.

Age at Immigration

Several studies attest to the role that school-level factors (pupil–teacher relationship, classroom management, teacher instructional behavior, ability grouping, tracking, diversity, etc.) play in impeding the progress of immigrant students in school (Buckland, 2011; Crush & Tawodzera, 2011; Heckmann, 2008; Nusche, 2009; UNICEF, 2005). Interviews with school authorities showed the correlation between age at immigration and completion of basic school in Ghana. These interviews exposed that migrants who moved into Ghana at older ages were more prone to dropping out of school than migrants who migrated to Ghana at younger ages, who adjusted better to challenges in school, most notably language. School authorities cited examples of migrants who entered school at older ages and struggled to adjust to the school system, subsequently dropping out. Challenges associated with integration for migrants who entered at older ages often had to do with their placement in lower-than-expected classes. Teachers and head teachers gave accounts of how the placement of older migrants in classes with relatively younger classmates came with its own challenges (i.e. bullying, teasing, loneliness). These factors eventually pushed migrants out of school. Olivia, a teacher at the Shie Primary and Junior High School, posited:

> The biggest challenge we have with those who are not from Ghana is usually associated with the placement. Most of the people I have encountered come to Ghana when they are old. It is always difficult finding the right classes for them. The age gap between them and the class is sometimes more than four to five years. Teaching and managing them becomes very difficult and they eventually drop out of school even before we write the final exams.

Although most of the literature on age at the time of immigration and entering school is based on research conducted in the Global North (Basu, 2016; Beck, Corak, & Tienda, 2012; Corak, 2011; Goldner & Epstein, 2014), these studies showing a correlation between older age at the time of immigration and school noncompletion are consistent with the findings of this study of conditions in Ghana, notwithstanding differences characterizing the South-South migration setting. There is evidence that with respect to intra-West African migration the age of children at the time of immigration has a similarly negative impact on school completion. The age of immigration does not act in isolation but rather combines with other factors, such as language barriers and grade-level placement, among others.

Cultural/Religious Values

There is extensive research on the linkage between immigrants, schools, religion, and culture. Most of this work focuses on how religion and the sociocultural values of immigrants might make them likely candidates for dropping out of school (Adelman & Taylor, 2015; Greenfield, 2006; Heckmann, 2008; OECD, 2015). Data from this work further confirms these studies that demonstrate sociocultural values can serve as a barrier to education (Adelman & Taylor, 2015; Greenfield, 2006; Heckmann, 2008; OECD, 2015). Findings from this study show religion and culture prevent West African immigrants in Ghana from enrolling in schools. Unlike previous research that assigns religion and culture as factors that may force one to quit school (Adelman & Taylor, 2015; Greenfield, 2006; Heckmann, 2008; OECD, 2015), in Ghana religion and sociocultural values prevented immigrants from enrolling in schools in the first place. In some instances, parents and children placed little value on schooling as a vehicle for achieving their goals and for the future. Parents and children cited the incompatibility of schooling with their beliefs and values, and some migrants perceived schooling as an actual threat to their culture, value systems, and norms. These migrants had conflicting views on the advantages of education. The research revealed these migrants were mostly from Niger. These were migrants who had been out of school in their countries of origin even before arriving in Ghana. During the interviews these migrants frequently referred to formal education as a "western concept" that was at variance with their beliefs. Formal education was described as foreign. Per the narrations of the migrants, the value and norms that guided their behavior in the societies they were coming from placed little value on formal education. More premium was given to learning the Quran. Issah Balkas of Niger explained:

> For us we usually do not take our children to school apart from taking them to Madrassa [Qur'anic or Arabic school] to be able to read the Quran and write in Arabic. When a child is born, two or three years he or she is given to an alpha [Mallam] to start teaching him or her how to read the Quran. When the child is about six or seven he or she is assigned some work to do. This could either be commercial or domestic. In the case of a boy, he is asked to start herding goats, sheep, cattle, and camels. And in the case of a female, she is assigned domestic chores until puberty when she gets a husband. That is the way we do things.

He further added:

> We do not agree with western education. It clashes with our culture and traditional values. We think western education will undermine our cultural values. Many examples abound of people who have sent their children to school in towns and cities only to return to disrespect our culture. This makes us careful in sending our children to school. We prefer they go to Madrassa where we know they will be safe and learn what is important for us.

Agali, a Nigerien migrant, also confirmed:

> Besides Arabic, we do not do any kind of education. This has been there since our great grandparents. It has been there from generation to generation that we do not go to school. Our primary concern when it comes to education is to be able to read the Quran. That is all. Even in Niger I was not going to school.

When asked whether his short duration of stay (four months) had something to do with his inability to go to school, he retorted strongly, "I told you before, for us we do not go to school."

This position taken by migrant parents brings to the fore the portrayal of formal education as the incontrovertible good by which knowledge can be transmitted. It also shows the limited sense in which the processes of learning are defined, excluding any event that happens outside the confines of the classroom. The arguments put forth by migrants for not going to school only reinforce existing debates between formal and informal education. For this, Strauss (1984) advises a shift in focus on the formal or informal education debate. Rather there should be emphasis on the cognitive process rather than the categorization of the learning processes.

Gender Norms and Values

Gender is a critical feature of migratory movements in West Africa, as there has been a marked increase in the number of women moving across the region (Adepoju, 2008). The vulnerability levels fluctuate based on the roles and status accorded women by society. Children involved in migration within the West African region are prone to vulnerabilities that vary along gender lines (Regional Mixed Migration Secretariat [RMMS], 2017). Substantial gains have been made over the past 20 years with respect to female education in Ghana and, by extension, sub-Saharan Africa. That notwithstanding, research suggests the gender gap in education is most pronounced in sub-Saharan Africa. These educational discrepancies against women have hinged on the beliefs and attitudes of societies in Africa (Dube, 2015). These gender norms place girls' domestic contribution to the home above their personal education. Some migrants interviewed claimed to be coming from settings that frowned on educating their female children. This was the practice in their societies of origin, and they replicated it in their new country of residence. Milhas Hassan, a migrant parent, stated:

> Back home in Niger my daughter [pointing to her daughter] was not going to school. I fear that when I take her to school and she mixes with the opposite sex when she is of age, something bad could happen and bring shame to me and the entire family. You know women are not supposed to be mixed with boys so she can be safe. Because of that I prevent her from going to school. She has two other brothers who have completed basic education.

Sixteen-year-old Fatou also added:

> I have not been in Ghana for long. It has been close to five months. I am here with my husband to look for better opportunities. I got married three years ago. I got betrothed to my husband when I was 10 years and when I turned 13 my father married me off. I was never in school in Niger. For us, it is only boys who sometimes go to school. We stay at home, do the house chores, and keep the home.

This confirms the claim by Chavatzia, Engel, and Hastedt (2016) that immigrant girls comprise the most vulnerable group least likely to be enrolled in school. The prominence of gender norms and values in the research findings, and the dearth in research dedicated to the gendered aspects of migration and education within the Ghanaian context, is noteworthy, especially in the current global and local scheme of things where there is increased focus on getting all educated, including the most vulnerable. These findings have implications on the agenda for gender equity in education. This also derails the progress being made to achieve gender equality as mentioned in the SDGs and all the other major international frameworks.

Economic Reasons

Migrants also cited cost and lack of affordability as a reason for keeping their children out of school in Ghana. Migrants who cited economic reasons to explain their inability to enroll children in schools fell into two main groups. The first group were those who had at one point accessed schools in Ghana but could not sustain funding because of the costs involved and, thus, had to drop out. The second group were those who cited their struggles in making ends meet as the reason for not enrolling children into Ghanaian schools in the first place. The second category of migrant children was made up of those who were enrolled in school prior to migrating but stayed out of school after migrating due to economic reasons. As one migrant parent, Rahima, explained:

> I am Nigerian. I have been in Ghana for over fifteen years. I have four children. Two are in school and the other two are not in school. Those who are not in school are 17 years and 14 years respectively. They were initially in school but dropped out because I could not finance the education of all of them. They were older and had been in school for a while so they had to give way so the younger ones would also have their turn. Life is difficult for us here as we struggle to even feed ourselves.

Teachers and head teachers confirmed how many migrants dropped out of school due to economic challenges. They spoke more about the unaccompanied migrant children as those who often dropped out of school. According to one teacher:

I had one guy who was a Nigerian. He was working and schooling at the same time. Initially he was a good boy. He was repeated. He disagreed and stopped school. He is now in town. He was initially a good student, spoke good English but has a tonation. The work took away his attention. He didn't write all his exams.

Unaccompanied Child Migrants

Much of the existing research on migration regards children as passive movers who only move in reaction to their parents' decisions to migrate. This idea of the child as a passive mover has been critiqued by Hashim (2004) and Whitehead, Hashim, and Iversen (2007) as a western concept that does not apply in other settings, especially West Africa. Unaccompanied child migration is common in Africa (Thorsen & Hashim, 2011). According to research done in the European Union member countries, unaccompanied children are one of the most vulnerable groups of children during migration (Eurochild, 2016). "Out-of-school immigrant youth are more likely to be living away from their parents than are in-school immigrant youth in every age group" (Hill & Hayes, 2007, p. 37).

According to the interviews conducted in this study, the reasons for migrating ranged from migrating in search of family members who had migrated earlier to migrating in search of better job opportunities. The quest to survive on their own took precedence over any other desire, as the safety net provided by family in their countries of origin was no longer available. Engaging in economic activity no longer became a matter of choice but a matter of survival. Thus, schooling was perceived by migrants as interfering with their quest to work and earn a living to survive.

As Boateng, a head teacher, said:

These migrants come into the country alone in search of better economic opportunities or to find a kinsman who had travelled earlier. They also on many occasions migrate to work as house helps. Due to the lack of support from either parents or family, they therefore have to work to survive, making it difficult for them to go to school or stay in school.

Ibu, a migrant child from Nigeria, explained:

I have been in Ghana for a while. I joined some people from my town. I am alone in Ghana and work at a car garage. I am learning to be a mechanic. The little money I get from the job is what I live on. It will be difficult for me to stop the job and continue school since in my country I used to go to school. In Ghana, it is impossible for me to go to school. I have no one here as I explained to you earlier.

The data from the field also revealed that, although unaccompanied child migrants traveled independently of any third party, the nature of kinship and social network ties that exist in West Africa often means that migrant children traveling alone nevertheless have networks of support on which they can rely. These findings reinforce similar conclusions drawn from previous research done in the area (Adepoju, 2008; Alber, Häberlein, & Martin, 2010; Thorsen & Hashim, 2011). The research uncovered that the out-of-school migrants were those without the support of kinsmen and social network. The unaccompanied migrant without network and social support was therefore more prone to stay out of school than those unaccompanied migrants who found support from kinsmen in their countries of present stay.

Begging Child Migrants

Migration functions as an economic coping or survival strategy for many families. Moreover, children are critical participants in the execution of this strategy. This often leaves children exposed to the ills associated with the decision to migrate, including the necessity to engage in street begging. The research revealed that migrant children engaged in begging in Ghana tend to fall into two categories. One group was comprised of children who had never been to school—whether in their countries of origin, in Ghana, or in another host country. These were mostly children from Mali and Niger who were found on the major streets of Accra in the company of parents and other siblings. Through the interviews, these migrant families described their motivation for coming to Ghana as a search for a better life and improved economic prospects. Many of these migrants were escaping drought conditions in their countries of origin. They placed no value on formal education and were also not open to new ideas. The children were used as instruments in soliciting for alms, as most parents perceived that people were more inclined to give to children than to adults. "It is easier for people to pity children and give them something than older people," Abala, a 17-year-old migrant, explained. Nigerien migrant parent Sekou said:

Since we have no work doing in Ghana we all beg. Our children also do beg. People are usually kind to the children. That's how come we sometimes sit back and allow them to beg. Proceeds from the begging is what we use to survive in Ghana. Life back home was very challenging. We therefore decided to come to Ghana to beg. We had been informed by our tribesmen who had migrated to Ghana earlier that it was better to be here. We used to rear cattle and raise other animals back home. We had severe drought that destroyed our farming. Our children never go to school.

Fati, a migrant child, explained:

My sister and I do beg for our parents. I do not know about western education. We have never been to such schools before. I prefer to live in Niger because that is my home country and have more friends there. We are here just for better living conditions.

Buckland (2011) asserted the importance of formal institutional nodes and social network nodes in influencing decisions taken by migrants. The lack of formal institutional support for migrants in Ghana meant they were more inclined to be influenced primarily by the social network nodes to which they belonged. These groups of migrants, who the researcher observed, stayed within very close-knit kin networks with other migrants from the same culture and, thus, were more likely to be impacted by the negative school-going habits of fellow kinsmen caught in the out-of-school-going net.

The second group of children found to be engaged in street begging were migrants who accompanied elderly or visually impaired parents or guardians. Migrant children in this context served as guides. These migrant children were not only accountable for their lives but the lives of the elderly who also depended on them. The interviews revealed that many of these children previously attended school in their countries of origin but were forced to abandon school in order to accompany their guardians or parents. This group of migrants were mostly found around the major mosques in Accra. These mostly Muslim migrants preferred the mosques as they believed almsgiving was an important part of the Islamic faith. Nigerien migrant parent, Moussah Aboubakar, explained:

As you can see I am old and my son is the one you see [pointing to his son of about 8 years]. He helps me on daily basis. He runs errands for me. That was why I brought him to Ghana. He was going to school back home in Niger. He was doing both the Arabic and the French schools.

Yaro, a ten-year-old Nigerien migrant, also explained:

> I was born in Niger. It has been over one year since we came to Ghana. I used to attend school in Niger but because my father is a beggar and blind, I am the only one who takes care of him. I have other siblings. They are at Sowtuom. They are there with my mother. They attend school. We all cannot be in school so I sacrifice to take my dad around. I am the eldest child. I cannot really say anything about school in Niger.

The father of Yaro (who is visually impaired) confirmed the reason behind Yaro's inability to attend school:

> It's true that school is good. I agree with you, but someone also must sacrifice. And once he is the eldest he is the one who sacrifices. As for Arabic school he does attend, but when it comes to secular education he doesn't. Through the begging I do, I may buy a sewing machine so he can learn a trade so he can fend for himself. I came to Ghana for the tranquility.

This group of migrant children was usually affected by the lack of family or network that allowed other family members to run errands and take care of the elderly or the disabled. The lack of family support in their new country of residence meant that their very survival depended only on what they did to survive.

Tahiru, a child migrant, narrated:

> Back home I used to go to school. We had many people home to take care of my grandfather. In Ghana, I am only here with him, and as you can see I am all he has. I cannot go to school and leave him behind. He cannot do anything on his own.

Seasonal Migration as a Barrier to Enrollment into Schools

The educational disadvantages confronting children who travel with parents engaged in seasonal migration are enormous. The literature on barriers to school access confronting these children is extensive (Deep, 2017; Hadley, 2010; Mosse et al., 2002; Smita, 2008). Deep (2017) further argued that the nature of the migration makes it difficult to account for such children, and they are therefore effortlessly left out of school. The temporary nature of seasonal migration easily leads to a break in attendance of school. Abala, a 17-year-old migrant from Niger, stated:

> I have been in Ghana with my father for about five months. This is not the first time we have come to Ghana. We do come from time to time. Since I started travelling with my father, I have had to stop school in my home country. When we come we don't stay for long. We have a farm back home we work on. When the farming season is over, we always come to Ghana. We have been doing this for about four years. When we come to Ghana we move from one town to the other trying to find something to do. We sometimes beg, help people in the market, and anything that will give us some money to take back home.

Tau, a Nigerian child migrant, explained how the temporary nature of migrating with the father has led to a break in school-going habits:

> We kept moving all the time with my family. It has been three years now since I went to school. The last time I went to school was in Nigeria. I was about two years short of completing the basic school. I have stayed out of school for three years and don't know where to start from after all these years. I think it is better I continue with the shop assistant job I am doing other than going back to school.

The nature and type of migration also affected the migrant child's schooling. Migrants who kept moving from one country to another for relatively short intervals were also kept out of school. Samba, a migrant parent from Mali, explained:

> This is the third country I have been to in the past two years. I am originally from Mali. Before coming to Ghana, I lived in Togo and Burkina Faso. I came directly from Togo to Ghana. I didn't stay for more than six months in either Togo or Burkina Faso. I have been migrating with my family in search of better opportunities. My children are two (boy and girl). They were all in school in Mali till we decided to migrate in search of a better standard of living two years back. I have not been able to send them to school because we have barely settled in any country since we started migrating. I know the importance of education and will definitely send them back to school if we finally get to settle in Ghana.

Bayo, a migrant child from Togo, also explained:

I am in Ghana with my parents. We came to Ghana two years ago from our hometown Togo. I don't live with them now. In Accra, I am on my own. My parents are at Aflao. Since we arrived in Ghana, we have been moving to several towns as we try to find what will work best for us. I had to leave the Volta region to Accra in search of a better job. In Togo, I used to help my parents in a shop. I used to attend a French school in Togo and was in class six. In Ghana, we keep moving from one place to the other. This is making it difficult for me to enroll in a school. I am keen on going to school, and once I get to find a permanent home in Accra, I will go to school.

Decision-Making and Education

Migration decisions taken by individuals are not done in isolation but in and between different groups of people. International migration is not only affected by extraneous elements but reinforced by relations between movers and stayers (Faist, 1997). The research on Ghana shows that the perceived economic benefits of migration were always prioritized at the expense of children's education. The effect of migration on the education of the migrant child was hardly, if ever, considered when deciding to migrate. The decision of whether to migrate or not was made on behalf of the migrant child by the parents and guardians. Most migrants interviewed explained that they had no choice other than migrating. With most migrants coming from places where society was organized on kinship ties, individual freedoms were curtailed through social groups in the form of conformity to societal norms. Child migrants in many cases had been socialized to accept the responsibilities they had to undertake during migration and offered little resistance, even when it affected their chances of attending school. Migrant children in many of the interviews agreed with their parents or guardians when it came to their decision not to send them to school.

CONCLUSION

The findings of this research show that factors that influence and determine whether migrant children are in or out of school are multifaceted. Migrant children who are outside the school system in Ghana do not constitute a monolithic group and, therefore, efforts aimed at assuaging their plight should be targeted, taking into consideration the disparate variables affecting their situation. The results of interviews conducted revealed that none of the migrant children in this study who were out of school had been denied access based on their legal status. The existing literature is awash with findings showing that migrants without the necessary documentation, especially in countries in the Global North, have difficulty accessing schools (Buckland, 2011; Crush & Tawodzera, 2011; Nusche, 2009; PICUM, 2012). However, this research on Ghana reveals that, in the absence of a clear policy direction to guide migrant education, legal status and documentation appear to have a lesser, if any, impact on enrollment.

The existing literature on out-of-school migrants is heavily centered on those who drop out. However, the research undertaken in Ghana reveals that the prevalence of out-of-school migrants is more likely the result of decisions not to enroll in schools. The international migrant child's decision not to go to school in Ghana is less caused by school-level issues. This finding is a major contrast to work done by Makarova and Herzog (2013) on the hidden reasons why migrants stay out of school. Their work concluded that school-level factors have more prognostic ability in explaining why immigrants may choose to stay away from school than social background, a position this research sways from.

A survey of previous research on migrant education suggests that scholarship treats unaccompanied migrants as a monolithic group. This project speaks to the obvious negative implications of the strategy associated with previous scholarship by identifying several subgroups within the larger body of unaccompanied migrants. The unaccompanied child migrant without network support remains the most prone of the child migrants to be out of school. There are different constructions of what education means to parents and children engaged in intra-regional migration in Ghana. The meaning of education for parents and migrant children goes beyond the formal school to include Islamic education, household roles, as well as other forms of economic activity. As argued by Hashim and Thorsen (2011), education has thus become a socialization process regardless of whether it happens at home or outside the home.

Education is an investment that has opportunity costs beyond the direct costs involved. Thus, where the decision to invest in children's education comes with the cost of not being able to have children contribute economically (begging, working, etc.), migrant parents and children often decide otherwise. The decision not to enroll in school is made, as doing otherwise undermines the underlying reason for migrating in the first place.

REFERENCES

Adelman, S., & Taylor, L. (2015). Immigrant children and youth in the USA: Facilitating equity of opportunity at school. *Education Sciences, 5*(4), 323–344.

Adepoju, A. (2008). *Migration in sub-Saharan Africa*. Uppsala, Sweden: Nordiska Afrikainstitutet.

Alber, E., Häberlein, T., & Martin, J. (2010). Changing webs of kinship: Spotlights on West Africa. *Africa Spectrum, 45*(3), 43–67.

Awumbila, M. (2017). *Drivers of migration and urbanization in Africa: Key trends and issues*. New York, NY: United Nations.

Bartlett, L. (2015). *Access and quality of education for international migrant children*. Paris, France: United Nations Educational, Scientific, and Cultural Organization (UNESCO).

Basu, S. (2016). *Age-of-arrival effects on the education of immigrant children: A sibling study*. New York, NY: Western Economic Association International Conference.

Beck, A., Corak, M., & Tienda, M. (2012). Age at immigration and the adult attainments of child migrants to the United States. *Annals of The American Academy of Political and Social Science, 643*(1), 134–159. Retrieved November 12, 2017, from https://ncbi.nlm.nih.gov/pmc/articles/pmc3478675

Braun, V., & Clarke, V. (2006). Using thematic analysis in psychology. *Qualitative Research in Psychology, 3*(2), 77–101.

Buckland, S. (2011). *Lost in transition: The barriers to educational access for school-age Zimbabwe migrant children in South Africa and the influences of institutional and social networks on overcoming them* (Doctoral thesis). Retrieved February 19, 2017, from http://sro.sussex.ac.uk/id/eprint/7522/1/Buckland%2C_Stephanie.pdf

Burra, N. (1995). *Born to work. Child labour in India*. New Delhi, India: Oxford University Press.

Chavatzia, T., Engel, L., & Hastedt, D. (2016). *Where are the immigrant girls?* Amsterdam, Netherlands: The International Association for the Evaluation of Educational Achievement.

Christianakis, M. (2010). Lessons for life: Roma children, communal practices, and the global marketplace. *Perspectives on Urban Education, 8*(1), 11–18.

Corak, M. (2011). *Age at immigration and the education outcomes of children*. Ottawa, Canada: Institute for the Study of Labor (IZA).

Crush, J., & Tawodzera, G. (2011). *Right to the classroom: Educational barriers for Zimbabweans in South Africa*. Cape Town, South Africa: Southern African Migration Programme (SAMP).

Deep, S. (2017). Seasonal migration and exclusion of children in school education. *International Journal of Advanced Educational Research, 2*(4), 1–7.

Dube, T. (2015). Gender disparities in educational enrollment and attainment in sub-Saharan Africa. *Journal of Educational and Social Research, 5*(3), 279–284. Retrieved November 12, 2017, from https://papers.ssrn.com/sol3/delivery.cfm/ssrn_id2656544_code1795413.pdf?abstractid=2656544&mirid=1

Eurochild. (2016). *Turning the tide for children on the move.* Brussels, Belgium: Author.

Faist, T. (1997). The crucial meso-level. In T. Hammar, G. Brochmann, K. Tamas, & T. Faist (Eds.), *International migration, immobility and development* (pp. 187–217). Oxford, UK: Berg.

Ghana Statistical Service. (2013). *The 2010 population and housing census: National analytical report.* Accra, Ghana: Author.

Goldner, S. C., & Epstein, G. S. (2014). Age at immigration and high school dropouts. *IZA Journal of Migration, 3*(1), 19. Retrieved November, 12, 2017, from https://link.springer.com/article/10.1186/s40176-014-0019-2

Green, P. (2003). The undocumented: Educating the children of migrant workers in America. *Bilingual Research Journal, 27*(1), 51–71.

Greenberg, E., Adams, G., & Michie, M. (2016). *Barriers to preschool participation for low-income children of immigrants in Silicon Valley: Part II.* Washington, DC: Urban Institute.

Greenfield, P. M. (2006). Applying developmental psychology to bridge cultures in the classroom. In S. I. Donaldson, D. E. Berger, & K. Pezdek (Eds.), *Applied psychology: New frontiers and rewarding careers* (pp. 135–152). Mahwah, NJ: Lawrence Erlbaum Associates.

Guba, E. G., & Lincoln, Y. S. (1994). Competing paradigms in qualitative research. In N. K. Denzin & S. Lincoln (Eds.), *Handbook of qualitative research* (pp. 105–117). Thousand Oaks, CA: Sage.

Hadley, S. (2010). *Seasonality and access to education: The case of primary education in sub-Saharan Africa.* Brighton, UK: University of Sussex, Consortium for Research into Educational Access Transition and Equity (CREATE).

Hashim, I. (2004). *Working with working children: Child labour and the barriers to education in rural northeastern Ghana.* Brighton, UK: University of Sussex.

Hashim, I., & Thorsen, D. (2011). *Child migration in Africa.* New York, NY: Zed Books.

Heckmann, F. (2008). *Education and the integration of migrants challenges for European education systems arising from immigration and strategies for the successful integration of migrant children in European schools and societies.* Bamberg, Germany: European Forum for Migration Studies.

Hill, L., & Hayes, J. (2007). *Out-of-school immigrant youth.* San Francisco, CA: Public Policy Institute of California.

Majgaard, K., & Mingat, A. (2013). *Education in sub-Saharan Africa. A comparative analysis.* Washington, DC: International Bank for Reconstruction and Development/The World Bank.

Makarova, E., & Herzog, W. (2013). Hidden school dropout among immigrant students: A cross-sectional study. *Intercultural Education, 24*(6), 559–572. Retrieved November 12, 2017, from http://tandfonline.com/doi/full/10.10 80/14675986.2013.867603

Mosse, D., Gupta, S., Mehta, M., Shah, V., Rees, J., & Team, K. P. (2002). Brokered livelihoods: Debt, labour migration and development in tribal western India. *The Journal of Development Studies, 38*(5), 59–88.

Nusche, D. (2009). *What works in migrant education? A review of evidence and policy options.* Paris, France: Organisation for Economic Co-operation and Development.

Organisation for Economic Co-operation and Development (OECD). (2015). *Helping immigrant students to succeed at school and beyond.* Paris, France: Author.

Organisation for Economic Co-operation and Development (OECD). (2016). *Migration integrating refugees and other migrants into education and training.* Paris, France: Author.

Platform for International Cooperation on Undocumented Migrants (PICUM). (2012). *Undocumented children: Barriers to accessing social rights in Europe.* Brussels, Belgium: Author.

Ratha, D., & Shaw, W. (2007). *South-South migration and remittances.* Washington, DC: World Bank.

Regional Mixed Migration Secretariat (RMMS). (2017). *Mixed migration in West Africa data: routes and vulnerabilities of people on the move.* Copenhagen, Denmark: Danish Refugee Council, Regional Mixed Migration Secretariat.

Sabates-Wheeler, R. (2009). *The impact of irregular status on human development outcomes for migrants.* New York, NY: United Nations Development Programme.

Schapiro, K. (2009). *Migration and educational outcomes of children.* New York, NY: United Nations Development Programme.

Smita, S. (2008). *Distress seasonal migration and its impact on children's education.* Retrieved November 12, 2017, from http://sro.sussex.ac.uk/1869

Stevenson, A. D., & Beck, S. A. (2017). Migrant students' emergent conscientization through critical, socioculturally responsive literacy pedagogy. *Journal of Literacy Research, 49*(2), 240–272. Retrieved June 30, 2018, from http:// journals.sagepub.com/doi/abs/10.1177/1086296x16683418

Strauss, C. (1984). Beyond 'formal' versus 'informal' education: Uses of psychological theory in anthropological research. *Ethos, 12*(3), 195–222.

Thorsen, D., & Hashim, I. M. (2011). *Child migration in Africa.* Uppsala, Sweden: Zed Books.

United Nations Conference on Trade and Development (UNCTAD). (2017). *Economic development in Africa report 2018. Migration for structural transformation.* New York, NY: United Nations.

United Nations Development Programme (UNDP). (2009). *Human development report 2009. Overcoming barriers: Human mobility and development.* New York, NY: Author.

United Nations Educational, Scientific and Cultural Organization (UNESCO). (2010). *Education for all global monitoring report: Reaching the marginalized.* Oxford, UK: Oxford University Press.

United Nations Educational, Scientific and Cultural Organization Institute for Statistics (UIS). (2017). *More than one-half of children and adolescents are not learning worldwide.* Montreal, Canada: Author.

United Nations Educational, Scientific and Cultural Organization Institute for Statistics (UIS) & Global Education Monitoring Report (GEMR). (2016). *Leaving no one behind: How far on the way to universal primary and secondary education?* Montreal, Canada and Paris, France: Author.

United Nations International Children's Emergency Fund (UNICEF). (2005). *The rights of all children in the context of international migration.* New York, NY: Author.

United Nations International Children's Emergency Fund (UNICEF). (2017). *Education uprooted: For every migrant, refugee and displaced child, education.* New York, NY: Author.

Whitehead, A., Hashim, I. M., & Iversen, V. (2007). *Child migration, child agency and intergenerational relations in Africa and South Asia.* Retrieved November 12, 2017, from https://www.researchgate.net/publication/237336827_Child_Migration_Child_Agency_and_Intergenerational_Relations_in_Africa_and_South_Asia_1

Irregular Migration as Survival Strategy: Narratives from Youth in Urban Nigeria

Lanre Olusegun Ikuteyijo

Background to the Study

The phrase "giant of Africa" is associated with Nigeria due to its large population—which constitutes one-sixth of the continent's total—and also because of its geopolitical significance and the size of its economy. However, the prevalence of extreme poverty in Nigeria and other West African countries functions as a major push factor for youth migration in the subregion. In 2018, World Poverty Clock reported that Nigeria has more people living in extreme poverty than any other country in the world. Additionally, in the third quarter of 2016, the National Bureau of Statistics (NBS) (2016) revealed that the overall unemployment rate had risen to 13.9%, with the youth unemployment rate having risen to 25% from 24% in 2015. These economic trends, coupled with other variables such as political instability and rising waves of conflict, have led to an increasing number of youths in certain categories leaving Nigeria for other countries perceived to hold greater promise.

L. O. Ikuteyijo (✉)
Department of Sociology and Anthropology, Obafemi Awolowo University, Ile-Ife, Nigeria

© The Author(s) 2020
M. L. McLean (ed.), *West African Youth Challenges and Opportunity Pathways*, Gender and Cultural Studies in Africa and the Diaspora, https://doi.org/10.1007/978-3-030-21092-2_3

Nigerian youths, defined here as individuals aged 15 to 35, constitute the largest population in a growing flow of migrants from Global South countries in search of a better life in Europe and other major destination countries (De Haas, 2008). Much of this movement is in violation of the migration norms[1] of destination countries. Defining *migration norms* as all policies and laws that govern the movement of people from one country to another, this chapter will hereafter refer to movement that contravenes these norms as *irregular migration*. The terminology to encapsulate irregular migration has undergone critique by various scholars and policy makers over the years (see Ikuteyijo, 2013). Labels such as illegal migration, undocumented migration, unauthorized migration, and clandestine migration are among the many that have been used. According to Ikuteyijo (2013), debates arose over different political and ideological viewpoints surrounding these descriptive terms. For instance, Koser (2005) criticized the use of "illegal" to qualify migrants for two reasons. First, the term "illegal" connotes criminality, whereas most irregular migrants are not criminals. This was corroborated by the UN Special Rapporteur on the Rights of Non-Citizens, which recommended that countries of destination refrain from treating immigrants (even those without valid documents) as criminals (as cited in Koser, 2005). Second, defining irregular migrants as illegal would amount to denying their humanity and the rights to which they are entitled, irrespective of their status (Guild, 2010; Ikuteyijo, 2013).

Irregular migration occurs outside the regulatory norms of the origin, transit, or destination country and can refer to three groups of migrants: those who arrive in a clandestine fashion (i.e., enter and stay illegally in the considered country), those who arrive legally (for instance, on the basis of tourist or student visas) and then overstay the period for which their visa/permits are valid, and asylum seekers whose claims have been rejected and who have not left the country as required (Ikuteyijo, 2013). The criminalization of irregular migration involves punishments ranging from imprisonment to outright deportation.

Apart from economic push factors, the trend toward the securitization and militarization of borders as a measure to check illegal entry into countries of the Global North has been identified as another major driver of

---

[1] Historically, these norms, which stipulate documentation and other requirements, have been subject to change. For instance, moving from Nigeria to the United Kingdom required no visa until the introduction of the entry visa requirement soon after independence.

irregular migration. Securitization includes the use of modern security infrastructure, such as the closed-circuit television for surveillance. The continued criminalization of irregular migration is seen as another factor that incentivizes perpetrators to devise means of evading security agents (Davitti & Ursu, 2018).

The migration of the youth is also precipitated by the recruitment of foreign labor by Global North countries where the twin factors of an aging population and declining birth rate are at play (Akinyemi & Ikuteyijo, 2009). Other pull factors that affect youth migration, especially at the international level, include prospects for getting a better education, increasing earning power, and improving living conditions through access to better infrastructure and public amenities.

The bulk of irregular migration in Nigeria occurs among youth aged 18 to 35. Members of this age cohort tend to be mobile, as most are unmarried and have the energy to relocate, unlike older people, who are more likely to be married, with more commitments and less energy to withstand the rigors of migration (Adepoju & Hammar, 1996; Ikuteyijo, 2012). Irregular migration can involve acute hardship, such as wilderness trekking and crossing waterways in unsafe vessels. The Mediterranean Sea has become one of the most popular routes for irregular migrants in recent times (Brenner, Forin, & Frouws, 2018). In 2016, over 20,000 youths involved in the Mediterranean Sea crossing were reported to be from Nigeria (Nwalutu, 2016; Ojeme, 2016). In addition, in the first quarter of 2017, hundreds of irregular Nigerian migrants were deported from various destinations, including Italy, Libya, and South Africa. Overall, in comparison to other countries in sub-Saharan Africa, irregular migrants from Nigeria dominate migration to Europe and North America and represent 25.5% of all West African migrants living in Organization for Economic Cooperation and Development (OECD) countries (De Haas, 2008).

While the bulk of previous studies have concentrated on trends of irregular migration and factors that motivate it (Adepoju, 2000; De Haas, 2008; Haugen, 2012), less attention has been paid to acquiring a socially embedded understanding of the experiences of irregular migrants. This study aims toward closing that gap by contributing to the understanding of what motivated youths found to be susceptible toward irregular migration—that is, youths in four major Nigerian cities who fell into one or more of these categories: they were unemployed, in their final year in a tertiary education institution, or on the mandatory national youth service.

The study also explored the experiences of returnee irregular migrants in these four locales.

MIGRATION IN POSTCOLONIAL NIGERIA

The postcolonial migration era in Nigeria, the period from independence in 1960 through the early 2000s (Adepoju, 2010), witnessed the highest volume of labor migration from various parts of the country to the main administrative and urban economic centers. Likewise, the number of destinations, both for internal and international migration, was greater than during the precolonial and colonial eras. The postcolonial era can be described as the most eventful of the three epochs (i.e., before, during, and after colonialism) in the sense that a number of major forces shaped the history of migration, not only in Nigeria but across Africa. Since the period after independence, migration in Nigeria has been characterized by emigration as well as substantial amounts of internal migration (mostly rural to urban) (Meagher, 1997). For instance, during the oil boom years in Nigeria (1970s to early 1980s), Nigeria assumed the status of a significant destination country for immigrants from other West African countries, and immigrants accounted for almost 2% of the population (Shaw, 2007).

The extent to which immigration during this period was accurately measured is unclear (Black, Ammassari, Mooillesseaux, & Rajkotia, 2004). The major index of immigration was unskilled workers from neighboring countries. The consensus of the literature is that, in the 1970s and 1980s, very few Nigerians would likely have opted to emigrate because domestic working conditions were attractive and internationally competitive (Black et al., 2004). However, the euphoria of the oil boom did not last, and the government of Nigeria expelled many foreigners in 1983 under the guise of "national security." Afolayan (1988) reported that one of the excuses given by the Nigerian government was the fact that most of the foreigners, especially Ghanaians, were engaged in illicit activities like street begging and prostitution.

Other major events of the postcolonial era that affected the course of migration in Nigeria include the establishment of more administrative centers, with the creation of new states and the Abuja Federal Capital territory and, most notably, the civil war which lasted for three years from 1967 to 1970. Ikuteyijo (2013) found that another key factor that determined migration flows in Nigeria was the lopsided development in the creation of more employment opportunities and infrastructural facilities in urban centers at the expense of the rural areas. This is perhaps one of the most significant impacts of Nigeria's postcolonial migration history, as the effects are still observable today.

Youth migration also took on another dimension in the postcolonial era as young people sought advanced educational opportunities outside the borders of the country. The mass exodus of Nigerian students could be explained by the twin factors of declining standards of education in the country (Jumare, 1997) as well as increased incidences of "escaping" to the Global North to avoid the impact of structural adjustment austerity measures and attendant political instability. Most young Nigerians who went abroad to further their education after the 1970s did not return to the country. This was a sharp contrast from what was obtainable in the colonial era (Adegbola, 1990; Adepoju, 1991; Afolayan, 1998). In fact, according to Rachael Reynolds (2002), in the late 1990s and early 2000s there were more Nigerian academics in the United States than in Nigeria, with many not assuming jobs in relevant fields and working instead as taxi drivers, factory workers, or in other unskilled or low-skilled occupations.

However, the migration of Nigerian youth to other countries in the postcolonial era was not limited to the educated class alone but was rather, as has been described, "highly diverse" (Blench, 2004, p. 7). The mass exodus was facilitated by cheap air tickets and the possibility of legal entry without visas.

Human Trafficking as a Form of Irregular Migration

Human trafficking is the third most profitable criminal enterprise globally, after drug trafficking and illegal arms transactions (International Labour Organization [ILO], 2003; United Nations Office on Drugs and Crime [UNODC], 2011). It has also been described as the modern form of slavery, which, like older forms, involves the trading of human beings as commodities. The United Nations Office on Drugs and Crime (UNODC) defines human trafficking as

> recruitment, transportation, transfer, harbouring or receipt of persons, by means of threat or use of force or other forms of coercion, of abduction, of fraud, of deception, of the abuse of power or of a position of vulnerability or of the giving or receiving of payments or benefits to achieve the consent of

a person having control over another person, for the purpose of exploitation. (UNODC, 2011, p. 7)

The United Nations estimates that 2.5 million people are in forced labor (including sexual exploitation) at any time as a result of trafficking (Goldin, Cameron, & Balarajan, 2011).

Although, human trafficking cases can have varying dimensions, there are certain characteristics that mark them out: people are abducted or recruited in the country of origin, transferred through transit regions, and then exploited in the destination country (International Organisation on Migration, 2007). Also, trafficking can be classified in terms of space and movement in two ways: internal and international trafficking. While internal trafficking takes place within the borders of a country, international trafficking involves movement of victims outside the borders. In some cases, however, the internal may lead to international trafficking, as in the case of young women and children who are recruited from remote rural areas and moved to urban centers, before being moved out of the country. This takes the form of step migration.

Human trafficking differs from human smuggling in two ways. First, whereas human trafficking can take place within or outside national boundaries, human smuggling is always about movement across boundaries. Also, while human trafficking may involve some elements of coercion, fraud, or deception, human smuggling is usually more voluntary, and the participants are often aware of the purpose and legal implications of the movement. The issue of consent has been a subject of major debate, as underage children cannot give consent. Also, the consent of parents is often obtained under false pretenses, for instance, by traffickers who promise that children will have access to education or vocational training, and a better life, at the ultimate destination (Ikuteyijo, 2013).

Human trafficking has tremendous negative effects on the victims, the countries which serve as primary sources for human trafficking, the receiving countries, and even the global community. Many trafficked persons die prematurely in the process of trafficking, while the future of those who survive it becomes uncertain as they are denied the opportunity for proper mental and physical development. Also, many of the children and young persons who could have contributed positively to the growth and development of their countries were denied this opportunity. This has an indirect way of negatively affecting the development of the countries that are the primary sources for trafficking in persons.

Network Theory

In migration discourse, network theory explains migration dynamics at the micro level, including how connections among actors influence migration decisions. For instance, it explains how individual migrants are linked with friends or family members and provided with information about job opportunities, both before and after arrival at their destination. Other theories may explain the interactions between push and pull factors and their influence on the decision to migrate but fail to account for why migration persists even after these factors have diminished. The movement of people from one place to another often leads to the establishment of a process of "cumulative causation" (Brown & Bean, 2006) or what Massey (1987) has termed "chain migration." The study of networks, particularly those linked to family and households, permits understanding migration as a social product—not as the sole result of individual decisions made by individual actors, or as the sole result of economic or political parameters, but rather as an outcome of all these factors in interaction (Boyd, 1989). Because most migrants do not know about the relative price of labor between their own country and country of destination, they rely on information from friends and relatives, which often signals opportunities in the labor markets of destination countries (Sassen, 1995). The network theory is relevant to the explanation of how potential trafficked victims are recruited. In most cases, this recruitment is done through close social networks of friends, relatives, and other acquaintances,

The network also provides an important means through which migrants acquire social capital, that is, the repertoire of resources such as information, material assistance, as well as social support that flow through social ties (Brown & Bean, 2006)—which could either be kin, communities, or institutions like churches, mosques, or other professional or religious groups. Network theory is especially useful for analyzing irregular migration because it helps us to understand how migrants get to be introduced into processes, as well as how relationships are sustained over time.

Political Economy Theory of Migration

The political economy theory of migration encompasses a larger framework than the network theory: it explains the interplay of factors affecting migration flows and, thus, is considered to be a more holistic macrotheory. In some literature, political economy theory of migration and international migration theory are equated because they share similar features (Brown & Bean, 2006). The political economy theory of migration highlights three principal categories of international migration, namely micro, meso, and macro levels. The micro level focuses on factors influencing individual decisions to migrate, analyzing how potential migrants weigh up the various costs and benefits of migrating (Boswell, 2002). They include the values an individual places on migration as well as his/her expectations of the benefits accruable from such a venture. The micro level is all about the individual migrant.

The meso level of explanation locates migration flows within a complex system of links between people. Two concepts are particularly important for meso theories, namely systems and networks. Migration is assumed to occur within a migration system, and this could be explained in terms of how people are linked by economic, political, and cultural ties as well as by migration flows. Thus, the conditions generating movement are understood as the dynamics of relations between two or more people, rather than a set of objective indicators. The social networks include both social as well as symbolic ties which could either be strong or weak. The contents of such ties, however, include transaction obligations and reciprocity. It also entails the control of information among the group as well as access to the resources of others (Brown & Bean, 2006).

The macro level, which is the context in which migration occurs, emphasizes the structural, objective conditions which act as push and pull factors for migration. This could be explicated in terms of economic, political, and cultural settings. In the case of economic migration, pull factors would typically include economic conditions such as unemployment, low salaries, or low per capita income relative to the country of destination. Pull factors would include migration legislation and the labor market situation in receiving countries. The macro level also encompasses political variables such as laws aimed at regulating spatial mobility and other national or international migration norms. Macro level push factors would include involuntary displacement, which could be due to state repression, fear of generalized criminal violence, or civil war (Boswell, 2002; Crisp, 1999; Taylor, 2000; Usher, 2005). The situation in some parts of Nigeria like Jos and Maiduguri,[2] as well as outside the country in other parts of

---

[2] The Jos crises were mostly ethno-religious in nature, and these crises have been ongoing for years, since the 1980s up until 2018. The crises in Maiduguri are mainly caused by the Boko Haram terrorists, and this began from 2002 to 2018 and still persists.

West Africa (e.g., Liberia), and especially in the Middle East, where violence has displaced many individuals, and families could serve as points of reference for push factors on the political platform.

DATA AND METHODS

Research Design

This study was inspired by the concept of interpretivist research design, which emphasizes the collection of data in the naturalistic setting. The study, therefore, attempted to make sense of the phenomenon of irregular migration in terms of meanings that actors, in this case youths, bring to it. This was accomplished by the collection of a variety of data using personal experience, life history, and interviews, which described the meanings and problematic moments in the lives of the research participants (Denzin & Lincoln, 2005). Except as otherwise stated, where quoted in this chapter the language as actually used by participants (including slangs, colloquial speech, proverbs, etc.) is retained in its original form.

Location of the Study

The study was carried out in four major cities in Nigeria: Lagos, Ibadan, Ile-Ife, and Benin City. The choice of these cities was informed by their characteristics in relation to irregular migration. Lagos State is the commercial capital of Nigeria and the most cosmopolitan city in the country. The state also boasts an international airport, which is the busiest in the country. Apart from the location of the airport, the city of Lagos has many other accessible land and sea routes in and out of the country. For instance, the Apapa Sea Port is an exit route, while the land borders at Badagry, Idi Iroko, and Seme provide opportunities to exit Nigeria by land. Ibadan is a famous nodal city which connects the other parts of the country with Lagos State. Ibadan also hosts the premier University of Ibadan (the first in Nigeria) and other landmarks which make the city attractive to migrants from other parts of the country. Ile-Ife is often referred to as the center of civilization as it boasts a number of institutions, such as the Obafemi Awolowo University (formerly University of Ife) as well as other important sites and landmarks. Benin City is the capital of Edo State and is well known as the hub of human trafficking in migration literature. In addition, all these cities have one common feature: the presence of a federal university and a large population of youth.

Study Population

The study targeted youths who were unemployed, those in their final year at a tertiary-level education institution (i.e., public universities and public and private polytechnics), and those engaged in Nigeria's compulsory National Youth Service Corps (NYSC). Youths who fell in one or more of these categories were prone to view migration as a survival strategy in light of Nigeria's high unemployment and bleak economic prospects for wage earners. Also included were youths who had already been involved in irregular migration and had returned to the country either voluntarily or via deportation. In this study, youths who fall into these categories are collectively referred to as "youths susceptible to migration."

Sampling and Data Collection

The purposive sampling technique was used to select participants for the study. To select participants for focus group discussions, a pre-survey questionnaire was administered to youths susceptible to migration (as defined above). Separate focus group discussions were held for males and females, and in all 11 focus group discussion sessions were held. The inclusion criteria included whether participants were familiar with the process of irregular migration, a factor determined by asking questions about their first-hand experiences or knowledge of the irregular migration experiences of family members and acquaintances. The focus group discussions were facilitated using both vignette and free listing methods to obtain data on the attitude of youth toward irregular migration. Some of the thematic outlines of the focus group discussions included motivation to migrate, role of social networks, migration experience, and so on.

To reach the returned youth migrants, the snowballing or referral method was used. The referrals were at both individual and institutional levels. At the individual level, persons who knew youths who fell under the category of returned migrants referred the researcher to them, while some other returned migrants were sourced through the National Agency for Prohibition of Trafficking in Persons and other Related Offences (NAPTIP). The returned migrants constitute the hard-to-reach or "invisible" population since, unlike the other categories of youth who were more accessible, the returned migrants had to be located through referrals. A total of 7 returnees were captured for data collection, plus an additional 63 youth who had not yet left the country but were susceptible to irregular migration.

Ethical Considerations

In a study of this nature, there were a number of substantive ethical issues to be addressed. Practical steps were taken to protect the integrity of participants and to ensure that the study did not have a harmful impact on them. For instance, they were guaranteed anonymity and confidentiality of their responses. Hence, pseudonyms are used to identify the individuals whose narratives are quoted in this chapter. Given the fact that returnee migrants constitute the invisible or hard-to-reach categories because of the circumstances surrounding their departure, they were all informed about the aim of the research, and pseudonyms were used to represent their views. In addition, their informed consent was sought before the commencement of the interviews, and they were free to discontinue with the interview at any point. Other ethical considerations were followed strictly, including disclosure of identity and maintaining the confidentiality of all participants.

Sociodemographics of Participants

Besides the 63 study participants who were considered susceptible to migration (students in their last year of tertiary education, unemployed youth, and youth corps members), the study included 7 individual returnee irregular migrants who were purposively selected. It is commonplace for qualitative studies to consist of relatively fewer samples than quantitative studies. What is missing in terms of numbers is gained in terms of depth of information sought from participants (Creswell, 2003; Tashakkori & Teddlie, 1998). Through interviews, their life histories were collected with a view to analyzing their experiences during migration. Selected cases for the key in-depth interviews comprised three females and four males who had left the country in an irregular manner.

The age range of the returnee migrants was between 19 and 39 years. The three young women left from Benin City, Nigeria, to go to Italy and Libya, while the four young men emigrated to Switzerland, Belgium, Libya, and Gambia, respectively. The majority of the returnees were unemployed secondary school dropouts who cited inability to cope and lack of support as reasons for dropping out of school. Also, a majority of the selected cases were from polygynous families (with their fathers marrying more than once, an average of three wives). Furthermore, most of the cases were from large families, with the most having 19 children in the family and the least having 7 children. The number of children a family has may have implications on the quality of care and attention received by children in that family. Lastly, all selected cases were deported from destination or transit countries, with the exception of only one who returned to Nigeria after fruitless efforts to cross to Europe from Algeria.

The age range of other categories of respondents—those unemployed, serving in the NYSC scheme, or in their final year in a tertiary institution—was from 15 to 35 years. The majority of these individuals (89%) were single, and more than half (55%) were male. In terms of religion, Christianity was the dominant religion among the respondents, as 73% of them were Christians.

RESULTS AND FINDINGS

Awareness and Attitude of Youth to Irregular Migration

Youth who constituted the vulnerable groups (final-year students in tertiary institutions, youth corps members, and unemployed youth) were asked a number of questions to determine their familiarity with the concept of irregular migration. The majority of the participants said that they understood the meaning of irregular migration. Ironically, most of them demonstrated ignorance of formal immigration procedures, as more than half of them did not have a valid passport, which is the basic, minimum requirement for international migration. However, most of them knew someone personally who had traveled out of the country through illegal means like forging a passport, patronizing unauthorized agents, and traveling to "Europe by road"—as irregular migration is referred to in the popular idiom. Most of the youths showed positive attitudes toward irregular migration, stating that the end would justify the means. They demonstrated a consensus of opinion that migrants were far better off than those who stayed behind because they had access to a better quality of life. As Bola, a 29-year-old female unemployed youth from Osun State, asserted: "Sincerely, those who migrate outside the country often live far better than we in Nigeria. They enjoy constant power supply, good weather, eat good diet and to a reasonable extent, they are secured." Along these same lines, Joseph, a member of the National Youth Service Corps from Oyo State reported: "We value money, not integrity, here in Nigeria, so youth want to go abroad to make money. When they come back, they will have integrity."

The positive attitude toward irregular migration expressed by most of the young people in the study rested on a shared belief that life is better abroad. It was also tied to a shared perception of "success" as being able to travel abroad. Hence, most of the youth did not consider irregular migration as a crime but as just being practical (or as one respondent put it, "diplomatic") or "smart." Most of them were of the opinion that those who traveled abroad tended to return "better" than they were when they left, and that, therefore, traveling abroad by "whatever means" was justified.

Reflecting this point of view, Efosa, a 25-year-old male Youth Corp member from Benin City, observed:

To me, I cannot see any criminality in adopting any means whether irregular (illegal) or regular (legal) to go abroad. There is a difference between being "criminal" and being "diplomatic." Those who leave Nigeria by irregular means are just being diplomatic. Irregular migration is not a crime.

George, a 19-year-old undergraduate from Lagos, said

I know some people who have travelled abroad and when they got there they were doing odd jobs. The reason most people traveled is that because in our country things are very difficult. People graduate but no jobs, so they want to leave and try their luck outside.

Similarly, Gabriel, a 27-year-old male final-year student in Lagos, reported:

I have an uncle who traveled by ship to Germany. Looking back today, he is not regretting it because he is doing well. He told me it's worth it because what he is enjoying there could not be obtained in Nigeria.

Besides the individual young person's awareness or understanding of irregular migration, the motivation to migrate was also key to understanding the dynamics of the irregular migration experience. Therefore, participants (especially the returnee migrants) were also asked what motivated them to migrate.

Motivation to Migrate

Returnee migrants were asked what factors motivated them to leave the country when they did. A look through the responses given by all the respondents to this question echoed the push factors inherent in the Nigerian society. As young men and women who were not sure of what their future in the country could be, they all ventured into the alternative line of action that is leaving the country for greener pastures abroad. The quest to make ends meet constitutes the major motivation for all the respondents. All of them were at the time of departure not satisfied with their respective statuses, economically and academically. Yakubu, a 39-year-old male returnee migrant back from Gambia, noted:

> After seeing some people who had traveled and returned to live flashy lifestyle or maybe he or she has sent some cars home to their families and from there you begin to develop the interest of traveling too. You begin to nurse and plan to go. So as you are planning then you meet the connection men.

Francis, a 20-year-old male returnee migrant back from Libya, who was motivated by the information available to him about job and life prospects in Europe, had this to say:

> I was hearing some of my friends saying they wanted to travel at the barbing saloon. So I just decided to go with them. I had the mindset of going to hustle and make it. I am a footballer and I believe that when I get to Italy, I will survive.

Juliet, a 30-year-old female returnee migrant back from Italy, reported that her quest for better education was used as bait for her to be trafficked to Italy. She noted:

> During the first term holiday in my SS one, a family friend told my parents that he would take me to Italy to continue my education. My parents succumbed to the idea because they felt that in Italy my education would be unhindered and my prospect of getting a job after school was higher than in Nigeria.

A similar situation happened in the case of Gina, a 19-year-old female returnee migrant from Libya, who had dropped out of secondary school in Nigeria due to the inability to pay her school fees. She reported that she had to drop out of school since there was no funding for her education. She was introduced to the syndicate who promised to help her secure good employment in Paris. She was informed that there were opportunities for hairstylists; hence, she hurriedly enrolled in a school to acquire the skills of hairdressing. However, she was taken to Abuja under the guise of obtaining her international passport, and from there she was trafficked to Libya. Another participant, a 21-year-old female returnee from Libya, shared a similar story, as her quest to further her education coupled with the inability of her parents to sponsor her dream led to her falling victim to human trafficking.

The absence of an effective social security system in Nigeria, whereby indigent youth can still meet their educational aspirations, is another key motivation for migration. Some of the respondents had poor economic backgrounds, and the pressure of having to fend not only for themselves but also for their younger relatives made them easy prey for agents of irregular migration. In most cases, the youth (especially women) were promised greener pastures abroad only to later realize that they had become victims of human trafficking.

The next theme explored was respondents' perceptions about how migration could serve as a survival strategy in the absence of essential services and an enabling environment for youth to meet their basic needs and thrive in Nigeria.

Migration as Survival Strategy

Both the youth who were susceptible to migration and those who were returnee migrants agreed that irregular migration was a viable strategy for youth to survive Nigeria's economic downturn. The idea that migration offers a more comfortable life was widely held among the participants. Most expressed the belief that irregular migration promised economic benefits. For instance, Adisa, a 21-year-old participant, said that the unfavorable exchange rate between the Naira and other foreign currencies was sufficient incentive to leave the country. Migration was also seen as a way of being helpful to their family members. Daniel, a 24-year-old unemployed respondent, offered the example of someone he knew who had left Nigeria for Spain and was living a much better life and was able to financially assist his family after his return. He maintained this stance despite the fact that in Spain his acquaintance was reportedly doing menial jobs, or work that the migration literature describes as the 3Ds: dirty, dangerous, and demeaning.

RETURNEE EXPERIENCES DURING MIGRATION

As a baseline for assessing the actual experience of irregular migration against the expectations of youth who were susceptible toward and inclined to migrate, the study also interrogated the experiences of returnee youth migrants.

Returnee migrants were asked to relate their experiences on the journey, and quite a number of facts were revealed. Persons who were smuggled had the liberty to do what they wanted in the course of the journey. For instance, they had to engage in a number of menial jobs to survive, and they also had access to the money earned in the process. Some of them had to disguise their identity (e.g., by wearing veils or hijab) anytime they were going to buy things from the market. The men had to engage in some menial jobs that their self-esteem would have prevented them from doing in Nigeria. Yakubu, a 39-year-old male returnee migrant from Gambia, reported that he had to work as a shoe cobbler and later as a barber in the destination country. He maintained that these were some of the jobs he would not do in Nigeria.

Sullivan, a 37-year-old returnee male migrant who had traveled to Switzerland, said he worked as a morgue attendant and also served as a drug courier just to make ends meet. In most cases, the returnee migrants embarked on the journey through the land route, and they all reported having to go through long and tortuous trips in the desert. Francis, a 20-year-old male returnee back from Libya, reported that in the course of the journey they were moving from one place to another and ended up spending hours in the desert in the middle of the night. He reported that several fellow migrants were lost in the desert. Juliet, a 30-year-old female returnee migrant from Italy, reported that some of the girls died at sea in the course of the trip. She remembered that about 160 girls were moved in three "Zodiac ships" (possibly a reference to a maritime company), and two of the ships suddenly developed mechanical faults in the middle of the sea. Six of the girls reportedly died before the ship could be rescued. The surviving girls were eventually picked up by prospective patrons or employers, illicit or otherwise, when the ship finally berthed in Madrid.

ROLE OF SOCIAL NETWORKS

A number of studies have explained the role that migration networks play in stimulating migration streams between a specific country of origin and countries of destination (Boyd, 1989; Faist, 2000; Haug, 2008). The role of social networks in irregular migration has been studied extensively (Brown & Bean, 2006; Massey, 2003). Social networks serve as sources of information as well as provision of supports to migrants in terms of finances or other logistics. Respondents were asked what role social networks, particularly friends and relatives, played in their movement. The majority of the returnee migrants had the support of their parents and friends in the course of the journey. Yakubu, a 39-year-old male returnee migrant back from Gambia, recalled that while in Gambia (a transit country) another irregular migrant got a job in a Scandinavian country and had to return to Nigeria to source money for the trip. He said:

> When I was in Gambia, there was a driver living in the same house with me who had a driver's license. Many of us who were transit migrants came together and used his driver's license to apply for job in one Scandinavian country. One of us was so lucky to be selected and he quickly came back to Nigeria to inform his parents who gave him money to process the necessary travel documents and he got the visa and travelled.

Francis, a 20-year-old male returnee migrant back from Libya, reported that he financed his journey through the sale of his father's house. He said:

> My father's house was sold and I used my share to facilitate my travel to Libya. My father had four wives and seventeen children. I am the seventh child. I know many people who had used the sea route; many of my friends have gone through the route. Before they left Nigeria, I knew and about two weeks after they left, an Italian phone number called me and they told me they got there (Italy) safely. Many boys in my area have gone through the sea.

Not uncommonly, the decision to migrate does not rest with the individual but, rather, with family members. Often, it is the family that decides who travels and how to support him or her. Yakubu, a 39-year-old male returnee migrant back from Gambia, recalled:

Relatives and friends play very supportive roles; for example, my elder brother called me one day and said there was a man in his church who helps young people who want to travel out. The man is a musician who helps people to travel out with his band. My brother provided the money for passport and gave the man some money on my behalf. He gave the man about 150,000. I went with the man to play at an occasion which was allegedly taken to the embassy. After a while, the effort was thwarted and I am not sure he has collected his money from the man.

Sullivan, a 37-year-old male returnee from Switzerland, also noted that he sent money home through Western Union when he was in Switzerland. He noted that he realized that the money he was sending home had given him a higher social status among his peers, even when none of them had an idea of what he was doing to survive abroad. This statement corroborates the perspective of intending migrants who expressed the opinion that migration added to the migrant's social status at home.

OTHER FINDINGS

The narratives from participants in this study revealed the motives and experiences of youth who were either inclined toward, or had already engaged in, irregular migration as a strategy to escape Nigeria's economic hardships. The majority of the participants perceived irregular migration as a "great opportunity." This perception explains the general positive attitude toward irregular migration among youth who were susceptible to migration.

Most of the youths expressed fear of the future and viewed irregular migration as a survival strategy to escape an existence of poverty and powerlessness in Nigeria. This attitude, however, was also influenced by radio, TV, music, and other popular culture and media representations of destination countries as El Dorado. "Been to," the popular term for people who have visited foreign continents, especially Europe and America, attributes a level of social status. There is also the phenomenon of naming a Yoruba child who was conceived or born abroad "Tokunbo," meaning "from overseas." The presence of a returnee migrant, especially from Europe and America, at social gatherings adds glamor and prestige. In such gatherings, musicians and other praise singers often eulogize migrants, not mindful of the source of income or nature of work the migrants are engaged in abroad. At the other end of the spectrum are popular songs such as "This Is Nigeria" by rapper Falz The Bahd Guy and "Nigeria Jaga Jaga" by Eedris Abdukareem, which offer critical social commentary on life in Nigeria. Falz's hit song, a takeoff on Childish Gambino's "This is America," spotlights issues such as political corruption, drug addiction, and unscrupulous preachers. In contrast to representations that celebrate lifestyles in Europe and North America, these lyrics portray Nigeria as a place anyone who could would want to leave.

Additionally, the study revealed that, although the youths demonstrated a high knowledge of the processes of irregular migration, they had very little knowledge, and displayed ignorance, about official migration laws, regulations, and procedures. For instance, the majority of students enrolled in their final year at various tertiary education institutions and who wanted to travel abroad did not have passports. Similarly, the study participants had little, if any, knowledge of employment prospects and labor regulations (work permit requirements, terms and conditions of service, etc.) or rights of migrants in destination countries. The lack of knowledge displayed by the participants in the study, including returnees, suggests opportunities to introduce curricula in secondary schools that would provide a more realistic, data- and information-based assessment of economic opportunities abroad and accurate information about the requirements, risks, and potential rewards of emigration.

Returnee migrants had bitter tales to tell, as what they expected was different from what they experienced in the journey. The youth participants in the study most often decided to leave Nigeria in search of greener pastures based on speculative information about availability of jobs in the countries of destination and without adequate information on the labor norms in those countries. The realities of irregular migration were usually a far cry from the expectations of the migrants. Most of the migrants resorted to the 3Ds (dirty, demeaning, and dangerous) (Adepoju, 2003; Wolffers, Verghis, & Marin, 2003) kind of work to survive at the destination. The migration experience of returnees was also gendered. Male returnees paid their ways through the journey using travel syndicates, while the young women were tricked into embarking on trips.

Overall, the role of social networks was crucial, as most of the migrants were motivated by or relied upon social networks to embark on the journey. The study revealed the impact of this factor as most of the respondents (vulnerable and returnee migrants) recounted the important roles played by relatives abroad. The returnee migrants all reported that they were "lured" to migrating by either friends or relatives, and youths who had yet to migrate also reported that their sources of information about migration were mostly friends and relatives. In most cases, these sources painted exaggerated pictures of reality in destination countries. This factor supports findings in the literature on migration networks and the nature of communications between migration networks in sending countries and diaspora communities in the countries of destination. The findings suggest that destination country networks tend to paint a positive picture of living conditions in order to save face (Boyd, 1989; Faist, 2000; Haug, 2008).

CONCLUSION

The study examined the experiences of returnee youth migrants who left Nigeria through irregular channels, as well as the perceptions of other youths who were susceptible toward migration, that is, youths who were unemployed, in their final year at a tertiary-level education institution (public universities and public and private polytechnics), and those engaged in Nigeria's compulsory National Youth Service Corps (NYSC). These youths' collective perception of irregular migration as survival strategy to escape harsh economic conditions in Nigeria was not borne out by the experience of the youths who actually left the country and returned. Furthermore, many of the returnees were stigmatized by friends and relatives and thus failed to improve their social as well as economic status.

Nigeria was the first African country to domesticate the Palermo Protocol prohibiting human trafficking and smuggling (Ikuteyijo, 2018), but there are apparent gaps in these policies. Government efforts focus mainly on punishment and enforcement against trafficking, while fewer efforts have been focused on rehabilitation, resettlement, and reintegration of returnee migrants. More proactive measures are needed to address the issue of irregular migration, especially in the form of human trafficking and smuggling.

In terms of level of awareness of the processes and forms of irregular migration, the youths demonstrated a very high awareness level about avenues to engage in irregular migration, which was corroborated by the focus group discussions. The study also showed that most of the youths had positive attitudes toward irregular migration for the sake of making ends meet, expressing the view that "the end justifies the means."

However, the majority of the youth participating in the study, both those susceptible toward migration and returnee migrants, demonstrated a high level of ignorance about the requirements of legal means of migration. For instance, among the final-year students in tertiary institutions, the majority of those who wanted to travel abroad did not have passports, which is the minimal requirement for international migration. They also exhibited ignorance of other key information such as labor regulations and rights of migrants in destination countries.

The majority of the respondents got their information about destination countries from informal sources like friends, relatives, and social media. Most of this information is exaggerated or wholly inaccurate. This suggests an opportunity for secondary school-based curricula about the rights of migrants and international migration norms and procedures.

In terms of the experiences of returnee irregular migrants, the study revealed that circumstances leading to their decision to leave the country resulted from influence and active support from family members. Many of the youth returnee migrants in the study reported that their parents were not only aware of their plans to migrate irregularly, but also provided them with financial and other support to embark on the irregular migration journey. All the female returnee migrants reported that they left the country with the knowledge of their parents. Although, in some instances, the women were taken out of the country under the guise of securing better education and employment, some parents were privy to the activities of the illegal syndicates involved in the trafficking and/or abducting of their daughters and yet still endorsed them. There is therefore the urgent need to also educate parents.

The study also revealed the role of social networks in irregular migration. Most of the returnee migrants had the support of people within their respective networks, such as friends, relatives, and, in some cases, organized criminal elements. The youth reported a high level of collaboration among international criminal syndicates, which in some cases included government officials.

The study found that for youth who are susceptible toward migration, the increasing youth unemployment rate in Nigeria is a major push factor. Between 2002 and 2005, over 200,000 students graduated from various universities in Nigeria and over 70% of them were added to the figure of unemployed youths in the country (Nigerian Bureau of Statistics, 2010). This trend, coupled with growing security challenges in Nigeria, explains the surge in irregular migration that Nigeria has been witnessing in the recent past, particularly among the youths. The situation is exacerbated by the strict visa regimes introduced by most major destination countries, which push Nigerian youth to clandestine migration practices. The combination of variables create opportunity for criminal cartels to capitalize on the desperation of susceptible youths.

REFERENCES

Adegbola, O. (1990). *Demographic effects of economic crisis in Nigeria: The brain drain component.* Paper presented at the Conference on the Role of Migration in African Development Issues and Policies for the 90s, Union for African Population Studies, Nairobi. In Adepoju (Ed.), *South-north migration: The African situation.* Le Grande-Saconnex, Switzerland: International Organization for Migration (IOM).

Adepoju, A. (1991). South-north migration: The African experience. *International Migration Review, 29*(2), 205–222.

Adepoju, A. (2000). Issues and recent trends in international migration in Sub-Saharan Africa. *International Social Science Journal, 52*(165), 383–394.

Adepoju, A. (2003). Continuity and changing configurations of migration to and from the Republic of South Africa. *International Migration Review, 41*(1), 3–28.

Adepoju, A. (2010). *The future of migration policies in Africa.* A background paper of the World Migration Report. Geneva, Switzerland: International Organisation for Migration (IOM).

Adepoju, A., & Hammar, T. (1996). *International migration in and from Africa: Dimensions, challenges and prospects.* Dakar, Senegal & Stockholm, Sweden: Population Human Resources and Development in Africa (PHRDA) & Stockholm Center for Research in International Migration and Ethnic Relations (CEIFO).

Afolayan, A. A. (1988). Immigration and expulsion of ECOWAS aliens in Nigeria. *International Migration Review, 22*(1), 4–27.

Afolayan, A. A. (1998). *Emigration dynamics in Nigeria: landlessness, poverty, ethnicity and differential responses.* Brookfield, VT: Ashgate Publishing Limited.

Akinyemi A., & Ikuteyijo, L. (2009, January). *Emigration of health professionals in Nigeria: Review and evidence on determinants, patterns and trends.* Paper presented at the Inaugural Scientific Conference of the Network of Migration Researchers in Africa (NOMRA), Lagos State, Nigeria.

Black, R., Ammassari, S., Mooillesseaux, S., & Rajkotia, R. (2004). *Migration and pro poor policy in Africa* (Working Paper C8). Brighton, UK: Sussex Center for Migration Research.

Blench, R. (2004). *Position paper: Migration.* London, UK: Department for International Development (DFID).

Boswell, C. (2002). *Addressing the causes of migratory and refugee movements: The role of the European Union* (New Issues in Refugee Research Working Paper No. 73). Geneva, Switzerland: United Nations High Commissioner for Refugees.

Boyd, M. (1989). Family and personal networks in international migration: Recent developments and new agendas. *International Migration Review, 23*(3), 638–670.

Brenner, Y., Forin, R., & Frouws, B. (2018, August 22). *The 'shift' to the western Mediterranean migration route: Myth or reality?* Mixed Migration Center (MMC). Retrieved March 25, 2019, from http://www.mixedmigration.org/articles/shift-to-the-western-mediterranean-migration-route/#

Brown, S. K., & Bean, F. D. (2006). International migration. In P. Dudley & M. Micklin (Eds.), *Handbook of population* (pp. 347–382). New York, NY: Springer.

Creswell, J. W. (2003). *Research design: Qualitative, quantitative and mixed methods approaches* (2nd ed.). Thousand Oaks, CA: Sage.

Crisp, J. (1999). *Policy challenges of the new diasporas: Migrant networks and their impact on asylum flows and regimes* (New Issues in Refugee Research Working Paper No. 7). Geneva, Switzerland: United Nations High Commissioner for Refugees.

Davitti, D., & Ursu, A. (2018). *Why securitising the Sahel will not stop migration* (FMU Policy Brief No 02/2018). Nottingham, UK: University of Nottingham, Human Rights Law Centre.

De Haas, H. (2008). *Irregular migration from West Africa to the Maghreb and the European Union: An overview of recent trends* (Vol. 32). Geneva, Switzerland: International Organization for Migration.

Denzin, N. K., & Lincoln, Y. S. (2005). Introduction. The discipline and practice of qualitative research. In N. K. Denzin & Y. S. Lincoln (Eds.), *The Sage handbook of qualitative research* (pp. 1–32). Thousand Oaks, CA: Sage.

Faist, T. (2000). Transnationalization in international migration: Implications for the study of citizenship and culture. *Ethnic and Racial Studies, 23*(2), 189–222.

Goldin, I., Cameron, G., & Balarajan, M. (2011). *Exceptional people: How migration shaped our world and will determine our future.* Princeton, NJ: Princeton University Press.

Guild, E. (2010) *Criminalization of migration in Europe: Human rights implications* (Issue paper). Strasbourg, France: Council of Europe, Commissioner for Human Rights.

Haug, S. (2008). Migration networks and migration decision-making. *Journal of Ethnic and Migration Studies, 34*(4), 585–605.

Haugen, H. Ø. (2012). Nigerians in China: A second state of immobility. *International Migration, 50*(2), 65–80.

Ikuteyijo, L. (2012). Illegal migration and policy challenges in Nigeria. *Africa Portal, Backgrounder, 21*, 1–10.

Ikuteyijo, L. (2013). *Patterns and processes of irregular migration among youths in southwest Nigeria* (Unpublished doctoral dissertation). Obafemi Awolowo University, Ile-Ife, Nigeria.

Ikuteyijo, L. (2018). Between prosecutors and counsellors: State and non-state actors in the rehabilitation of victims of human trafficking in Nigeria. In K. Hiralal & Z. Jinnah (Eds.), *Gender and mobility in Africa: Borders, bodies and boundaries* (pp. 139–157). New York, NY: Palgrave Macmillan.

International Labour Organization (ILO). (2003, March 24). *The trafficking of women and children in southern African region.* Presentation of the International Labour Organization, Geneva, Switzerland.

International Organisation on Migration. (2007). *Irregular migration from West Africa to the Maghreb and the European Union: An overview of recent trends.* Geneva, Switzerland: Author.

Jumare, I. (1997). The displacement of the Nigerian academic community. *Journal of Asian and African Studies, 32*(1–2), 110–119.

Koser, K. (2005). *Irregular migration, state security and human security.* Geneva, Switzerland: Global Commission on International Migration.

Massey, D. S. (1987). Understanding Mexican migration to the United States. *American Journal of Sociology, 92*(6), 372–403.

Massey, D. S. (2003, June 4–7). *Patterns and processes of international migration in the 21st century.* Paper presented at the Conference on African Migration in Comparative Perspective, Johannesburg, South Africa.

Meagher, K. (1997). Shifting the imbalance. The impact of structural adjustment on rural urban population movements in Northern Nigeria. *Journal of Asian and African Studies, 32*(1–2), 81–92.

National Bureau of Statistics (NBS). (2010). *Statistical factsheet.* Retrieved October 21, 2012, from www.nigerianstat.gov.ng

National Bureau of Statistics (NBS). (2016). *Unemployment/underemployment report, Q3, 2016.* Abuja, Nigeria: National Bureau of Statistics.

Nwalutu, M. O. (2016). *From Africa to Europe, youth and transnational migration: Examining the lived experiences of Nigerian migrant youth in Malta* (Doctoral thesis). University of Toronto, Canada.

Ojeme, V. (2016, October 28). 22,500 Nigerians cross Mediterranean Sea, in 2016 says EU. *Vanguard Newspapers.* Retrieved October 6, 2018, from https://www.vanguardngr.com/2016/10/22500-nigerians-cross-mediterranean-sea-2016-says-eu-2/

Reynolds, R. (2002). An African brain drain: Igbo decisions to emigrate to the US. *Review of African Political Economy, 29*(92), 273–284.

Sassen, S. (1995). Immigration and local labour markets. In A. Portes (Ed.), *The Economic sociology of immigration* (pp. 87–127). New York, NY: Russell Sage Foundation.

Shaw, W. (2007). *Migration in Africa: A review of economic literature on international migration in 10 countries.* Washington, DC: World Bank.

Tashakkori, A., & Teddlie, C. (1998). *Mixed methodology: Combining qualitative and quantitative approaches.* Thousand Oaks, CA: Sage.

Taylor, J. E. (2000). Migration: New dimensions and characteristics, causes, consequences and implications for rural poverty. In K. G. Stamoulis (Ed.), *Current and emerging issues for economic analysis and policy research*. Rome, Italy: Food and Agriculture Organization.

United Nations Office on Drugs and Crime (UNODC). (2011). *Issue paper: Smuggling of migrants by sea*. Geneva, Switzerland: United Nations.

Usher, E. (2005). *The millennium development goals and migration*. Geneva, Switzerland: International Organisation for Migration (IOM).

Wolffers, I., Verghis, S., & Marin, M. (2003). Migration, human rights, and health. *The Lancet, 362*(9400), 2019–2020.

World Poverty Clock. (2018). The percentage of Nigerians living in extreme poverty could increase by 2030. *World Poverty Clock Blog*. Retrieved March 27, 2019, from https://worldpoverty.io/blog/index.php?r=12

Untold Stories: Newark's Burgeoning West African Population and the In-School Experiences of African Immigrant Youth

Michael Simmons and Mahako Etta

INTRODUCTION

Notwithstanding the current political discourse, immigration to the United States is not a new phenomenon. More than 70 years ago, as he endeavored to write the history of immigration in the United States, Oscar Handlin (1951) astutely observed that immigrants are American history. Indeed, the history of the United States is the story of the movement of peoples from around the globe, each bringing with them a unique set of customs and beliefs. While each group of new arrivals to the shores of the United States has brought an extensive collection of talents and abilities,

M. Simmons
Joseph C. Cornwall Center for Metropolitan Studies, Rutgers University-Newark, Newark, NJ, USA
e-mail: michael.simmons@rutgers.edu

M. Etta (✉)
Rutgers University-Newark School of Public Affairs and Administration, Newark, NJ, USA
e-mail: metta@scarletmail.rutgers.edu

© The Author(s) 2020
M. L. McLean (ed.), *West African Youth Challenges and Opportunity Pathways*, Gender and Cultural Studies in Africa and the Diaspora, https://doi.org/10.1007/978-3-030-21092-2_4

not all have arrived under the same set of circumstances, nor have their stories been equally represented in the retelling of the nation's migratory history. Arguably, in no case is this as true as it is for those arriving to the United States from the African continent.

There is a long history of African presence in the Americas. During the transatlantic slave trade in the sixteenth through nineteenth centuries alone, it is estimated that more than 12 million forced African migrants were transported to the United States (Segal, 1995). Early census data indicate that, as a result of forced migration, people of African descent accounted for close to one-fifth of the US population by the end of the eighteenth century (Anderson, 2015). Historical records indicate, and DNA testing has since confirmed, that many of those brought to the United States during the European slave trade originated from Western Africa. In fact, the presence of the Igbo peoples—a population from modern-day Nigeria—was so significant in parts of colonial Virginia that leading historian of slavery in North America Ira Berlin (1998) has referred to the region of the United States as "Igbo Land" to mark the African cultural influence that is still felt in the area today. Through the advent of genetic testing, today there are scores of African Americans, including celebrities ranging from Oprah Winfrey to Isaac Washington, who have traced their ancestry to West Africa (Halter & Johnson, 2014).

Beyond the transatlantic slave trade, the mass movement of people of African descent continued to characterize the experiences of Black Americans well into the first half of the twentieth century. During the Great Migration—sometimes differentiated into three time frames from 1865 to 1896, again from 1910 to 1940, and finally from 1940 to 1970—it is estimated that more than six million Blacks left the South for better opportunities in the northern and western regions of the United States (Mathieu, 2009). In total, the Great Migration represents one of the largest internal mass movements of individuals in US history (Lemann, 1991). Often missed in the analysis of the Great Migration is how similar the experiences of Black migrants were after their arrival to the northern and western parts of the United States to that of international immigrants coming to the United States. Like many international immigrants, Black migrants were confronted with linguistic and cultural adjustment challenges upon their arrival to their new designations. Additionally, the motivations for resettlement, including the "push" factors associated with the desire to leave behind the social and economic limitations of one environment and the aspirational "pull" factors associated with the promise of greater social and economic mobility, were another similarity shared by Black migrants and international immigrants. Interestingly, recent research by Alexander, Leibbrand, Massey, and Tolnay (2017), using census data from 1940 to 2000, found that second-generation migrants leaving the South exhibited higher economic mobility and educational attainment than those who remained in the South and frequently outperformed their native counterparts.

Changing Demographic Makeup of the US Immigrant Population

Although African immigration to the United States in general, and to the state of New Jersey in particular, is a fairly recent development, commencing in earnest in the 1980s, the population's growth in the United States can be traced to national immigration policies enacted some 20 years earlier in the 1960s. Throughout much of Newark's early history, immigrations from Europe were the primary driver of population growth in Newark and other cities around New Jersey. In fact, the state's proximity to Ellis Island, the United States' most important early immigrant port of entry, placed New Jersey at the epicenter of the country's early European immigrant history. Quickly, New Jersey became a designation of choice for the new arrivals. In Newark alone, the city's Italian population grew from 400 in 1880 to over 25,000 by 1920. Starting with the census of 1840 and continuing to the present, New Jersey has had one of the highest proportions of foreign-born populations (U.S. Census Bureau, 2014; Shaw, 1994).

At the turn of the twentieth century, immigrants made up more than a quarter of New Jersey's population. However, after World War I, economic uncertainties and rising xenophobic attitudes culminated in the passing of the National Origins Act of 1924. The act instituted national quotas and effectively limited immigration to the United States to individuals of Western and Northern European descent. In the 1960s, unprecedented economic growth and more inclusive social attitudes as a result of the Civil Rights Movement helped to set the stage for more progressive immigration policies. For instance, weeks after the passing of the Voting Rights Act of 1965, the Immigration and Nationality Act become the law of the land. Two of the more significant features of the act was the abolishment of the national origins preferential quota system that favored those of European descent and the creation of the family unification clause, enabling family members of permanent residents and naturalized citizens easier access to emigrate to the United States. Few individuals at the time understood the transformative impact the new immigration legislation would have on the demographic makeup of the country. Many assumed at the time of its enactment, as did the bill's cosponsor, Congressman Emanuel Celler, that

> there will not be, comparatively, many Asians or Africans entering the country … Since the people of Africa and Asia have very few relatives here, comparatively few could immigrate from those countries because they have no family ties to the U.S. (U.S. Congress, House of Representatives, 1965, pp. 21, 758)

While it would be decades before its full impact would be felt, the legislation helped to usher significant changes to the ethno-racial landscape of the United States. Due to the 1965 legislation, the percentage of immigrants admitted under the family unification provision increased from around 14% in the mid-1960s to 70% by 1980 (Njue & Retish, 2010). As reflected in Table 4.1, in 1970 the US foreign-born population represented less than 5% of the total population, its lowest level in the twentieth century. In each of the subsequent decades, the foreign-born population increased as a percent of the total US population from 6.2% in 1980, to 13.5% in 2016 (Grieco & Trevelyan, 2010; Zong, Batalova, & Hallock, 2018). Moreover, demographically the foreign-born population shifted from being comprised of those of European descent in the 1970s to being

Table 4.1   US foreign-born immigrant population

Year	Size of immigrant population (millions)	Immigrant share of total US population (%)
1970	9.6	4.7
1980	14.1	6.2
1990	19.8	7.9
2000	31.1	11.1
2010	40.0	12.9
2016	43.7	13.5

Source: Migration Policy Institute (MPI) (2017b) tabulation of data from the United States Census Bureau 2010 and 2016 American Community Surveys (ACS), and 1970–2000 decennial Census data

made up of individuals immigrating from Latin American countries by 2016 (Grieco et al., 2012; Zong et al., 2018).

The increase in the foreign-born population was even more dramatic in New Jersey. The state's foreign-born population increased from 8.9% in 1970 to nearly 22% by 2016 (Matthau, 2017). Currently, there are approximately 1.9 million immigrants living in New Jersey, due in part to the growth of the non-European immigrant population in urban centers like Newark. Similar to national trends, Newark's foreign-born population is made up largely of new arrivals from South America. However, the fastest-growing population of Newark's foreign-born population are individuals emigrating from Africa, particularly from West African countries, which is also in line with national trends.

Voluntary African Immigration to the United States

Unlike the United States' extensive history of forced African migration, the voluntary resettlement of Africans[1] to the United States is a relatively new development. Estimates suggest that between 1900 and 1950 only 31,000 Africans lived in the United States (Gordon, 1998). Even after the Immigration and Nationality Act in the 1960s, a first in a series of immigration reforms that would change the cultural landscape of the United States, African immigration continued to lag behind immigration patterns of individuals from other regions of the world. Despite sweeping changes to US immigration policies, previously established French and British colonial ties made Europe a more likely destination for Africans than the United States. Even in the case of Africans who did come to the United States, such as Kwame Nkrumah, the first prime minister of Ghana, or Nnamdi Azikiwe, the first president of Nigeria, the tendency was to come to the United States for educational opportunities and eventually return home. Consequently, in 1970 the foreign-born African population in the United States was only 80,000, accounting for less than 1% of the nation's foreign-born population. However, African immigration has roughly doubled in each of the subsequent decades since 1970, with an increase by 29% for sub-Saharan migration alone between 2010 and 2015 (Zong & Batalova, 2017). Today, there are approximately 2.1 million foreign-born

---

[1] It should be acknowledged that depicting migration as voluntary can be problematic, given that migration that happens as a result of war, natural disaster, political persecution, or economic hardship could be considered a form of forced migration.

Africans residing in the United States, representing close to 5% of all US immigrants. The increase in the number of immigrants coming from the African continent, coupled with recent declines[2] in Caribbean migration, has led demographers to conclude that by 2020 the number of Africans migrating to the United States will surpass those coming from the Caribbean (Capps, McCabe, & Fix, 2011).

Today, new arrivals from the African continent represent the fastest-growing population of immigrants to the United States (Anderson, 2017). Interestingly, the growth of African relocation to the United States has corresponded with a decline in African immigration to Europe. As immigration policies in the United States were becoming more open during the later half of the twentieth century, the opposite was taking place in Europe, where legislation sought to discourage migration from former African colonies. For instance, 1970s French legislation ended legal migration from the continent, while starting in the 1960s and continuing into the 1980s and 1990s, US legislation became more inclusive of African immigrants. The 1986 Immigration and Control Act, for example, expanded pathways for citizenship for undocumented immigrants, ultimately granting amnesty to over 30,000 Africans. Later, the 1990 Immigration Act created the Diversity Visa Program (commonly referred to as "the lottery") and broadened citizenship opportunities for those from underrepresented countries of origin (Halter & Johnson, 2014). Notwithstanding the recent exponential growth of African immigrants, public policy attention and media commentary has continued to focus almost exclusively on immigrants from Mexico and Central America, the United States' largest immigrant community.

The rapid growth of African immigration to the United States over the past 50 years has not been without some distinct patterns regarding migrants' countries of origin and their final designation once they arrive in the United States. The West African region, particularly the countries of Nigeria and Ghana, has been the leading region of origin for African migrants coming to the United States. In total, 36% of African immigrants have come from West Africa, followed by 29% from East Africa and 17% from North Africa. Within the United States, a quarter of all African immigrants have settled in the Northeast, drastically changing the

---

[2] It is not fully known why Caribbean migration has declined, although some, including sociologist Kevin Thomas (Thomas, 2011), have pointed to the recent economic recession in the United States as a contributing factor.

immigrant population makeup of the region. In total, 27% of the foreign-born population of people of African descent in the United States reside in the New York-Newark-Jersey City metropolitan area, with foreign-born Blacks making up 28% of the total Black population in the region (Anderson, Lopez, & Rohal, 2015). Nationally, the state of New Jersey has the fifth-largest African-born population, behind the more populous states of New York, California, and Texas, as well as the similarly sized state of Maryland (Gambino, Trevelyan, & Fitzwater, 2014).

In New Jersey, where close to 20% of the state's residents are made up of those who are born outside of the country, the state's immigrant population is concentrated in urban centers (Grieco et al., 2012). In Newark alone, the city's 77,873 foreign-born residents represent more than 25% of the city's population and close to 4% of the state's foreign-born population. Moreover, New Jersey's African immigrant population has increased by 76% since 2000, mainly due to new arrivals from North and West Africa (Anderson, 2015; U.S. Census Bureau, 2014). Following this trend, and as shown in Fig. 4.1, Newark's African immigrant population has increased by 76% since 2000, primarily due to immigration from Ghana and Nigeria. In fact, the New York-Newark-Jersey City metropolitan area is the home of the largest population of African immigrants in the country, which provides a natural pathway for new immigrants to settle in the area through the family unification provisions first introduced in the Immigration and Nationality Act of 1965 (Edward, 2010; Halter & Johnson, 2014).

Newark, New Jersey is made up of 5 political wards and 20 distinct neighborhoods. As reflected in Figs. 4.2 and 4.3, overall Newark's immigrant population is concentrated in the city's North and East Wards. This is particularly true for the city's burgeoning South American and Caribbean foreign-born communities. Conversely, the city's African immigrant population is concentrated in the city's South, Central, and West Wards. Within the city's wards, and displayed in Fig. 4.4, the largest percentage of immigrants with African ancestry reside in the Lower Clinton Hill neighborhood in the city's South Ward. African immigrants make up 8% of the total population of Lower Clinton Hill, followed by 7.7% of the Springfield neighborhood in the Central Ward, and 7% of the Westside neighborhoods in the West Ward (Statistical Atlas, 2018).

Recent Trends in Region and Country of Birth for Newark Immigrants

Today, most immigrants living in Newark were born in South America. The number of South American immigrants continues to rise, growing by 26% from 2000. However, immigrants from Central American and Africa have grown at exceptional rates. Immigrants from the Central American countries of Mexico and Honduras are growing faster than immigrants from any other country. Once prolific in Newark, numbers of European immigrants have plummeted since 2000.

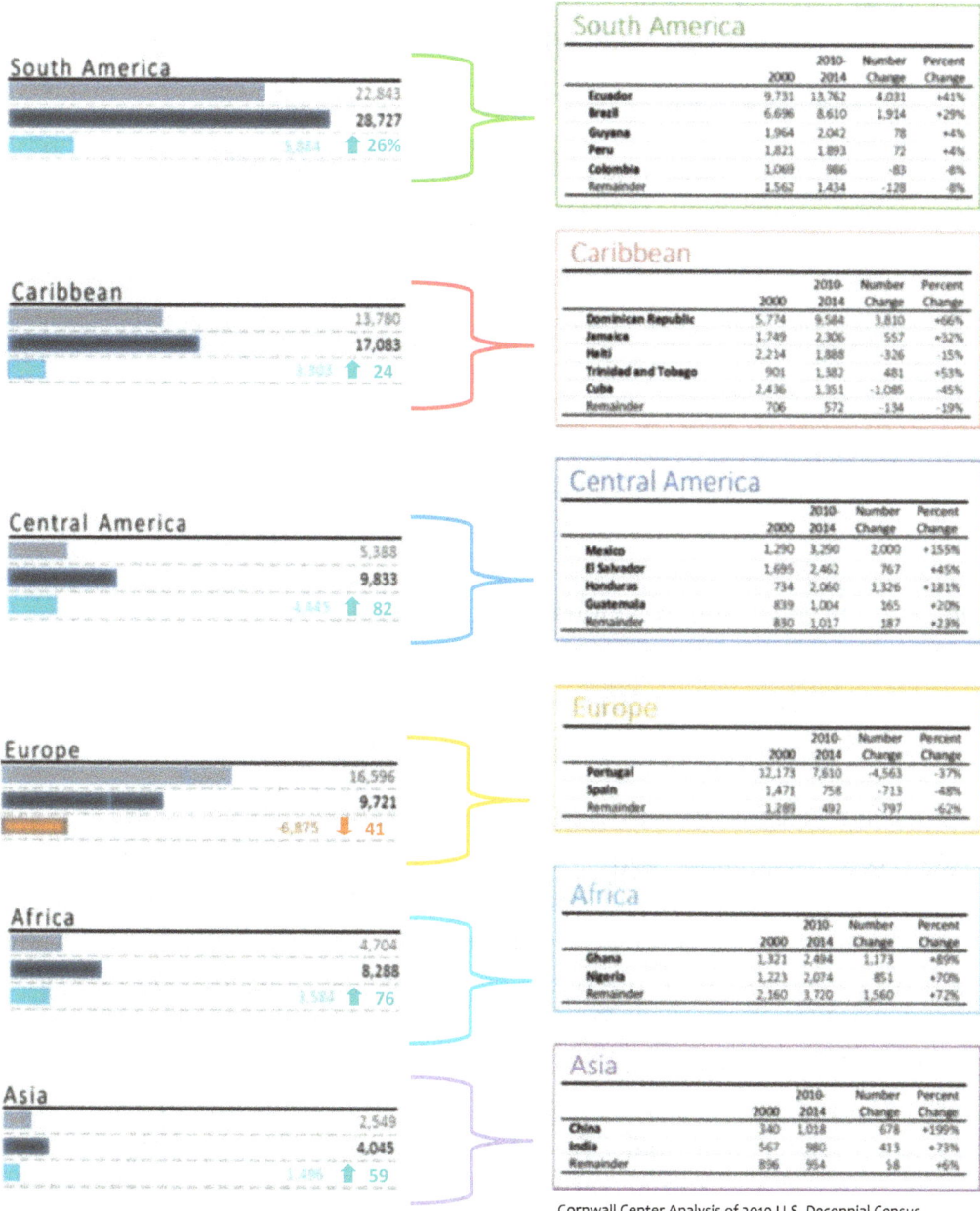

South America

	2000	2010-2014	Number Change	Percent Change
Ecuador	9,731	13,762	4,031	+41%
Brazil	6,696	8,610	1,914	+29%
Guyana	1,964	2,042	78	+4%
Peru	1,821	1,893	72	+4%
Colombia	1,069	986	-83	-8%
Remainder	1,562	1,434	-128	-8%

Caribbean

	2000	2010-2014	Number Change	Percent Change
Dominican Republic	5,774	9,584	3,810	+66%
Jamaica	1,749	2,306	557	+32%
Haiti	2,214	1,888	-326	-15%
Trinidad and Tobago	901	1,382	481	+53%
Cuba	2,436	1,351	-1,085	-45%
Remainder	706	572	-134	-19%

Central America

	2000	2010-2014	Number Change	Percent Change
Mexico	1,290	3,290	2,000	+155%
El Salvador	1,695	2,462	767	+45%
Honduras	734	2,060	1,326	+181%
Guatemala	839	1,004	165	+20%
Remainder	830	1,017	187	+23%

Europe

	2000	2010-2014	Number Change	Percent Change
Portugal	12,173	7,610	-4,563	-37%
Spain	1,471	758	-713	-48%
Remainder	1,289	492	-797	-62%

Africa

	2000	2010-2014	Number Change	Percent Change
Ghana	1,321	2,494	1,173	+89%
Nigeria	1,223	2,074	851	+70%
Remainder	2,160	3,720	1,560	+72%

Asia

	2000	2010-2014	Number Change	Percent Change
China	340	1,018	678	+199%
India	567	980	413	+73%
Remainder	896	954	58	+6%

Cornwall Center Analysis of 2010 U.S. Decennial Census and 2010-2014 5-year A.C.S. data.

Fig. 4.1   Recent trends in region and country of birth for Newark immigrants

Immigration in Newark's Neighborhoods

Where do foreign-born residents live?

- With the exception of the South Ward, immigrants' presence are felt in neighborhoods in every Ward of the city.

- Foreign-born residents are particularly prevalent in Neighborhoods throughout the East and North Wards.

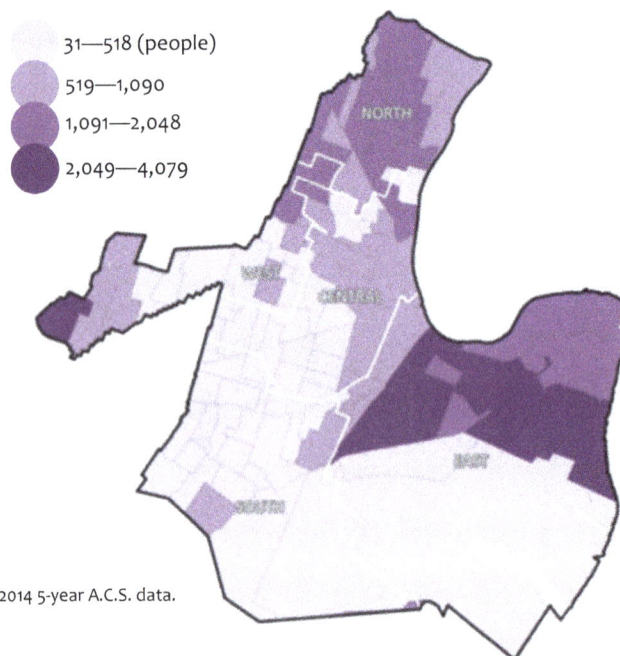

31—518 (people)

519—1,090

1,091—2,048

2,049—4,079

Cornwall Center Analysis of 2010-2014 5-year A.C.S. data.

Fig. 4.2   Immigration in Newark's neighborhoods

UNDERSTANDING NEWARK'S AFRICAN YOUTH IMMIGRANT EXPERIENCE

Previous research on the African immigrant community in the Bronx, New York, may offer some insight into the population growth of the Newark community. In her oral history, sociologist Jane Edward (2010) noted that along with the opportunity to reunite with family members currently living in the United States, African immigrants in her study who perceived that the United States was a place of opportunity and a gateway to economic upward mobility made that a part of the decision to emigrate to the United States. Increasingly, as African immigrants invest in and take advantage of educational opportunities and find economic success, the emigration of additional relatives to the United States often involves younger family members. Consequently, a natural outcome from the growth of the immigrant community in the United States has been the corresponding rise in the immigrant youth population. Since the 1980s, the children of immigrants have become the fastest-growing segment of

Region of Birth in Newark's Neighborhoods

- Immigrants from counties in the same world region tend to settle in close proximity to one another, forming pockets or enclaves throughout the city.

- South American immigrants are widespread in neighborhoods throughout the city's East Ward.

- Pockets of Caribbean immigrants are found in the city's North, West, Central, and South Wards

- African immigrants are typically found in parts of the city's West, Central, and South Wards.

- A contingent of Asian immigrants is found in neighborhoods near downtown and University Heights.

- Central American immigrants are found just north of downtown and in the extreme west of the city.

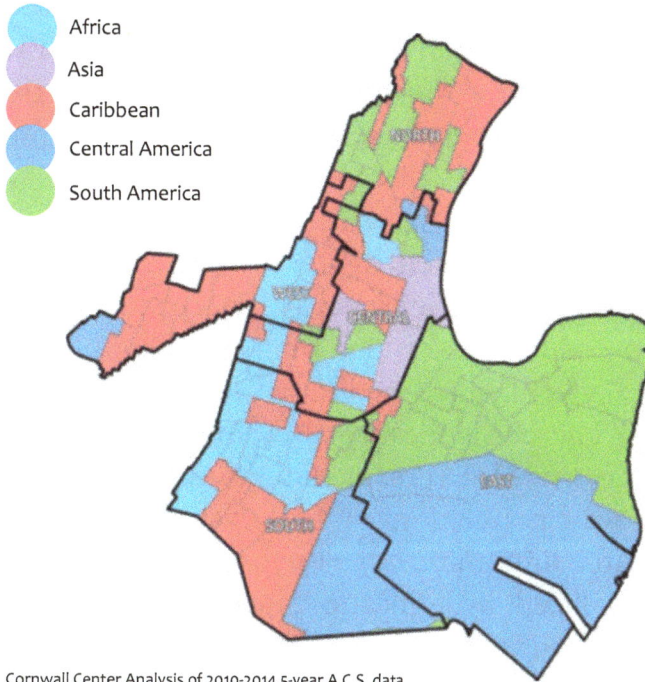

Legend:
- Africa
- Asia
- Caribbean
- Central America
- South America

Cornwall Center Analysis of 2010-2014 5-year A.C.S. data.

Fig. 4.3 Region of birth in Newark's neighborhoods

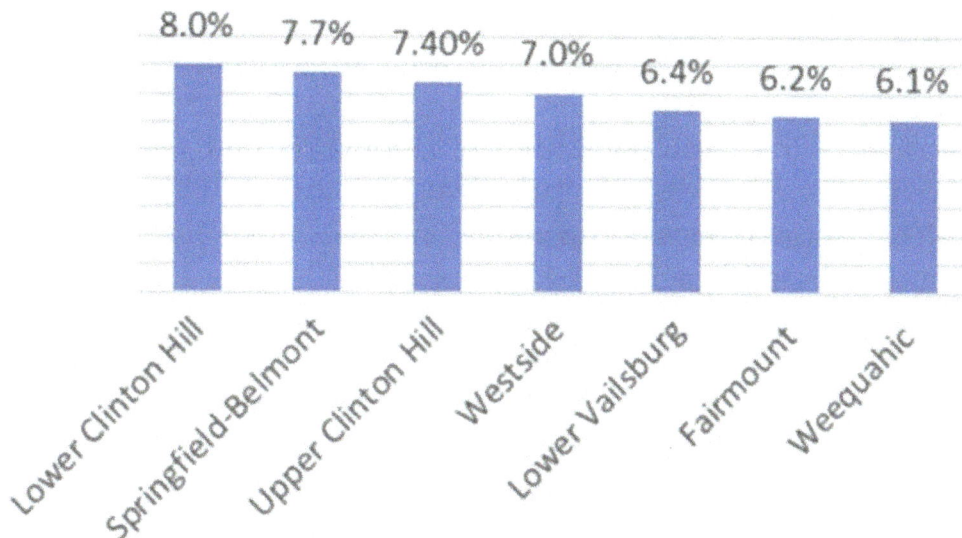

Bar chart values: Lower Clinton Hill 8.0%, Springfield-Belmont 7.7%, Upper Clinton Hill 7.40%, Westside 7.0%, Lower Vailsburg 6.4%, Fairmount 6.2%, Weequahic 6.1%

Fig. 4.4 Newark communities with the highest percentage of African immigrants: percentage of total population (Data from the United States Census Bureau accessed on the Statistical Atlas (2018) website in April of 2018)

the youth population in the United States, accounting for close to one-quarter of all children by 2015. Today, there are more than 18 million immigrant children in the United States, with 62% of them clustered in California, New York, New Jersey, Florida, Illinois, and Texas. In total, 37% of children in New Jersey are born to immigrant parents (Migration Policy Institute, 2017a).

African immigrants are found in communities across New Jersey but remain concentrated in the state's urban centers. For communities like Newark, the large increase in African students can be particularly demanding on educational and community-based institutions—each of which are typically challenged by limited financial resources and social support systems. The challenges faced by immigrant young people can not only go unmet, but also remain hidden from the larger public. School officials with large populations of African students and nonprofit leaders within the African community, however, are often positioned to understand the challenges faced by educational and community-based systems that serve African youth.

West African Students Within the Educational System

An emerging narrative within scholarly research and popular literature posits that African immigrants are the new "model minority" in the United States. Within social science research, McCabe (2011) and Zong and Batalova (2017) reported that adult African immigrants are more likely to have college degrees than both other immigrants in the United States and people who are native born. Similarly, Anderson et al. (2015) and Gambino et al. (2014) showed that African immigrants have higher rates of advanced degrees than Asian immigrants or US-born citizens. In recent years, popular media has frequently highlighted the accomplishments of African students, such as Kwasi Enin, Priscilla Samey, and Ifeoma White-Thorpe, in ways that equally celebrate their scholastic achievements in being accepted into multiple Ivy Leagues colleges and that acknowledge their West African heritage.

Still others suggest that the experiences of young African immigrants are more nuanced than the model minority narrative would suggest. Ukpokodu (2018) called attention to the fact that many African immigrants reside in urban communities of color where "savage inequalities" continue to impact the academic achievement of students. Using a content analysis of scholarly literature of African immigrant students in K-12 schools, Ukpokodu reported a lack of data to substantiate the model minority claim. Moreover, in their examination of African and African American student interactions in a public high school, Traoré and Lukens (2006) discovered that misperceptions about the continent permeated virtually all aspects of the educational setting in their study, which adversely impacted students' relationships with other students and their ability to bond with their teachers. The authors concluded that arguably the darkest thing about Africa is the United States' ignorance of it. The prevailing notion that Africa is backward and Africans are primitive, diseased, and uneducated at times created uneven teacher expectations about what African students are capable of achieving and undermined the ability of African and African American students to develop positive relationships.

To understand the challenges faced by Newark's African youth immigrant population, this research uses a case study profile of a West Ward Newark high school that has experienced a recent increase in West African immigrant students. As a research tool, case studies are particularly useful to gain a more granular understanding of a complex set of events. Often exploratory in nature and typically using a limited number of individuals as subjects, case studies allow the researcher to "investigate contemporary real-life phenomenon through detailed contextual analysis" (Zainal, 2007, p. 2). The case study includes a series of stakeholder interviews with school personnel (principal, teacher, director of student support services) and the director of a college preparation program who serves as a prominent community partner to the high school. Due to the recent influx of West African students, the local high school has implemented a series of proactive academic and social programming measures to address the needs of African students and their families.

The interviews revealed important insight into the opportunities and challenges faced by institutions attempting to serve West African youth. Within the educational context, school personnel reported that in recent years there has been an increase in the number of African immigrant students who are arriving to the United States for the first time as teenagers. With a student population of just over 1200 students, the high school principal estimated that in recent years the first-time enrollment of West African students aged 16 to 17 years has been close to 100 students annually—easily outpacing the enrollment rates of other immigrant youth. Like many school districts around the country, Newark Public Schools currently do not have a reporting system in place to disaggregate students beyond broad racial and ethnicity categories to trace Black students' country of origin or recent African immigration status. For instance, district schools rely on information polling of their student populations. Informal surveying of the West African student population conducted by the school's student support services office suggests that the majority of the local high school's West African students have emigrated from Nigeria and that a substantial number of the students are Muslim. Furthermore, general data obtained from students suggest that greater access to social and economic upward mobility was the primary reason their families immigrated to the United States.

Because of the lack of student tracking data on students' recent African immigration status, school officials found that their immediate challenge was in recognizing that the demographics of their school was in fact changing. For school officials, this revelation happened during several end-of-the-year school-sponsored family outreach events. According to the principal:

> We really were able to understand the West African presence in our community in ways that were staggering around two large events that we hosted last year. The first one was a Thanksgiving dinner. We hosted a Thanks giving dinner for the community and saw so many people come out...a lot of them in traditional African wear, they came out as families. We fed three hundred plus people for dinner on the night before Thanksgiving last year. And a lot of them this was their first experience of Thanksgiving in America ... [Another] event was a coat giveaway, working with a local non-profit organization. We ... collected 450 coats, and those coats disappeared in one hour. The vast majority of the coats were taken by new families that had arrived to this part of the city. And we understood that they were families because they asked for coat sizes that range from one-two-year-old kids all the way up to the kids that we have here. So through those events, [it] opened a window, open our eyes and open a window of opportunity for further partnerships with community outreach organizations that can support new immigrant families.

In her attempt to provide precollege programming to high school students, the external community partner's realization of the growing presence of African immigrant students was more subtle. According to the community partner:

I don't know if it was ever a case that we saw a big influx of African immigrants at one particular time, so much as it was a gradual process over the years. It was a matter of creeping in a little bit at a time. As our programming became more focused and the college content became more focused, students and their families that wanted our programming sought us out to take advantage of our content.

Even still, the lack of a systematic process has meant that school officials have struggled in addressing the unique cultural challenges imposed by the changing community demographics. In addressing this issue, the director of student support stated:

It's work in progress [meeting the needs of immigrant students]. Progress primarily because I think … we've just had an Aha moment. I know for me since I've been in this position this year, it's been like, oh my God, I didn't realize we had so many [West African students] and now they're coming in droves. And so now I kind of feel like my charge probably over the summer is to really think about what systems are we going to have in place. Because right now I feel like we're being very reactionary, right? Because we didn't know that this was going to happen or is happening, so we're just responding the best we can to it...we just need to make more concerted efforts... this is a real thing, you know, what do we have in place to serve our students.

While discussing a catalytic event that led to a paradigm shift for him, the school principal pointed to an interaction with the school's growing African immigrant Muslim population. He reflected on how an exchange with students regarding prayer led to an expansion in student programming:

A lot of our students happened to be Muslim Nigerians. And based on some of their requests, some of them had been leaving school to go to *Jummah* on Fridays. After consideration and [internal] discussion, we identified a Muslim [teacher] here at my school who is willing to lead an advisory that would satisfy the requirement for *Jummah* on a Friday. So on Fridays during our mentoring hour [school time where teachers are encouraged to mentor students and provide socio-emotional support] we now have an hour of power where young people have a place that they can go that is convenient where they can pray as they're expected to on Fridays.

Although additional work is needed, school officials point to the example displayed by the Muslim students, and others like it, where students petitioned for greater school-wide acknowledgment of students' cultural diversity, as the impetus for the creation of the school's monthly Multicultural Day. The director of student support services stated:

[F]or us as a guidance team...what I've tried to really promote and push [is] having [immigrant students] feel that sense of pride. Because...they want to assimilate and...disconnect from their background. And...any movement away from that is what they're looking for. [T]hrough our actions and our words [we] encourage students to be comfortable with differences ... I think that we as a school [have] made a tremendous effort in making [our immigrant population] feel like [this school is their] home and like they're valued and appreciated. For example, today is multicultural day [so] they went on a trip to go see Blank Panther, which in and of itself is an important cultural expression. We try to celebrate diversity in big and small ways, so for instance, we always have flags [of different countries around the world] up. [T]oday, I'm wearing my Haitian outfit ...for students and staff alike to...see a part of who we are...The more the demographics started to change...the more we wanted everybody to feel like they belong. [H]aving certain days like today where...everybody came in [in] their gear and really celebrated...our babies in that way..is what...helps make it for them.

The community precollege partner has viewed cultural exchange programming as an essential part of the ability of her organization to instill pride in native-born Black students and African immigrant students. In arranging teleconference communications between the students in her program and African students on the continent, the precollege program director discussed how the communications have helped to facilitate a cross-cultural exchange to help Black students gain a better understanding of their African heritage and see their African immigrant peers in an improved light:

We held teleconferences every year with our program participants. It was a way to bring out a sense of pride for kids who are African coming from different countries where they were a little shy and whatever. But it also helped the African American students to see Africa in a better light, which is so critical to their own personal development. We found that when the African American students gained a better understanding of Africa they gain a better appreciation of African immigrant students.

The science teacher detailed how for both African and African American students in Newark, living in the United States can rob individuals of the ability to see themselves in important roles. In detailing his formal years growing up in Nigeria, and time spent as a young adult visiting extended family living in Europe, the teacher stated:

So, if you were to go to England it would not be strange to be serviced by a Nigerian doctor or a doctor of West African heritage right? But here in America, when you see an African American doctor, you sit up a little bit straighter because like, well here it's an anomaly. Despite the image of America as a place of chance and opportunity, it is at the same time so confining to our students. So, I admit I struggle with getting my native-born students to see their possibility than I do for my West African students, and I think that while there are many factors, not hav[ing] ever seen yourself in the roles that I'm trying to get you to envision for yourself is at least part of the issue.

The final two themes that emerged from the conversations with school personnel focused on the academic preparation of their West African student population and the need for additional research focused on the broad social needs of the burgeoning population. First, school personnel expressed general agreement that the West African students are the more academically engaged segment of the student population. The school principal remarked:

We have kids coming here, not saying maybe I'll go to college, they are saying I want college and only that. So, this is the kind of hunger that's fascinating and it's what we as educators have been wishing for all the along. Can I get a population that's just hungry for education? We see this population as a core part of the change in our academic offering. We know that programmatically, what we will offer [our] kids in the future is different because now we have a group of students who are, who are crying and demanding and begging for it [education].

Based on the overwhelming interest of the school's West African student population, the high school is looking to fully revamp its academic programming through several partnerships with Newark-based colleges and universities. The expanded programming will include additional dual college credit course offerings, from the current limit of 25 slots to accommodate upwards of 100 more students. According to the principal:

Honestly, we did not have as great a need for math and engineering [college course] offerings before our West African immigrants arrived, and now that they're here and they're saying I want this, we feel the need to expand our academic programming. … We have written a grant with that focus on college access and college success. We didn't specifically name our West African kids, but we wrote it literally, I'm telling you, with the thinking that came out of the need of what we saw from this hunger for more and more college kinds of offerings.

Moreover, in her review of transcripts of recently arrived West African students, the director of student support services opined that West African students enter the high school with more advanced academic achievement levels than their native-born counterparts. In her experiences, the student support administrator contended that the traditional US high school model of assessing credit accumulation by number of hours students receive seat-time instruction does not fully recognize the talents of recently arrived West African immigrant students. According to the school official:

[West African Students], they're coming from a position of strength and they don't even know it, you know, and I think that's kind of the thing that we don't talk about because they come with these amazing transcripts and you're fascinated because you're like, you need to be in college right now, right. And yet, you know, due to our system, you have to go through this high school process. And for me, I feel like it needs to be a whole revamping of how we look at education period because, and don't let me get started on my little soap box, but if we were to use this population as a platform to have that conversation, we would ask, "Are we really servicing our children for the next step?" because there's no reason why some of these babies have to go through some of these classes.

Rather than a seat-time model to measure academic proficiency, the student support administrator advocated for a competency-based system where academic reporting and advancement center around students' demonstration of knowledge and skills. The administrator added:

Understand, I'm not talking about a GED, I mean a regular high school diploma with all of the respect associated with the degree. The GED is looked upon negatively, unfortunately. Otherwise, I feel like it's a kind of a disservice that we're here trying to use transcripts to match what students' experience is and use it as a measure of perceived mastery within a content area. We do that as opposed to just maybe testing… you are tested as an eleventh grader let's put you in eleventh grade or you are a twelfth grader... let's put you in the twelfth grade... versus sitting here and measuring students' seat-time.

Next, the high school principal expounded on the critical moment presented by the burgeoning West African population in Newark and how there remains so much more the school and the larger community can do to address the social needs of African immigrants. The principal concluded in offering:

> Now I have to think about systems that also are design[ed] to conduct meaningful outreach of our West African population. Who is the staff that I hire to make sure that when a family comes in, they see somebody or hear somebody that they can build this relationship, a trusting relationship with? This is a problem I understand is important for my school, but also for the city as a whole. We don't always understand this, but it is traumatizing when people don't see themselves in the social, educational, and social systems that they are asked to exist in.

CONCLUSION

Voluntary African immigration to the United States is a relatively new phenomenon, with much of the growth taking place during the later half of the twentieth century. Since the 1970s, the number of Africans migrating to the United States has nearly doubled in each subsequent decade. Today, Africans represent the fastest-growing group of immigrants in the United States, as well as the state of New Jersey. Much of the growth of the African immigrant population in New Jersey has been the result of individuals coming from West Africa. Currently the state of New Jersey has the fifth-largest population of native-born Africans in the country, with much of the growth fueled by demographic changes in the state's urban centers (Gambino et al., 2014). Leading the way in this population growth is the city of Newark. Anecdotal evidence suggests that new West African immigrants relocating to Newark are doing so though family unification provisions that enable family members of permanent residents and naturalized citizens expanded access to emigrate to the United States.

Moreover, US Census data shows that Newark's African immigrant population is concentrated in the city's North and East Wards. Within the city's wards, the largest percentage of immigrants with African ancestry reside in the Lower Clinton Hill neighborhood in the city's South Ward, followed closely by the Springfield neighborhood in the Central Ward, and 7% in the Westside neighborhoods in the West Ward. Within Newark's West Ward, a local high school has attempted to address the unique needs of its expanding population of West African students. Exploratory interviews with school personnel suggest that West African youth are displaying a very high academic proficiency, leading school personnel to create a number of additional scholastic and social support services. Academically, school personnel anticipate expanding dual credit college offerings for the next school year. Furthermore, the school has implemented cultural diversity programming into their school calendar.

Attention to Newark's growing adolescent West African immigrant population provides the city with an excellent opportunity to learn from and provide more targeted support to an important subset of immigrant youth. Currently within the city of Newark there are a panoply of sophisticated youth-serving efforts underway that are designed to expand educational and employment avenues for the city's youth population. This programming includes, but is not limited to, the Newark City of Learning Collaborative, a collective impact initiative seeking to increase the postsecondary attainment of Newark residents from the current 18% to 25% by 2025. On the other end of the spectrum is Newark's Opportunity Youth Network, an innovative partnership between the Newark Public School system, city officials, university partners, and a collection of high-functioning community-based organizations seeking to stem the tide of young people who leave school prior to graduating from high school. Moreover, there is the Newark 2020, a coalition made up of community stakeholders from the employment, academic, nonprofit, and governmental sectors seeking to increase employment opportunities for Newark residents. Just as these important efforts are providing such needed services to Newark residents, the Newark Public Schools will be returned to local control for the first time in nearly a quarter of a century. Local control means that local residents and governmental officials will have more authority in determining the educational programming and tracking educational progress of the city's more than 35,000 students. In each of the instances outlined above, increased awareness of and targeted services to Newark's burgeoning West African immigrant population offers an important avenue for greater positive youth outcomes.

As such, based on the insight gleaned from this study, the authors recommend that future consideration in Newark should be given to:

- Development of a system to disaggregate student school level race/ethnicity data to reflect students and their parents' immigrant status in order to understand the academic performance of immigrant students; and
- Development of a qualitative research initiative to explore the social interactions of West African immigrant youth, including challenges and opportunities regarding social acculturation and students' secondary academic achievement.

REFERENCES

Alexander, J. T., Leibbrand, C., Massey, C., & Tolnay, S. (2017). Second-generation outcomes of the Great Migration. *Demography, 54*(6), 2249–2271.

Anderson, M. (2015, April 9). *A rising share of the U.S. Black population is foreign born*. Washington, DC: Pew Research Center.

Anderson, M. J. (2017, February 14). *African immigrant population in the U.S. steadily climbs*. Washington, DC: Pew Research Center. Retrieved May 15, 2018, from http://www.pewresearch.org/fact-tank/2017/02/14/african-immigrant-population-in-u-s-steadily-climbs

Anderson, M., Lopez, M. H., & Rohal, M. (2015). *A rising share of the U.S. Black population is foreign born; 9 percent are immigrants; and while most are from the Caribbean, Africans drive recent growth*. Washington, DC: Pew Research Center.

Berlin, I. (1998). *Many thousands gone: The first two centuries of slavery in North America*. Cambridge, MA: The Belknap Press of Harvard University Press.

Capps, R., McCabe, K., and Fix, M. (2011). *New streams: Black African migration to the United States*. Washington, DC: Migration Policy Institute.

Edward, J. (2010). *Bronx African American history project's (BAAHP) African immigrant research* [White paper]. New York, NY: Fordham University.

Gambino, C., Trevelyan, E. N., & Fitzwater, J. T. (2014). *The foreign-born population from Africa: 2008–2012* (Report Number ACSBR/12-16). United States Census Bureau. Retrieved April 20, 2018, from https://www.census.gov/library/publications/2014/acs/acsbr12-16.html

Gordon, A. (1998). The new diaspora – African immigration to the United States. *Journal of Third World Studies, XV*(1), 79–103.

Grieco, E. M., & Trevelyan, E. N. (2010). *Place of birth of the foreign-born population: 2009* (ACSBR/09-15). Washington, DC: US Census Bureau.

Grieco, E. M., Trevelyan, E., Larsen, L., Acosta, Y. D., Gambino, C., de la Cruz, P., et al. (2012). *The size, place of birth, and geographic distribution of the foreign-born population in the United States: 1960 to 2010* (Population Division Working Paper Number 96). Washington, DC: US Census Bureau.

Halter, M., & Johnson, V. (2014). *African & American: West Africans in post-civil rights America*. New York, NY: NYU Press.

Handlin, O. (1951). *The uprooted: The epic story of the great migrations that made the American people*. Boston, MA: Little Brown.

Lemann, N. (1991). *The promised land: The great Black migration and how it changed America*. New York, NY: Alfred A. Knopf.

Mathieu, S., (2009) *The African American great migration reconsidered, OAH Magazine of History, 23*(4), 19–23. Retrieved October 2009, from https://doi.org/10.1093/maghis/23.4.19

Matthau, D. (2017). *NJ used to have more immigration than today*. Retrieved May 2, 2018, from https://nj1015.com/nj-used-to-have-more-immigration-than-today/.

McCabe, K. (2011). *African immigrants in the United States*. Washington, DC: Migration Policy Institute. Retrieved May 9, 2018, from http://www.migrationinformation.org

Migration Policy Institute (MPI). (2017a). *Children in U.S. immigrant families*. Retrieved April 20, 2018, from https://www.migrationpolicy.org/programs/data-hub/charts/children-immigrant-families

Migration Policy Institute (MPI). (2017b). *U.S. immigrant population and share over time, 1850–present*. Retrieved April 20, 2018, from https://www.migrationpolicy.org/programs/data-hub/charts/immigrant-population-over-time

Njue, J., & Retish, P. (2010). Transitioning: Academic and social performance of African immigrant students in an American High School. *Urban Education, 45*(3), 347–370.

Segal, R. (1995). *The Black diaspora: Five centuries of the Black experience outside Africa*. New York, NY: Farrar, Straus and Giroux.

Shaw, D. V. (1994). *Immigration and ethnicity in New Jersey History*. Trenton, NJ: New Jersey Historical Commission, Dept. of State.

Statistical Atlas. (2018). *Ancestry in Newark, New Jersey*. Retrieved April 20, 2018, from https://statisticalatlas.com/place/New-Jersey/Newark/Ancestry

Thomas, K. (2011). *A demographic profile of Black Caribbean immigrants in the United States*. Washington, DC: Pennsylvania State University and Migration Policy Institute. Retrieved March 15, 2018, from https://www.migrationpolicy.org/research/CBI-demographic-profile-Black-caribbean-immigrants

Traoré, R., & Lukens, R. (2006). *This isn't the America I thought I'd find: African students in the urban U.S. high school*. Lanham, MD: University Press of America.

U.S. Census Bureau. (2014). *Sex by age by nativity and citizenship status (Black or African American alone). Universe: People who are Black or African American alone: 2010–2014 American community survey 5-year estimates*. Retrieved April 20, 2018, from https://factfinder.census.gov/faces/tableservices/jsf/pages/productview.xhtml?pid=ACS_14_5YR_B05003B&prodType=table

U.S. Congress, House of Representatives. (1965, August 25). *Congressional record, 89th Congress, 1st Session*. Washington, DC: U.S. Government Printing Office.

Ukpokodu, O. N. (2018). African immigrants, the 'new model minority': Examining the reality in U.S. k-12 schools. *Urban Review, 50*(1), 69–96.

Zainal, Z. (2007). Case study as a research method. *Journal Kemanusiaan, 5*(1), 1–6.

Zong, J., & Batalova, J. (2017, May 3). *African immigrants in the United States*. Migration Information Source. Retrieved May 2, 2018, from http://www.migrationpolicy.org/article/sub-saharan-african-immigrants-united-states

Zong, J., Batalova, J., & Hallock, J. (2018, February 8). *Frequently requested statistics on immigrants and immigration in the United States*. Migration Information Source. Retrieved May 2, 2018, from https://www.migrationpolicy.org/article/frequently-requested-statistics-immigrants-and-immigration-united-states

PART II

Agency and Aspirations

CHAPTER 5

"To Become Somebody in the Future": Exploring the Content of University Students' Goals in Nigeria

Dabesaki Mac-Ikemenjima

INTRODUCTION

What ends do young people in sub-Saharan Africa aspire to? What economic, social, political, and environmental factors shape their aspirations? Research on aspirations has gained traction globally during the last four decades, with varying emphasis on production and reproduction of different types of life outcomes and the roles of structure and agency in the formation of aspirations, strategies, and potential for their achievement (Weiss, 2012; Hart, 2013). Recent research in this area, particularly in the field of international development, includes an emerging body of work exploring the relationship between aspirations, wellbeing, and youth transitions to successful adulthood (Copestake & Camfield, 2010; Davids, Roman, & Kerchhoff, 2017). This interest in youth aspirations stems firstly from a desire to understand the lives of young people, their developmental experiences and trajectories, and their values (Honwana, 2012). Secondly, it

D. Mac-Ikemenjima (✉)
Ford Foundation, Lagos, Nigeria
e-mail: d.mac-ikemenjima@fordfoundation.org

© The Author(s) 2020
M. L. McLean (ed.), *West African Youth Challenges and Opportunity Pathways*, Gender and Cultural Studies in Africa and the Diaspora, https://doi.org/10.1007/978-3-030-21092-2_5

103

stems from an interest in drawing on what youth value in designing policies and programs and measuring their life outcomes as an axis of policy evaluation (te Lintelo, 2012).

Youths' goals are closely aligned with the ways in which they act and the things they prioritize. Goals show the directions in which youth might want to take their lives, and give an indication of how they contend, incorporate, and deal daily with structural or systemic factors that might affect, prevent, enable, or disrupt the achievement of their goals (Locke & te Lintelo, 2012; Vigh, 2006). Furthermore, goals provide the grounding for understanding young people's resilience and how they deal with threats and challenges to their wellbeing, how they mitigate risks, and how they assess their lives (Emmons, 2003). A young person's goals can be influenced by factors within their environment, and these could be related to constructs such as materialism, altruism, biological drive, or simply survival instinct (Honwana, 2012; Massey, Gebhardt, & Garnefski, 2008).

Moreover, from a theoretical standpoint, understanding goals helps researchers to connect youths' past, present, and future expectations at various stages of their lives. Scholars have made these connections in varying ways, through theories that argue for the role of cultural capital and experience in the formation and pursuit of aspirations (Appadurai, 2004; Bourdieu, 1986) and human motivation (Kruglanski & Kopetz, 2009). In this milieu, there has also been an interest in how young people strategize to achieve their goals (Honwana, 2012). The study of goals often also includes an exploration of the strategies that youth adopt toward achievement, particularly in contexts where they face risks of stagnation and structural constraints (Honwana, 2012). While important, however, the strategies that youth adopt in pursuit of their goals are not an explicit focus of this chapter. The study presented in this chapter will help to illuminate an understanding of a specific group of youth who are studying within the geography of Nigeria's Niger Delta, and will enhance the understanding of the lives of this group of youth in an environment that is historically fraught with conflict and best known for its oil and the associated resource curse (Okonta & Douglas, 2003). It also contributes to the scholarship on youth living in conflict and post-conflict regions (Weiss, 2012; Sommers, 2010; Utas, 2012; Vigh, 2006).

An understanding of youth both as a concept and as a demographic group is crucial for enabling countries to avoid generational tensions attributable to resource scarcity and competing needs of different sub-population groups and positions them to attain the demographic dividend.[1] The need to mitigate such tensions is apparent given the increasingly limited resources and opportunities for youth to actualize their aspirations, a situation exacerbated by intensifying global inequality, a redefinition—and changing world—of work, resulting in shrinking numbers of unskilled jobs and concomitant opportunities in the formal sector. Compounding these structural constraints, state antagonism in the form of policies and regulations that criminalize the informal sector economic activities that youth tend to pursue for lack of alternatives—for example, restrictions on motorbike transport operators and street vendors, in cities such as Lagos and Kigali—further limits the space for young people to envision, and act toward achieving, life desires and ambitions (de Gramont, 2015; Rollason, 2017).

The aim of this chapter is to explore dimensions of youth aspirations from a sample of university students in Nigeria's Niger Delta by analyzing the content of their goals. It explores these goals, categorizes them, and contrasts them across gender. The analysis is drawn from research on goals, as a specific aspect of aspirations, and aims to show the different types of goals of students in a university in the Niger Delta. It offers insight into how university students in Nigeria see their futures, which could offer a baseline for further work exploring the aspirations of the general population of youth. The students' goals could have important implications for theorizing on youth goals in Nigeria, aiding in the design of educational, health, economic, and general youth policies and programs and facilitating the monitoring of such programs for effectiveness along with the evaluation of outcomes. Understanding youth goals would inform assessments of the degree to which policies and programs that target them either approximate or diverge from youths' expected or desired future lives (te Lintelo, 2012). In this way, goals and evidence of their satisfactory achievement, or progress made toward them, could serve as indicators of whether public policies and programs targeted to youth are consequential and responsive.

---

[1] The demographic dividend is the projected economic output a country is positioned to achieve due to changes in the structure of its population. Based on the experiences of countries in Southeast Asia, it is suggested that where a country has a large and productive working population, the majority of whom are youth, it is positioned to have better economic growth and development (see Bloom, Canning, & Seliva, 2003).

Understanding Youth Goals

In this study, *youth* is defined as any individual between the ages of 15 and 30. This definition derives primarily from the age range of the students in the study cohort, rather than convention or theory. This definition is, however, used with the cognizance that youth is a contested concept and lacks a common definition. For example, international organizations such as the United Nations Economic Commission for Africa (UNECA) (2009) define youth as those aged 15 to 24, and the African Union (2006) uses the ages 15 to 35. In Nigeria, the National Youth Policy defines youth as any individual between the ages of 15 and 29 (Federal Republic of Nigeria, 2019).[2] Despite this, the country's national youth service sets an upper age limit of 30 for participation. In this chapter, university students are treated as a subcategory of youth and, thus, a part of the wider population of youth. As used in this chapter, youth refers to the wider population of young people aged 15 to 30 in the region, whereas *students* is used when referring to the study participants whose goals are described.

The goals of these university students are analyzed as specific aspects of their aspirations. As distinguished from goals, aspirations are a broader category comprising all the things that young people desire to be or have, including things they are working toward achieving and things that they simply wish for (Staats & Partlo, 1993). In this sense, aspirations are seen as being mainly cognitive, which may or may not result in action and may or may not be actively pursued (Ibrahim, 2011). Perhaps with this idea in mind, Copestake and Camfield (2010) define an aspiration as "perceived importance or necessity of goals" (p. 618). On the other hand, goals are understood as desired future states toward which people are working (Kruglanski & Kopetz, 2009). One key distinction between goals and aspirations is the emphasis of goals on action. Goals are linked to actions toward achievement; as such, they are more pragmatic in their outlook and orientation. In this respect, goals have been analyzed in relation to personal projects and plans (Little, 1983). Goals are also distinguished in the literature from other aspirations-linked concepts such as ambition and hope (Ibrahim, 2011).

The possible selves theory (Markus & Nurius, 1986) provides a useful organizing framework that illustrates the centrality of action in the conception of goals as distinct from aspirations. The possible selves theory analyzes individuals' disposition in relation to their envisaged potential

[2] At the time of this study, the National Youth Policy (2009) defined youth as individuals aged 18 to 35. This was changed in mid-2019 with the adoption of the new youth policy by the government.

future selves and is focused on how people's behaviors are shaped by what they want to have or become, as well as what they do not want to have or become and, therefore, avoid (Markus & Nurius, 1986). In a sense, this theory is an extension of the approach and avoidance achievement literature—where behavior is directed by either positive/desirable or negative/undesirable potential outcomes (Massey et al., 2008), and shows that people typically move toward their desired end states and withdraw from undesired ones (Markus & Nurius, 1986).

Possible selves theory also illustrates the ways in which different goals are linked, forming an important way of thinking about instrumental and terminal functions of goals. Instrumental goals are linked to other ends and may or may not be ends in themselves. For example, the desire to become financially stable may motivate a person to seek education or training or migrate, based on the belief that those actions would enhance their prospects for upward social and economic mobility. These goals are often precursors to other envisaged outcomes in a person's life and underpin decisions on education, migration, and other important life choices. On the other hand, terminal goals are those that are considered as end states in themselves, which are not necessarily linked to others. The dichotomous characterization of goals as found in the possible selves theory is somewhat similar to other ways of thinking about the concept as discussed in the sections that follow.

The goal content theory, one of five subtheories within the self-determination theory of motivation, is also a useful theoretical framework for understanding goals. This subtheory posits that goals are either intrinsic or extrinsic (Deci & Ryan, 2000). Intrinsic goals are those that are focused on one's self and relations with others such as community, romantic relationships, and personal growth. These goals are suggested to enhance the achievement of the three basic needs of autonomy, competence, and relatedness and increase the wellbeing of individuals (Deci & Ryan, 2000). On the other hand, extrinsic goals are outward looking and include material attainments, fame, and wealth, and are suggested to result in lower wellbeing, and possibly contribute to ill-being (Deci & Ryan, 2000). The goal content theory has been operationalized in exploring the specific goals of individuals in different contexts (Davids et al., 2017). The use of binary lenses in the analysis of goals somewhat limits the range of possible categories that can be deciphered from the variety of future expectations and plans that youth have for their lives.

In various attempts to operationalize the goal content theory, goals have been described in ways that extend beyond this binary and include multiple categories. An example is the aspirations index (Kasser & Ryan, 1993), which organizes people's aspirations into four categories of self-acceptance, affiliation, community feeling, and financial success. Emmons (2005) also organizes goals into four distinct categories: intimacy, spirituality, generativity, and achievement. This, he suggests, is consistent across a range of studies which also explore the concept of goals from the perspective of meaning, personal strivings, and life narratives (Emmons, 2005). In a similar vein, Gabrielsen, Ulleberg, and Watten (2012) developed a taxonomy of goals in Norway, based on interviews and focus groups, which has the same four categories. Some of the individual goals included in the categories of the above studies include having meaningful work, relationship with God, belief in the afterlife, having an intimate relationship, family, and achieving higher education, among others (Emmons, 2005; Gabrielsen et al., 2012). Further studies of youths' goals in Nigeria could therefore be guided by the notion of goals being multi-dimensional, diverse, and different for different categories of youth who live in and experience life from different perspectives.

Context of the Study

The Niger Delta is situated in the southernmost part of Nigeria, bordering the Atlantic Ocean. It has a population of 32 million people (or 22% of Nigeria's population) and produces almost all of Nigeria's oil, which contributes around 90% of the country's export earnings. The region is mostly known for its place in the resource curse literature, widespread violence, and entrenched mass poverty despite the region's oil wealth (Obi, 2009; Okonta & Douglas, 2003). The prevalence of violence in the Niger Delta is generally associated with restiveness of youth (Adebanwi, 2005). Thus, while there are many political, economic, and social analyses done on the region, these often focus on youth involvement in violence (Obi, 2006, 2009). Consequently, not much is known about the goals of the youth living in or associated with the region. Yet, restiveness could be linked to youth agency and aspirations, given that this can be seen as a form of protest against conditions which are not consistent with what the youth envision for their lives or as a strategy to survive prevailing conditions in their environment (Vigh, 2006). This type of conflict agency is well documented in the literature from elsewhere in Africa and illustrates the agency of youth in adopting strategies to adapt and navigate contexts of conflict and advance the achievement of their goals (Utas, 2005; Vigh, 2006).

Youth restiveness in the Niger Delta has often been linked to the desire for better distribution and allocation of resources for the sake of investments in social and economic outcomes (Adebanwi, 2005). The so-called resource control argument, with citizens of the Niger Delta demanding self-determination and direct management of their natural resources, comes from the need for more equitable mechanisms of benefits sharing of natural resources gains that lead to improved quality of life in the region (Adebanwi, 2005; Bryan & Ejumudo, 2014). A study conducted to explore the aspirations of youth in the Niger Delta found that youth in the region want better investments in education to improve their future opportunities, livelihood, and other aspects of human development such as health (Foundation for Partnerships Initiatives in the Niger Delta [PIND] and International Youth Foundation [IYF], 2011). These findings of the PIND and IYF study are consistent with much earlier, even dated, work on the Niger Delta, the UN's Human Development Report for the Niger Delta (United Nations Development Programme, 2006), which emphasized a central gap in the development of the region as being a result of the absence of systems to advance human capital development that should position the youth from the region for opportunities.

Like most in Nigeria, youth in the Niger Delta face many intractable challenges. During the 1980s, the region experienced, along with the rest of Nigeria, the stagnation of human capital development, occasioned by the World Bank mandated structural adjustment program, which significantly stunted the development of skilled manpower for the regional oil and gas economy (Anyanwu, 1992). Furthermore, in recent years, it was hit by Nigeria's jobless growth, during the boom years leading up to economic stagnation in 2007, and even further job losses in the recent economic recession (Ajakaiye, Afeikhena, Nabena, & Alaba, 2016). Nationally, the labor market participation rate of young university graduates has significantly declined since the 1970s, with as many as 22% of graduates being unemployed by official statistics, although this could be much higher (Akande, 2014). Youth unemployment and underemployment rates combined stood at 67.3% in the third quarter of 2017 (National Bureau of Statistics, 2017). There is also an increasing marginalization and stifling of young voices, with universities actively working to proscribe student activism. This is a major shift from the historical involvement of Nigeria's youth since the 1920s, and university student activism through the early 1990s, aimed at addressing economic and social imbalances that have an impact on individual lives and the wider society. Youth activists and student movements were vocal against Nigeria's adoption of the structural adjustment program and attendant cuts in resources to social services, or changes in policies which resulted in higher commodity prices.

While students' agency is still exercised through protests and the rejection of policies that affect them negatively, student movements have also become increasingly co-opted to advance political ends of university administrations and electoral candidates. Students have also participated in protests in which they were the ultimate victims, such as supporting university lecturers' strikes. While students/youth still have "social weight" (Rollason, 2017), in the political space, their voices are diluted by different intended political ends. Irrespective of the short-term or intermediate ends that students seek through protests, for the most part, their aim is to become "better persons in life," to become people who have achieved something, with economic, social, and political means to live the good life in Nigeria. A study commissioned by the World Bank as part of its Voices of the Poor project in 2000 found that people in different parts of Nigeria described a poor life as one that lacked electricity, water, education, health, self-esteem, and employment, among others (Ayoola et al., 2001). Inversely, the presence of these, reflecting people's goals, could be conceived as constituting the good life.

University students in Nigeria present an important population for a study on youth goals for a variety of reasons. Unlike other education systems in which university education is largely tuition based, public, federal, universities in Nigeria are tuition free (at least by the official federal government policy), which implies that almost every category of youth, including those that are economically and socially disadvantaged, can aspire to university education. This however does not discount the fact that those who are admitted to universities only represent a small portion (25%) of those applying to enter higher education, which makes them a relatively privileged group within the Nigerian context. Since 1999, following Nigeria's transition from military to civilian democratic rule, youth from more affluent backgrounds typically study either in local private or overseas universities. Thus, while university students may be generally perceived, accurately, as having more opportunities and potential, they face many of the same realities and share similar outlooks on the future, as their peers who do not pursue university degrees.

METHODS AND ANALYSIS

The analysis in this chapter draws on data collected from July 2012 to September 2013 as part of the author's doctoral study on the measurement of youth quality of life. That study entailed analysis of an extensive dataset comprised of six rounds of qualitative and quantitative data from undergraduate students aged 15 to 30. Fieldwork included the collection of qualitative and quantitative data using purposive sampling techniques—consistent with the process of data collection for the validation of new psychological measures, which samples those who meet preset criteria (in this case, primarily being students aged 30 and below). The process of data collection included initial interviews, with a follow-up with a select group of initial interviewees, focus groups, administration of a pre-pilot questionnaire, pilot questionnaire, final questionnaire, and further interviews with some of the final questionnaire respondents (see Mac-Ikemenjima, 2018, 2019 for a detailed description of the methodology). For this chapter, only qualitative information from two data sources—initial interviews and focus groups—are discussed in detail. These analyses and related results are augmented by some descriptive statistics from the quantitative data from the pilot survey.

A total of 23 initial individual interviews (13 males and 10 females) were held and broadly focused on the question "what are the things that you consider important to your life which you are working towards achieving?" This question is consistent with the conception of goals in the study which is linked to action. The initial set of goals identified using these interviews were then subjected to further exploration in 7 focus groups with a total of 43 participants (25 males and 18 females), where further issues which were missing from the initial data and their analyses were identified and included. Prior to the commencement of the study, ethical clearance was secured from the researcher's home university, the University of East Anglia, as well as the universities where data was collected. In addition, all participants were assured that data would be treated with confidentiality and anonymity and they were free to discontinue at any point.

The qualitative data was analyzed using a grounded theory approach. Grounded theory is an approach to data collection and analysis in which data is coded for theory or conceptually meaningful categories (Corbin & Strauss, 2008). Data for this study was coded using the three-step process of open, axial, and selective coding. The initial interview data was first analyzed to generate a set of broad categories through open coding. In this step, chunks of the data which relate to a general idea are labeled based on how they occur in the data. In this step, over 60 initial goal-related codes were developed. These were then subjected to focus groups, where participants both critiqued them and filled gaps in terms of meaningful goals that they considered missing, not adequately presented, or repetitive. This process allowed a broad set of participants to contribute to the review of the initial set of codes. Following these focus group discussions further open coding was undertaken with the new data.

This was followed by the axial coding stage of the analysis, in which relationships between several open codes were identified and similar codes were grouped to form a category. This second stage of the analysis formed the basis for determining the specific goal items that are discussed in this chapter. In the third stage of selective coding, the analysis identified theoretically and conceptually meaningful categories, which were mainly used as organizing categories for the several individual goal items that were developed in the earlier axial coding stage. The categories from the selective coding stage are described in the findings in this chapter. In the section on findings, relevant quotes from the qualitative data as they were analyzed in the open coding stage of the analysis are presented. In each case, the data has been anonymized using pseudonyms to maintain confidentiality.

Based on the analysis of the qualitative data, a set of 40 goals, described later as items, was developed and administered to 267 participants in the pilot study. The 40 items were explored based on two overarching questions: "how important is it to you?" and "how satisfied are you with achieving it?" In line with the aim of this chapter, which is exploring the content of students' goals, only the results of the importance question are presented. The use of importance scores is consistent with measures of aspirations such as the aspirations index and the adolescent life goals scale (Gabrielsen et al., 2012; Kasser & Ryan, 1996), where item importance is used as the basis for measuring goals, in addition to attainability.

WHAT GOALS DO YOUNG PEOPLE HAVE?

In this section, the goals identified by the students in the analysis are described. As indicated earlier, based on the analyses of the qualitative data, over 60 codes initially derived as areas important to the students were narrowed down to 40. Many of these goals related to students' education, relationships, opportunities for livelihood, and desire to have

Table 5.1 Demographic characteristics of survey respondents

Characteristic	n (%)[a]
Sex	
Male	101 (37.8)
Female	163 (61)
Missing	3 (1.1)
Year of study	
1	17 (6.4)
2	55 (20.6)
3	50 (18.7)
4	145 (54.3)
Age	(*M* = 24.53)
15–21	38 (14.2)
22–25	120 (44.9)
26–30	93 (34.8)
Missing	16 (6)
Marital status[b]	
Married	30 (11.2)
Single	232 (86.9)
Missing	5 (1.9)

Source: Author's analysis of fieldwork data

[a]*n* = 267

[b]Marital status is used here to imply whether the participant is married or unmarried at the time of the study and does not consider other types of relationship status

consumer or material goods. For purposes of the study, these goals are organized into four broad categories—achievement, relationships, generativity, and material goals—which are described in the subsections that follow.

Achievement Goals (Becoming Somebody)

The first category of goals is focused on personal achievement within the overarching idea of having a successful life. The notion of "becoming somebody" is defined here as attaining, through a systematic process, a steady progression to attaining the social markers of a successful life. These are often grounded in moral and philosophical considerations and are understood to be based on an ascendance to the next level of attainment. This progression may or may not include material achievement—as is the case of the material goals which I describe later—but are grounded in what may be becoming a responsible (i.e., independent and stable), honest, and upwardly mobile member of society. In certain societies in Nigeria, a person may possess material wealth but may not be considered to have become somebody if they do not meet the social and ethical markers. A person may attain financial wealth but may still not be considered to have become somebody if they do not have a university degree or if they attain wealth through corruption. The goals here embody the students' desire to have social and economic mobility and attain transition to social adulthood. The specific goals identified in the analysis for this category include: having higher educational qualifications, gaining financial independence, and obtaining postgraduate education.

Central to this category of goals is educational attainment, which is seen to be instrumental, offering a means to other ends, such as becoming a respectable person in the society through gaining the prestige that the possession of a degree offers or by becoming a professional in a defined area. As one 21-year-old male interviewee expressed, the inability to transition from education to this desired professional outcome could be a source of considerable stress:

> It gets frustrating when you spend your years in school, and you come out not having anything to do, anywhere to work even with your good grade or less grade you still don't have anything to do, it's frustrating and makes people want to do something stupid. … I wouldn't want to waste the whole resources in school and come out walking in the streets.

Despite their status as university graduates, students also recognize the nuances of the need to attain a "respectable" degree, achieved through high grade point averages "to come out with a 2.1, 2.2" (upper- and lower second-class degrees, respectively), as indicated by a 25-year-old female interviewee. Furthermore, students also discussed the importance of completing their degrees at "the right time" and studying "the right courses"—that is, courses perceived as offering opportunities in the labor market (e.g., medicine and engineering). Regarding the latter, students who were studying courses that were not among their original preferences said they were exploring avenues to change to their preferred courses. However, at the time of the study, none of the students who indicated this desire in the interviews had successfully changed to their preferred course.

The data also show that concern about opportunities in the labor market motivates students' desire to pursue graduate degrees. The perceived link between graduate education and labor market opportunities is illustrated by a 23-year-old male participant who observed that, for students who do not have social networks to rely upon, acquiring these additional credentials is a strategy to advance their chances of securing employment opportunities:

> Why I think it's important for me to take my educational level to masters before getting a job due to the fact of unemployment in this country, without masters or a PhD ..., you can hardly get a job as a BSc holder. ... Nowadays, ... if you don't have anyone even there's no how you can get [a job]. But once you are academically sound, you've gotten to certain level, they can easily consider you for employment in the country.

Contrary to conventional wisdom as reflected by expectations that international migration leads to a better life (Mains, 2013), in the interviews and focus groups conducted as part of this study, international migration for economic purposes was not a major factor. However, the quest for good *quality* higher education is a major influence on students' desire for international migration. The primary reason participants gave for intending to travel abroad was to receive a better-quality education owing, according to a 28-year-old male interviewee, to the "lack [of] those good facilities to study," which affect the "ability to acquire those things we are learning ... Sometimes lecture venues are not conducive. The school system and everything is bad." Although not specifically explored in this study, the absence of economically motivated migration goals among members of the study cohort of university students is an area worthy of further in-depth analysis.

Material Goals (Making It in Life)

As the title suggests, the category of material goals encompasses the desire for ownership of material and consumer goods. During the field data collection, it was common to hear the expression that a person has "made it." This phrase expresses the notion that the individual has attained specific markers of a successful life. These markers are varied and include having a highly or well-paid job, becoming a political official, purchasing consumer goods such as a car, and being able to build a house. It is typically based on specific material and status markers that describe a person's achievements relative to society's perception of what a person requires to be successful.

Making it in life relates to having tangible achievements that affirm a person's social and economic position. Some of the specific defining features of this category found in the analysis include being wealthy, having a powerful position in the society, and being famous. The goal of becoming wealthy is distinguished from that of being financially stable based on the degree of influence commanded by being wealthy, while being financially stable refers to simply being able to afford a basic life. One of the avenues that participants perceived as a path to the ownership of such wealth and affluence is becoming a politician. Many of the interview participants indicated an interest in becoming politicians. However, this did not seem to have general appeal among the majority of participants in the focus groups and survey. The item associated with this goal "to go into politics" was only endorsed by 41.9% of the participants as very or extremely important, with a much lower median and mode of 3 and 1, respectively, compared to all the other items which had medians and modes of between 4 and 5 (see Table 5.2).

Different reasons were given by the students for their interest in politics. Some of them were already involved in student union politics and indicated an intention to run for elected office upon graduating university. Two clear motivations for the students' interest in politics emerged from the analysis: the desire to become wealthy and powerful and the intention to contribute to social change through innovation—"abstract thinking and ideas"—in policy making (as indicated by a 28-year-old male interviewee). Being a politician is perceived to be one of the ways through which individuals make it in life, as the students believe that they will be afforded the opportunity to become wealthy. As illustrated by a 25-year-old male participant, becoming a politician is perceived as an avenue for personal enrichment because "politics is the highest payer in this country."

Another aspect of political life that was mentioned by only a few participants, but which stood out in the interviews and focus groups, is the desire to represent Nigeria to other countries in an ambassadorial or other capacity. The choice of this goal can be largely understood from the same prism of prestige, power, and wealth that other types of political offices are perceived to offer. Relatedly, some participants expressed the desire to be "well-known in the society" and to be respected because of the work that they have done or their contribution to society.

Table 5.2 Descriptive statistics of goal importance items (in order of importance)

Item	Goal importance rating frequencies % (n)						Md
	Not at all	A little	Average	Very	Extremely	Missing	
God	1.9 (5)	1.5 (4)	7.5 (20)	18.4 (49)	70.4 (188)	0.4 (1)	5
Career	0	3 (8)	7.1 (19)	24.7 (66)	64.8 (173)	0.4 (1)	5
Degree	0.4 (1)	1.1 (3)	9.7 (26)	22.8 (61)	65.2 (174)	0.7 (2)	5
Health	0.7 (2)	3 (8)	10.1 (27)	20.6 (55)	64.4 (172)	1.1 (3)	5
House	1.9 (5)	1.9 (5)	9 (24)	27.7 (74)	59.6 (159)	0	5
Support family	1.1 (3)	3 (8)	8.2 (22)	28.1 (75)	59.2 (158)	0.4 (1)	5
Live	1.5 (4)	1.9 (5)	8.2 (22)	29.2 (78)	58.4 (156)	0.7 (2)	5
Married	1.5 (4)	3.0 (8)	12.4 (33)	21.7 (58)	61.4 (164)	0	5
Knowledge	0.4 (1)	3.4 (9)	8.6 (23)	28.8 (77)	58.1 (155)	0.7 (2)	5
Peace	0.4 (1)	2.2 (6)	12.4 (33)	27 (72)	57.3 (153)	0.7 (2)	5
Job	1.5 (4)	2.2 (6)	7.9 (21)	18.4 (49)	66.7 (178)	3.4 (9)	5
Comfortable	0.4 (1)	3 (8)	7.5 (20)	29.2 (78)	57.7 (154)	2.2 (6)	5
Cumulative Grade Point Average (CGPA)	1.1 (3)	1.5 (4)	11.6 (31)	18.4 (49)	64 (171)	3.4 (9)	5
Needs	1.9 (5)	2.2 (6)	10.1 (27)	28.1 (75)	56.6 (151)	1.1 (3)	5
Financially stable	1.1 (3)	2.2 (6)	11.2 (30)	27.3 (73)	56.6 (151)	1.5 (4)	5
Social change	0.7 (2)	4.1 (11)	11.6 (31)	30 (80)	53.6 (143)	0	5
Masters	0.4 (1)	3.4 (9)	9 (24)	72 (27)	57.7 (154)	2.6 (7)	5
Happy home	1.9 (5)	3 (8)	9.4 (25)	18 (48)	64.4 (172)	3.4 (9)	5
Wealthy	0.7 (2)	3 (8)	14.2 (38)	30 (80)	51.7 (138)	0.4 (1)	5
Children	1.5 (4)	1.5 (4)	13.9 (37)	25.8 (69)	55.1 (147)	2.2 (6)	5
Role model	1.9 (5)	3.7 (10)	14.2 (38)	26.2 (70)	53.6 (143)	0.4 (1)	5
Prefer	1.1 (3)	4.9 (13)	13.1 (35)	29.6 (79)	50.6 (135)	0.7 (2)	5
Respect	0.7 (2)	2.6 (7)	13.9 (37)	36.7 (98)	45.3 (121)	0.7 (2)	4
Independent	4.1 (11)	2.2 (6)	11.2 (30)	33 (88)	48.3 (129)	1.1 (3)	4
Family support	3 (8)	2.2 (6)	15.7 (42)	25.1 (67)	52.1 (139)	1.9 (5)	5
Learning	0.7 (2)	3.4 (9)	12 (32)	30.7 (82)	49.8 (133)	3.4 (9)	5
PhD	1.1 (3)	4.1 (11)	17.6 (47)	27.7 (74)	47.6 (127)	1.9 (5)	4
Friends	1.5 (4)	4.5 (12)	13.5 (36)	39.3 (105)	40.1 (107)	1.1 (3)	4
Car	1.1 (3)	4.9 (13)	13.9 (37)	32.2 (86)	45.3 (121)	2.6 (7)	4
Vocational	3 (8)	4.1 (11)	17.2 (46)	32.2 (86)	42.7 (114)	0.7 (2)	4
Confide	3.4 (9)	5.6 (15)	13.1 (35)	31.8 (85)	44.6 (119)	1.5 (4)	4
Visit	1.9 (5)	4.9 (13)	14.2 (38)	31.8 (85)	44.2 (118)	3 (8)	4

(continued)

Table 5.2 (continued)

Item	Goal importance rating frequencies % (n)						Md
	Not at all	A little	Average	Very	Extremely	Missing	
Travel	0.4 (1)	3.7 (10)	17.2 (46)	34.1 (91)	41.2 (110)	3.4 (9)	4
Influential	1.9 (5)	5.2 (14)	13.5 (36)	40.8 (109)	37.1 (99)	1.5 (4)	4
Famous	3 (8)	4.5 (12)	14.6 (39)	33.7 (90)	41.6 (111)	2.6 (7)	4
Ambassador	4.1 (11)	4.1 (11)	16.5 (44)	28.5 (76)	44.2 (118)	2.6 (7)	4
Look	4.9 (13)	6 (16)	16.1 (43)	31.8 (85)	38.2 (102)	3 (8)	4
Study abroad	5.6 (15)	7.1 (19)	19.5 (52)	29.6 (79)	37.1 (99)	1.1 (3)	4
Business	4.5 (12)	6.4 (17)	18 (48)	36 (96)	31.5 (84)	3.7 (10)	4
Politics	22.8 (61)	11.2 (30)	20.2 (54)	21.7 (58)	20.2 (54)	3.7 (10)	3

Source: Author's analysis of fieldwork data

n = 257 to 267. NB: n varies across items due to missing responses. Responses were provided on a Likert-type scale (from 1 = not at all, 2 = a little, 3 = average, 4 = very, 5 = extremely)

Central to participants' conception of the good life, or making it in life, was the marker of wealth and money, as is illustrated by Brooke:

> Good life generally, like in Nigeria you hardly survive without money. Money is almost everything, so money should play a major role in a good life. It plays a major role. There are other things but money plays a major role. You need money for mobility, because if you have money you can actually move to somewhere. If you have money, you can look presentable. … Money is good; it's good in so many aspects.

Generativity Goals (Becoming a Voice)

Because they are closely related to helping others, and in some respects advancing social justice, the third category, generativity goals, are described as becoming a voice, rather than having a voice. These goals are understood in two ways. The first, on which there is a greater emphasis, relates to giving—supporting people in need both financially and materially, contributing to social change, and being a voice for the voiceless, those who are constrained or incapable of defending themselves. The second relates to giving back to family members, particularly parents and those who contributed to the students' education in some ways.

The desire or interest in addressing social issues was found to be influenced by the experiences of others whom participants witnessed and by participants' own experiences. In relation to witnessed experiences of others, this appears to drive the desire to help and to seek justice on behalf of those affected. This is illustrated by a 23-year-old male interviewee who highlighted the oppression he witnessed in his neighborhood as the main reason for his interest in helping others, citing police injustice as a specific example:

> I have seen social injustice from people towards people, that is from citizens towards fellow citizens, from government to citizens, from the rich to the poor, from the high-handed ones to the less privileged, and every time I see these things I just think "ah Osky, if you were here you would have done this, you know. You should have told that police man to leave."

The reference to state institutions, the police in the above example, also shows that students' desire to help others is, at least in part, driven by the perceived inadequacies of state institutions and responses to the problems that exist in the wider society. In the wake of youth protests in parts of North Africa such as Libya, Egypt, Tunisia, and elsewhere in the region, researchers have highlighted the factor of youth lack of trust in state institutions as a leading contributor to youth protests in Africa (Honwana, 2012). In addition, there is a long tradition of self-help established in parts of Nigeria, which has led to the development of community schools and other types of infrastructure such as community access roads. Negative experiences of young people also drive their desire to help others. For example, a 19-year-old female participant pointed out that the challenges that others in her environment face are like hers and this informs her desire to help:

> I don't like seeing people suffer. I'm not really from a very rich home so I know where I'm coming from and I know what my people are suffering. ... So, if I have the position to help them, I would help them. ... I came from the part of the country that you see so many things happening [as] you walk on the street, you see things what you are not supposed to be seeing...? You go around you meet people, you hear people cry, you hear people tell their stories and you are not really comfortable, you feel if you actually have something you know to help these people you can be able to help these people. ... People are suffering, and I think with my position if I have something to help them I should be able to help them.

Broadly, the desire to help others appears to reflect students' interest in contributing to wider social change. Several participants indicated that they were already engaged in activities to help others through the provision of free tutorials to their peers and through local nongovernmental organizations addressing important social issues. Students who stated this goal frequently cited the examples of establishing outreach groups to communities and schools and celebrating birthdays with children in orphanages. At least two interviewees discussed their involvement in community outreach/social work with youth in Port Harcourt, through the establishment of a community-based organization. These community groups typically engage in activities such as sex education, tutorials for secondary school students, and career advice.

Relationship Goals (Having Valuable Relationships)

The fourth category, relationship goals, refers to the desire to have meaningful connections with others. This includes close associations with those within one's family, having reliable and trustworthy friends, and being religious. Participants indicated that personal and communal relationships constituted an important aspect of how they envisioned their future lives. The goals discussed under this category include: the desire to have respectful and beneficial friendships; having a person with whom to discuss their personal problems, confide in, and seek guidance; being married; having children; being able to support their families; and "to have God."

The specific goals outlined in this category have both personal and cultural motivations and relevance. For example, as will be discussed in greater detail in a later section on gender differentiation, the data shows that young males and females' transition plans to marriage is defined in part by cultural expectations and norms. This potentially explains why the majority of the male students project their transition from university mainly as being able to secure employment or pursue graduate degrees, while some female respondents see their transitions as being directly to marriage. This could be partly attributed to the patriarchal nature of most societies in Nigeria, in which males are expected to be the primary financial providers in their families. Linked to the above is also the view that when a female marries, her financial or other needs become the responsibility of her future husband. This is illustrated by a 19-year-old female respondent who indicated that she would like to marry as soon as possible "because some load will be reduced from my father." In part, these kinds of relationships have been analyzed in the literature as adaptive and survival strategies (Utas, 2005). However, the anticipated benefits do not often materialize and many young women get stuck in relationships that offer limited benefits.

On the other hand, relationships perceived to be between people of the same religion are aligned with their need for affiliation. In most parts of Nigeria, Islam, Christianity, traditional religions, and sometimes Eastern religions, are practiced—although often the media and literature cast Nigeria as being a religious binary between Islam and Christianity (Sampson, 2014). Students in this study perceived religion as not only being important but also as a cardinal aspect of their lives. In a few interviews, students expressed "regret" or "remorse" for not being as actively religious as they would have liked, and thus expressed the desire to be "closer to God" or "return to God." As shown in the quantitative data in Table 5.2, "God" was categorized as one of the top items for importance among the goals listed, with more than 70% of participants rating it as extremely important.

References to God are often linked to the participants' spirituality, as illustrated by a 23-year-old female interviewee:

> My spiritual life is not the way I want it to be. I should have my time with God. To have your own time, it gives you insights. Everybody has his own guiding angel. To have your own time with God.

As they were described by the participants in the study, relationship goals are important for both the instrumental and terminal value that they offer. Some of these goals are viewed as ends in themselves, for example having children, whereas others are viewed as being instrumental to other ends, such as being married and having reliable friends.

How Important Are These Goals?

As described earlier, individual goals developed from the foregoing qualitative analysis were converted into items for the collection of additional quantitative data. The questionnaire developed through the qualitative analysis process was administered in a pilot study. A total of 267 students completed the instrument (see Table 5.1 for demographic characteristics). When the data from the 40 items using the question "how important is it to you?" were analyzed, they showed high-level endorsement of the goals by the participants. The results also showed that, consistent with the small sample of participants in the interviews and focus groups, these goals are highly valued by the students in the universities where data was collected. Table 5.2 shows the item-level responses and medians for each of the data points, which illustrates that most of them were endorsed at the highest level.

GENDER DIFFERENTIATION

The goals found in the analysis of the qualitative and quantitative data did not show significant differences between male and female students. Tests of statistical significance (Mann Whitney) did not find any statistically significant differences between male and female students (at 0.05 level) across the goal categories. However, one area where there was a difference in the qualitative data, in the sequencing of goals, is with respect to the goal to be married.[3] While marriage was identified as a next step for many female participants after completing their undergraduate studies, this was not the case for most of their male counterparts. The male participants cited the need for financial stability as the main reason for not prioritizing marriage immediately following their degrees.

As mentioned earlier, male students' prioritization of work or post-graduate education perhaps may stem from cultural norms that require them to be the primary income earners of their families (Olawoye et al., 2004). There appears to be an extension of the model of relationships in which females are expected to be entirely dependent on their male partners, or mainly take on the role of being house wives (Ntoimo, 2013). Some female participants (for instance, Chidinma, cited earlier in the section on relationship goals) pointed out that they preferred to be married while still studying or soon thereafter, citing the belief that marriage would improve their financial situation.

Research shows that the reasons young women marry in Nigeria include pressure to avoid the stigma associated with being single beyond a certain age and to acquire the social status associated with the perceived achievement of being married, and a desire for companionship and to have children. In some societies in Nigeria, being married accords a woman

---

[3] Marriage is used here to refer to heterosexual relationships between males and females. Although this differentiation was not explicitly asked, the researcher assumes the majority of the students referred to these types of relationships. This does not however discount the possibility that some students might have implied other types of marital relationships that do not fit the gender binary that is dominant in Nigeria.

certain social status and "respect," and having children elevates this even further, given the premium placed on childbearing (Uchendu, 2006). However, many young women, particularly urban and educated women, are choosing to remain single for various reasons, including the desire to first secure their financial independence, challenge the patriarchy, adhere to religious beliefs, and wait for the right partner (Ntoimo & Isuigo-Abanihe, 2011).

Discussion and Conclusions

This study finds that youth goals are culturally grounded, diverse, and multidimensional. The four categories of goals that emerged from the analysis presented in this chapter—achievement, material, generativity, and relationship—define the range of values that the students in the study wanted to achieve in their lives. For certain categories of youth who are similar in terms of their age or life stage, their goals can be similar irrespective of their gender or other markers of difference.

In analyzing the goals of the students, some additional questions emerged: Why are some obvious goals such as international migration, personal safety, and environment not prioritized by the students? What role do religion and culture play in the formation of the students' goals? These questions are discussed briefly in this section.

The first question reintroduces the instrumental and terminal functions of goals. In this regard, some goals, such as international migration, may be seen as means to other ends and therefore not considered specific goals in themselves. Consequently, despite the opportunities that may be perceived to be available via migration, the students did not indicate it as a goal. This is illustrated by the fact that when international travel was discussed in focus groups and interviews, it was mainly described in relation to vacations and overseas studies. The specific example of international migration is given as an example of "expected" goals not mentioned because it contradicts the high numbers who attempt to cross the Mediterranean into Europe (International Organisation for Migration, 2018).

Furthermore, it is interesting to find that despite their level of education, being university students, and perceived privilege, gender normative expectations still influence the goals of the students. This is seen in the replication of existing gender norms and stereotypes in the results where some female students prioritize marriage over further education. However, the above is said keeping in view that the essential composition of the participants' goals were similar across gender, and no statistically significant differences were found in their goal content.

The goals reported in this chapter are grounded in and defined by students' experiences, society, religion, and culture. This, however, fails to explain why some goals that should be locally relevant under the broad rubric of collective goals are missing, such as the preservation of the environment. Does this suggest that the students are increasingly individualistic, unaware of the impact of oil activities on the environment in the Niger Delta or unconcerned about the safety and security concerns daily expressed in the region? This question is further expressed given that students voiced a specific interest in participating in social change activities in the region. Why did these obvious questions of interest in the region not feature as prominently as those included in the four categories? These questions, and others such as the strategies the students are adopting in the pursuit of their goals, are not discussed in this chapter, but could be areas for further exploration.

This chapter sought to contribute to the body of work on youth aspirations by analyzing and describing the goal content of university students in the Niger Delta of Nigeria. Based on the analysis of qualitative and quantitative data, the study found and operationalized 40 goal items and validated these using descriptive results. The results offer an opportunity for policy makers and researchers to draw on the content of students' goals for program design and policy making. There is a wide array of issues that an analysis of goals generates, which can be translated into youth development policies (te Lintelo, 2012). Understanding the goals of youth could therefore enable the design of policies and specific programs that are more targeted in addressing students' instrumental goals and serve to tailor them in ways that help students achieve their terminal goals. For example, education programs may be strengthened to prepare youth better for employment opportunities. Furthermore, an understanding of the goals of young people could be taken as a dynamic process. This implies an ongoing process of research and analyses on how their goals may inform policy analysis and review on an ongoing basis rather than as a one-off exercise.

The similarities of young people's goals across gender also suggest that policies for youth can be broadly similar in their areas of focus. However, in areas where there are differences, policies should be appropriately tailored to meet youths' needs based on gender differences (Sommers,

2012). Approaching policy in this way will ensure that policies are dynamic, are continuously sensitive to the evolving priorities and needs of youth, and enable governments to channel resources to the aspects of young people's lives where they can make the most difference.

Finally, these results offer an opportunity for researchers to explore the goal content of young people, analyze the factors that affect, influence, and enhance the formation and pursuit of their goals, and explore further the extent to which goals influence youths' decision-making and the effects of specific types of goals on the ways in which young people live their lives. Researchers could also explore further the effects of culture and religion versus the role of globalization in shaping youths' goals.

REFERENCES

Adebanwi, W. (2005). The carpenter's revolt: Youth, violence and the reinvention of culture in Nigeria. *The Journal of Modern African Studies, 43*(3), 339–365.

African Union. (2006). *African youth charter*. Addis Ababa, Ethiopia: African Union Commission.

Ajakaiye, O., Afeikhena, J., Nabena, D., & Alaba, O. A. (2016). *Understanding the relationship between growth and employment in Nigeria*. Washington, DC: The Brookings Institute.

Akande, T. (2014). *Youth unemployment in Nigeria: A situation analysis*. Retrieved February 11, 2015, from http://www.brookings.edu/blogs/africa-in-focus/posts/2014/09/23-youth-unemployment-nigeria-akande

Anyanwu, J. C. (1992). President Babangida's structural adjustment programme and inflation in Nigeria. *Journal of Social Development in Africa, 7*(1), 5–24.

Appadurai, A. (2004). The capacity to aspire: Culture and the terms of recognition. In S. H. Davis & C. Jenkins (Eds.), *Culture and public action* (pp. 59–84). Stanford, CA: Stanford University Press.

Ayoola, G. B., Aina, M. B., Nweze, N., Odebiyi, T., Okunmadewa, F., et al. (2001). *Consultation with the poor*. Nigeria: Voice of the Poor. Retrieved February 11, 2015, from http://goo.gl/p8bzcY

Bloom, D. E., Canning, D., & Seliva, J. (2003). *The demographic dividend: A new perspective on the economic consequences of population change* (Population Matters). Arlington, VA: Rand.

Bourdieu, P. (1986). The forms of capital. In J. Richardson (Ed.), *Handbook of theory and research for the sociology of education* (pp. 241–258). New York, NY: Greenwood.

Bryan, K., & Ejumudo, O. (2014). Youth restiveness in the Niger Delta: A critical discourse. *SAGE Open, 4*(2), 1–12. https://doi.org/10.1177/2158244014526719

Copestake, J., & Camfield, L. (2010). Measuring multidimensional aspiration gaps: A means to understanding cultural aspects of poverty. *Development Policy Review, 28*(5), 617–633.

Corbin, J., & Strauss, A. (2008). *Basics of qualitative research* (3rd ed.). Thousand Oaks, CA: Sage.

Davids, E. L., Roman, N. V., & Kerchhoff, L. J. (2017). Adolescent goals and aspirations in search of psychological well-being: From the perspective of self-determination theory. *South African Journal of Psychology, 47*(1), 121–132. https://doi.org/10.1177/0081246316653744

Deci, E. L., & Ryan, R. M. (2000). The 'what' and 'why' of goal pursuits: Human needs and the self-determination of behaviour. *Psychological Inquiry, 11*(4), 227–268.

de Gramont, D. (2015). *Governing Lagos: Unlocking the politics of reform.* Washington, DC: Carnegie Endowment for International Peace.

Emmons, R. A. (2003). Personal goals, life meaning, and virtue: Wellsprings of a positive life. In C. L. M. Keyes & J. Haidt (Eds.), *Flourishing: Positive psychology and the life well-lived* (pp. 105–128). Washington, DC: American Psychological Association.

Emmons, R. A. (2005). Striving for the sacred: Personal goals, life meaning, and religion. *Journal of Social Issues, 61*(4), 731–745.

Federal Republic of Nigeria. (2019). *National youth policy: Enhancing youth development and participation in the context of sustainable development.* Abuja: Federal Ministry of Youth and Sports Development.

Foundation for Partnerships Initiatives in the Niger Delta [PIND], & International Youth Foundation [IYF]. (2011). *Niger delta region youth assessment.* Abuja, Nigeria: Author.

Gabrielsen, L. E., Ulleberg, P., & Watten, R. G. (2012). The adolescent life goal profile scale: Development of a new scale for measurements of life goals among young people. *Journal of Happiness Studies, 13*(6), 1053–1072.

Hart, C. S. (2013). *Aspirations, education and social justice.* London, UK: Bloomsbury.

Honwana, A. (2012). *The time of youth: Work, social change, and politics in Africa.* Sterling, VA: Stylus.

Ibrahim, S. (2011, September). *Getting priorities right! The role of aspirations in wellbeing analyses.* Paper presented at the European Association of Development Research and Training Institutes, York, UK.

International Organisation for Migration. (2018). *Mixed migration flows in the Mediterranean.* Geneva, Switzerland: Author.

Kasser, T., & Ryan, R. M. (1993). A dark side of the American dream: Correlates of financial success as a central life aspirations. *Journal of Personality and Social Psychology, 65*(2), 410–422.

Kasser, T., & Ryan, R. M. (1996). Further examining the American dream: Differential correlates of intrinsic and extrinsic goals. *Personality and Psychological Bulletin, 22*(3), 280–287.

Kruglanski, A. W., & Kopetz, C. (2009). What is so special (and non-special) about goals? A view from the cognitive perspective. In G. B. Moskowitz & H. Grant (Eds.), *The psychology of goals* (pp. 27–55). New York, NY: Guilford Press.

Little, B. R. (1983). Personal projects: A rationale and method for investigation. *Environment and Behavior, 15*(3), 273–309.

Locke, C., & te Lintelo, D. T. H. (2012). Young Zambians 'waiting' for opportunities and 'working towards' living well: Lifecourse and aspiration in youth transitions. *Journal of International Development, 24*(6), 777–794.

Mac-Ikemenjima, D. (2018). The role of qualitative methods in the measurement of youth quality of life in sub-Saharan Africa. *SAGE Research Methods Review*, 1–15.

Mac-Ikemenjima, D. (2019). *Measuring youth quality of life in Sub-Saharan Africa: Exploring the role of qualitative methods.* Basel, Switzerland: Springer Nature.

Mains, D. (2013). *Hope is cut: Youth, unemployment, and the future in urban Ethiopia.* Philadelphia, PA: Temple University Press.

Markus, H., & Nurius, P. (1986). Possible selves. *American Psychologist, 41*(9), 954–969.

Massey, E. K., Gebhardt, W. A., & Garnefski, N. (2008). Adolescent goal content and pursuit: A review of the literature from the past 16 years. *Developmental Review, 28*(4), 421–460.

National Bureau of Statistics. (2017). *Labour force statistics (Vol. 1): Unemployment and underemployment.* Abuja, Nigeria: Author.

Ntoimo, F., & Isuigo-Abanihe, U. (2011, December). *Determinants and consequences of spinsterhood in Lagos, Nigeria.* Paper presented at the Sixth African Population Conference, Ouagadougou, Burkina Faso.

Ntoimo, L. (2013). Patriarchy and singlehood among women in Lagos, Nigeria. *Journal of Family Issues, 35*(14), 1–29. https://doi.org/10.1177/0192513X13511249

Obi, C. (2006). *Youth and the generational dimensions to struggles for resource control in the Niger Delta.* Dakar, Senegal: Council for the Development of Social Sciences Research in Africa.

Obi, C. (2009). Nigeria's Niger Delta: Understanding the complex drivers of violent oil-related conflict. *Africa Development, XXXIV*(2), 103–128.

Okonta, I., & Douglas, O. (2003). *Where vultures feast: Shell, human rights and oil in the Niger Delta.* New York, NY: Sierra Club Books.

Olawoye, J. E., Omololu, F. O., Aderinto, Y., Adeyefa, I., Adeyemo, D., & Osotimehin, B. (2004). Social construction of manhood in Nigeria: Implications for male responsibility in reproductive health. *African Population Studies, 19*(2), 1–20.

Rollason, W. (2017). Youth, presence and agency: The case of Kigali's motari. *Journal of Youth Studies, 20*(10), 1277–1294. https://doi.org/10.1080/136 76261.2017.1324134

Sampson, I. T. (2014). Religion and the Nigerian State: Situating the de facto and de jure frontiers of state – Religion relations and its implications for national security. *Oxford Journal of Law and Religion, 3*(2), 311–339. https://doi.org/10.1093/ojlr/rwt026

Sommers, M. (2010). Urban youth in Africa. *Environment and Urbanization, 22*(6), 317–332.

Sommers, M. (2012). *Stuck: Rwandan youth and struggle for adulthood.* Athens, GA: The University of Georgia Press.

Staats, S., & Partlo, C. (1993). A brief report on hope in peace and war, and in good times and bad. *Social Indicators Research, 29*(2), 229–243.

te Lintelo, D. J. H. (2012). Young people in African (agricultural) policy processes? What national youth policies can tell us. *IDS Bulletin, 43*(6), 90–103.

Uchendu, E. (2006). Woman-woman marriage in Igboland. In A. U. Azodo & M. Eke (Eds.), *Gender and sexuality in African literature and film* (pp. 141–154). Trenton, NJ: Africa World Press.

United Nations Development Programme. (2006). *Niger Delta human development report.* Abuja, Nigeria: Author.

United Nations Economic Commission for Africa (UNECA). (2009). *African youth report 2009: Expanding opportunities for and with young people in Africa.* Addis Ababa, Ethiopia: Author.

Utas, M. (2005). Victimcy, girlfriending, soldiering: Tactic agency in a young woman's social navigation of the Liberian war zone. *Anthropological Quarterly, 78*(2), 403–430.

Utas, M. (2012). *Urban youth and post-conflict Africa: On policy priorities* (No. 4). Uppasala, Sweden: Nordiska Afrikainstitutet.

Vigh, H. (2006). *Navigating terrains of war: Youth and soldiering in Guinea Bissau.* New York, NY: Berghahn Books.

Weiss, B. (2012). *Street dreams and hip hop barbershops: Global fantasy in urban Tanzania.* Bloomington, IN: Indiana University Press.

CHAPTER 6

Making Lives, Making Communities: Deaf Youth in Benin

Carsten Mildner

Becoming Deaf

An adage of deaf rights movements that is commonly expressed in Benin says "les sourds peuvent tout faire sauf entendre": the deaf can do everything but hear. Physically, that is plausible and can serve as a good basis for equality claims and critique of discriminatory practices. But it is also true that, phenomenologically, the non- and hard-of-hearing experience family, community, and society very differently than the hearing, who to the deaf constitute an emic "other" that includes persons with other disabilities. Adhering to social models of disability (see Shakespeare, 2010), I do not intend to present deafness as an essential "differentness" (see Neubert & Cloerkes, 2001) that fundamentally separates deaf people from the presumably "normal." Rather, the differentness of deaf persons is socially constructed as well as fashioned by the deaf themselves, "looped," so to speak, through a continual process of change and adjusted perceptions (Hacking, 2011, p. 297f). The physiological aspect of deafness is—as with

C. Mildner (✉)
Bayreuth International Graduate School of African Studies (BIGSAS),
Bayreuth, Germany
e-mail: Carsten.Mildner@uni-bayreuth.de

© The Author(s) 2020

131

M. L. McLean (ed.), *West African Youth Challenges and Opportunity Pathways*, Gender and Cultural Studies in Africa and the Diaspora, https://doi.org/10.1007/978-3-030-21092-2_6

other disabilities—but one of many facets of being deaf. In Deaf studies, the normalization discourse is identified as reducing deaf people to their physiological impairment and forcing them into the standards of the hearing majority society (Davis, 1995). Deaf people themselves—in Benin and beyond (for Japan see Nakamura, 2006, p. 184, for Ghana see Kusters, 2015, p. 95)—practice a kind of segregation from within, othering themselves from the hearing by forming an exclusive peer group. This exclusive group is considered a deaf community, or as is critically discussed in the literature, a complex of "Deaf culture/community/world" (Kusters, 2015, p. 20)—a community of shared experience of social disability, of cultural similarity, and, most of all, of a shared language. In Benin, there is no unified, postulated, notwithstanding formalized, deaf community or culture, but there are several groups and spaces that serve as communities to the respective members.

This chapter explores how deaf youth in Benin can or cannot choose to enter these communities. In the first section, I identify and outline four major dimensions that frame the possibilities of being deaf in Benin: physiological, geographical, cultural, and social. As the discussion will show, these dimensions are immensely intertwined and entangled. To illustrate the possible interplay of these four dimensions in the lives of young Beninese during the period of transition from youth to adulthood, in the second section, I introduce three deaf individuals as case studies that will be preceded by a short discussion of youth concepts. All three young people are members of deaf communities, but their paths of entry, kinds of belonging, and appreciation of and by the respective communities are quite different. These case studies do not purport to cover all aspects and potentialities of moving through life as a deaf youth in Benin; but viewing them side by side yields a perspective on how the conditions and frames *can* work out for deaf young people. The phrase "making lives" in the title is inspired by Ian Hacking's (2011) "looping effect" and his thoughts on "making up people" (Hacking, 2002, pp. 99–114), emphasizing the inseparability of self-determining and being determined in the process of becoming a social person. In other words, "identity is a byproduct of modes of *inter*relationships" (Jackson, 1995, p. 118, italics in original) and therefore inevitably social (cf. Jenkins, 1996). Looking at this particular segment of West African youth, I explore some of the dynamics and challenges at stake for young deaf individuals seeking to take advantage of opportunities and overcome obstacles in making their lives.

Notes on Methods and Terminology

This chapter is based on ethnographic material gathered during 12 months of anthropological field research in 2016 and 2018 in Benin.[1] My research project broadly explores questions of identity, belonging, and community among the deaf in Benin, focusing on the interplay of the physical and social experience of deafness. I conducted participant observation in families, schools, workplaces, churches, festivities, and daily chores. This "thick participation" (Spittler, 2001) led to informal conversations and reflections, which were more common than recorded interviews. That is also because the documentation of interviews in sign language required setting up a video camera, which formalized the situation even more than the infamous tape recorder. I used the camera for longer narrative interviews, mostly with people I already knew quite well. I spoke, visited, and observed deaf people of practically all ages, who I got to know mostly through snowball sampling, with a slight gender bias toward male deaf persons. Most women I talked to were confident, interested, and open; I did not notice a particular restraint because they were interviewed by a male anthropologist, at least not after we got to know each other.

Readers who are familiar with Deaf studies will have noticed that I do not use the capitalized *D* when referring to the deaf in Benin. Deaf studies scholars and activists claim that being deaf is rather an experience of being a linguistic minority than an experience of disability. Therefore, Deaf culture and Deaf are written with a capitalized *D*, as you would capitalize other linguistic identity markers such as French, Fon, or Franconian (Ginsberg & Rapp, 2013; for further discussion see McIlroy, 2010; McIlroy & Storbeck, 2011, p. 498). The question of whether or not and how the deaf in Benin ascribe to "Deaf culture" is one that goes beyond the scope of this contribution. I chose to use a small *d* here as the conventional notion of Deaf culture is not widespread, and sign language is not a useful identifier of the deaf in Benin, as only a minority of the deaf know the Francophone West African variant of American Sign Language (ASL) (Kamei, 2006; Nyst, 2010). In countries where Deaf culture movements are strong—such as the United States (Lane, 2010, p. 83) or Japan (Nakamura, 2006, pp. 22, 185)—it is usually the hereditary born deaf who are seen as the truest, "purest" Deaf (Nakamura, 2006, p. 2), as their

[1] My field research was funded by Studienstiftung des deutschen Volkes and Bayreuth the International Graduate School of African Studies. I am very grateful to Hanna Lena Reich and the editors for their comments on this chapter.

first language is sign language. The rate of hereditary deafness in Benin, is, however, quite low—a factor that leads to a different physiological, and phenomenological, vantage point.

Physiological Dimension

The rate of hereditary deafness is very low in relation to deafness caused by illness or questionable medication during pregnancy; complications at birth; overdose of vaccination, antibiotics, or other medication of the newborn; complications of different diseases like malaria; and the most common cause, meningitis (Ette-Akre, 2012, p. 32; Vodounou, 2008, p. 62). Even though hearing loss is often attributed to witchcraft, curses, or breaching of taboos by the deaf person's parents (for Ghana see Kusters, 2015, pp. 108, 209), many hearing Beninese believe that deafness is hereditary. It could be that cultural and medical explanations are being conflated, or that both are equally respected and feared. On the physiological level, this means that parents tried to prevent their deaf children from marrying other deaf for fear of having deaf grandchildren (see also Kusters, 2015, p. 31). As hereditary deafness is usually recessive, this means that few deaf children experience having deaf parents (Aoki & Feldman, 1991). The core group that shares the "same" experience of generational and cultural deafness, thus, does not exist as such. Instead, there are several ways and moments in life to become deaf; therefore, there are manifold ways deafness plays out in a person's development.

Children who are born deaf or deafened prelingually, that is, before speech acquisition, have no experience of a spoken mother tongue. However, persons who are deafened postlingually, that is, after having acquired speech, usually around the age of two to three years, do have a general idea of what speaking is and that movements of the mouth produce sounds that are words that have meaning. The older a person is at deafening, the more she is familiar with language and might continue to speak for the rest of her life. A child or teenager who becomes deaf may acquire or learn a different social role as a deaf person and socialize into the deaf world. People who deafen after childhood or youth might not consider themselves deaf at all, as they deafened after being fully socialized in the hearing world. As that is a very individual experience—and sometimes a choice—there is no way of generalizing a certain age when this switch occurs. The French and Fon words for deaf—*sourd* and *tokounon*—

are applied to all kinds of severe hearing impairments and do not designate the degree of hearing loss.

The postlingually deafened, *les devenus sourds*, are potentially more able to learn lip reading in those languages they acquired before deafening than their prelingually deaf peers, *les sourds profonds* or *les nés sourds*. On the one hand, this makes the deafened more able to communicate with the hearing, to the extent that sometimes people would not even notice or believe that the person is deaf. Through lip reading and glimpsing into the hearing epistemology and ontology to varying degrees, the postlingually deaf have more access to the (hearing) world than their prelingually deaf peers.

Although a social approach to disability focuses on the constructivist aspects of disability and deafness, physiological dimensions have to be taken into account regarding their respectively different opportunities to actually become social in the first place. In an existential reflection of the question of essence and existence, Ian Hacking (2011) commented on the limits of social constructionism that "existence may precede essence for the lucky, but there is a vast dead weight of essence that presses down on most human beings" (p. 284). Those physiological impairments are deepened socially by the insufficient support from educators in deaf schools. Yet, the place where deaf people can learn to be social and to communicate is the school—the core space of community and identity construction. To get to school, however, you need to be somewhere there is a school.

Geographical Dimension

Ways of becoming deaf socially are shaped by the geographic location where a person happens to have been born. This refers to the rural-urban dualism and also to the sheer coincidence of growing up near or far from a deaf school.

In Benin, there are nine primary schools for the deaf: one in the capital Porto Novo, three in the biggest city Cotonou, two in the villages Sé and Pèporiyakou (near Natitingou), and one each in the towns of Allada, Bohicon, and Parakou. Most of these communities are in the south; only Parakou and Natitingou are located in the north. If a deaf child lives in a village in the north, she is thus not so likely to have access to, nor is her family likely to have knowledge of, deaf schooling and its opportunities. Due to the lack of qualified teachers, the schools do not necessarily offer quality education. However, it is in deaf schools that deaf children meet their deaf peers and sometimes realize for the first time that they are not the only deaf persons in the world, an important step for a deaf person's identity development (Vodounou, 2008, pp. 90, 93).

The schools constitute "deaf spaces" that serve not only as spaces of community and identification (Kusters, 2015), but also as "safe spaces" for deaf children. Although there is no widespread mockery of deaf people from adults, some deaf adults have childhood memories of being mocked by other children in the neighborhood. For instance, other children would take leaves in their mouths to communicate that the deaf children were viewed more like goats and other animals than as humans. Childhood experiences such as these distance the deaf child from the hearing world. Inside deaf schools, children are shielded from being denied their humanity. There is also the advantage that in the surrounding community deafness is less likely to be perceived as an anomalous condition attracting mockery. The fact that some schools are integrative and include both hearing and deaf children, or sometimes just some hearing siblings of deaf children, strengthens this effect.

Even if deaf children do not enter school, they can become part of a deaf community by meeting other deaf people. This is more likely in urban spaces than in the village, simply because the absolute number of deaf people in urban areas tends to be larger. In Parakou or Natitingou, where the schools have been established not much longer than ten years, there is a non-standardized way of signing among the deaf who were born before the schools existed. The deaf meet at deaf spaces such as deaf people's workshops or run into each other in the market or places where football matches are broadcast. The deaf community thrives most in Cotonou, where the first deaf school was created alongside the deaf church in 1977. Also, the two other primary schools and the *collège* (secondary school) facilitate contact and friendships. Furthermore, leisure activities and institutions like a deaf football club require a critical mass of people around the same age and gender that is more likely to exist in urban centers than in rural areas. The three individuals in the life story sketches all lived in Cotonou for the better part of their youth.

Cultural Dimension

Another factor in the rural-urban dualism is that beliefs in magic and witchcraft are becoming less dominant in the cities while they thrive in small towns and villages. The basic notion that "the dead are not dead" is widespread. Beninese people tend to say that this is a cultural reality rather than a religious belief. In any event, regarding the deaf, the supernatural explanations are relevant to the issue of stigma. In Benin, a child's deafness is oftentimes explained by her parents having been cursed by witchcraft or having violated some taboo or obligation toward the ancestors. Following this explanation, the deaf person herself is never the culprit but the passive victim. The ones who have failed to respect a taboo, the ones who were supposed to be punished or attacked, the guilty ones, are the parents and not the child. In theory, this means that it is not the deaf person who is stigmatized, and that deafness is nothing for the deaf person to be ashamed of. In sociocultural terms, deafness falls into the broad category of illnesses, mishaps, and disabilities commonly understood to be entangled with magico-religious practices. The downside is that, fearful of what others might think, some parents literally hide their deaf children away. I did not encounter deaf children who were being hidden away by their parents, but I heard many stories of activists and school employees who tried to convince parents to take their deaf children out in the open. Often these accounts involved parents of deaf children who were said to be rich and concerned that their child's deafness would be perceived as confirmation and evidence of immoral practices that made their wealth possible. This is a widespread view in some West African communities, where "[witchcraft] accusations were directed at those individuals and families who, in the pursuit of economic success, appeared most competitive, greedy, and individualistic in their social relations" (Scheper-Hughes & Lock, 1987, p. 24; see also Igwe, 2016).

Social Dimension

Arguably, with respect to the transition from youth to adulthood, the crucial experience that Beninese deaf have of their deafness is social. The more deaf children get in touch with other deaf children or institutions for the deaf, the more likely they are to enter a deaf community and grow to be deaf in the sense of a social being. But the creation of networks and community requires a certain number of deaf people who can get in touch. Particularly in rural contexts, though, the creation of and access to deaf communities is rarely possible.

The census data on disabled people is considered unreliable by the Fédération des Associations des Personnes Handicapées au Bénin (Federation of Associations of Disabled People in Benin), the umbrella organization representing people with disabilities and their interests on the national level. In 2003, Kiyaga and Moores stated that "there are neither reliable data nor reliable estimates of the number of school-age deaf children in sub-Saharan Africa. No country in the region has ever counted its deaf population in a census" (p. 21), which, to my knowledge, stands true to this day. The World Health Organization (2018) estimates that on a global scale "up to five out of every 1000 babies born are born with hearing loss or acquire it soon after birth." The cases that are caused later in childhood, adolescence, and adulthood have to be added to the 0.5%.

It is remarkable that in every village I visited in the north, I found one, two, or three deaf people, or at least heard stories about deaf inhabitants. There is no special education for deaf children in the village (except for the two village deaf schools in Sé and Pèporiyakou). Instead of going to school, they learn the gendered work as any other child would: the girls stay with their mothers, sisters, and other female relatives in the homestead, while the boys—after a certain age—follow their fathers and brothers to the fields. Most learning of village work is not acquired through explanation but occurs through observation and imitating. Parents and neighbors of deaf children I met in the villages assured me that the children were good workers.

Deaf children in the village barely go to school, but many hearing children do not attend the chronically understaffed and underfunded public village schools either; they too are expected to work. The lifeworld in the villages that is structured by age, gender, and work further undermines a feeling of "deaf similitude" (VanGilder, 2016, p. 148; see also Kusters, 2015, p. 92f). A deaf teenage boy and a deaf woman in her 30s would not necessarily have any shared spheres of life. Hence, given the likelihood that they each are experiencing different degrees of deafness, and that there is no standardized sign communication, what would motivate them to practice or create a shared identity?

In the towns—or in the deaf schools in Pèporiyakou and Sé—the situation is quite different. While the standard of education in the deaf schools is not particularly good, the deaf children learn to sign mostly in the breaks between or after class. The teachers—almost exclusively hearing individuals—have varying degrees of competence and interest in sign language. There is no special education nor a financial encouragement to teach in deaf schools. In the private schools, which are the majority, the teachers earn little more than the minimum wage of 40,000 FCFA (about $70) per month—if they are lucky enough to receive the salary at all. Teachers' salaries in the two public schools are higher, but the authorities do not employ enough teachers. Some substitutes are paid for directly by the parents of deaf pupils.

Similar opportunities are offered by the two deaf churches in Cotonou, where the congregations are made up of deaf teenagers and adults, some of whom have been to school and others who have not. Since the deaf churches were established, part of their mission has been to teach sign language, primarily for the sake of preaching the word of God (Kamei, 2006; Kiyaga & Moores, 2003; Nyst, 2010).[2]

Aside from those two institutions, churches and schools, there is the sphere of informal deaf space at the workshops of artisans, craftspeople, and purveyors. Deaf craftspeople often take deaf apprentices. Their workshops turn into deaf spaces, where deaf people work and learn, but also gather, chat, and socialize. These spaces are more numerous in cities than in smaller towns or rural settings.

By becoming part of these communities, deaf people have the profound experience of discovering that they are not alone in their condition—they are not the only deaf people in the world (see Nakamura, 2006, p. 19; Vodounou, 2008, p. 90). They can express ideas and get to know people that they can ask for advice, get information and—seemingly the most important thing—gossip. It is only in these communities that they can learn basic abstract concepts like the existence of Benin as a country among others, the meaning of religion, or other topics that cannot be discussed in rudimentary gestural communication with their family or neighbors. The prelingually deaf also get to know postlingually deaf who can explain to them how the hearing world and society works. As unifying as this community may potentially be, it also socially stabilizes the distinction I mentioned under the physiological dimension: the experience and knowledge of the postlingually deaf can lift them above the prelingually deaf and create paternalism and subordination.

Another crucial social aspect of becoming a deaf social being within the deaf community is hierarchy. Founders of schools, priests, and also those young deaf people who were the first to obtain higher education or are successful in economic activity are known and respected authorities that are sometimes even feared in the community. Being attached to one church, to one school, to one association, thereby to one head of either

---

[2] See also the articles by Andrew Foster on the website of the Christian Mission for the Deaf: www.cmdeaf.org

institution, might determine how one relates to other authorities—based on the relationship the respective authority has with the others—or if they relate at all. The question young deaf are faced with is how to integrate into these networks and hierarchies. Shall they take the place the respective authorities allocate to them, or shall they be "vanguards" and "vandals" (Abbink, 2005) and challenge the structure of the communities? These questions will be of importance in all three life story sketches that follow.

PATHWAYS TO BECOMING A DEAF ADULT

In the previous section, I have shown the versatility of "becoming deaf" in Benin and how that process is interconnected with both the sociocultural context and the physiological, individual experience. In this section, I examine how these challenges can be experienced or "navigated" (Vigh, 2006, 2010) by young people seeking their position in life and community. The notion of maneuvering and navigating captures the set of actions youth take to cope with difficult and obscure contexts, in order to make a living and make their lives (Christiansen, Utas, & Vigh, 2006).

Now, for the purposes of this study, whom do I categorize as *youth*? I do not intend to take on the challenge of developing a globally valid and inclusive perspective on youth (see Philipps, 2018, p. 1); nor do I wish to uncritically generalize and project youth models from the Global North (Philipps, 2018, p. 4) onto the setting in Benin. Instead, as used here, the term youth refers to persons considered *les jeunes* by members of the Beninese deaf communities included in this study: Deaf individuals who so identified, or were so identified, were in secondary school or apprenticeship, had not yet achieved professional and familial establishment and were roughly between 13 and 30 years of age.[3]

Age as such, however, is not crucial when defining young people—rather youth is an "imprecise group [of which] definitions compete according to circumstances, events or calculations" (Balandier, 1985, p. 87 as cited in Le Meur, 2008, p. 211). It depends on the achieved

---

[3] The United Nations Educational, Scientific and Cultural Organization (UNESCO) (2017) uses 15 to 24 years as the age brackets for youth and defines it as "a period of transition from the dependence of childhood to adulthood's independence and awareness of our interdependence as members of a community," that is, a time of finding one's place in community and society. For the African Union (2006), the words *youth* and *young people* refer "to every person between the ages of 15 and 35 years" (p. 3).

stages in life—for instance, graduation from primary school, receiving an apprenticeship diploma, foundation of a family, or settling professionally for the first time—"moving on to adulthood," as Le Meur (2008) notes in a case study on central Benin (p. 229). The notion of incompleteness is one that I witnessed being reproduced by the elders in the deaf community in Cotonou.

The idea of youth as a contingent category is carried further by Jean and John Comaroff (2005), who emphasize the historicity and volatility of the concept—noting that youth are not born but "made by historical circumstances. And rarely as they like" (p. 24; see also Christiansen et al., 2006, p. 11). The social construction of *youth* is just as true for *the deaf*. They face expectations they may choose to meet or not. In the literature, this tension is discussed in a polarity between subordination and rebellion, of being *Makers & Breakers* (Honwana & de Boeck, 2005; see also Abbink, 2005; Le Meur, 2008), of signifying hope and threat to established structures (Comaroff & Comaroff, 2005, pp. 20, 24; Martin, Ungruhe, & Häberlein, 2016).

Youth have been discussed as occupying "innovative, uncharted borderlands in which the global meets the local" (Comaroff & Comaroff, 2005, p. 27f), and as being between childhood and adulthood (Le Meur, 2008, p. 229; UNESCO, 2017). In such an unascertained position, they are in a situation of potentiality, being and not being. Reflecting on this liminality from the standpoint of disability, Patrick Devlieger (1999) proposes that disability be understood as an interstitial category, as disabled people "are situated (and situate themselves) in between the structural categories that define cultures" (p. 299). Deaf youth, then, can be considered to be in a double bind—a compounded intersectional situation.

Comaroff and Comaroff (2005) observe that navigating borders and structures of marginalization is a universal challenge for young people, but the ways in which they experience and face this challenge is not homogenized (p. 27; see also Philipps, 2018, p. 4). Likewise, there is no globally homogenous deaf culture (Erting, Johnson, Smith, & Snider, 1994; Friedner & Kusters, 2016; Monaghan, 2003), nor are national and regional deaf cultures and communities homogenous (Padden, 1980, p. 91). Orientations and navigation in these ambivalent and miscellaneous terrains are challenging for both youth and deaf, and maybe even more so for deaf youth (see also Friedner, 2015, p. 16, for orientations and conflicts of deaf youth in Bangalore). With the three life story sketches that follow, I will discuss a few shades of experience of deaf youth in Benin to show how different pathways unfold within the same arena of challenges and opportunities. All names are anonymized.

On the Edge of a Deaf Community: Élie

I met Élie for the first time in June 2016 when he was about 16 years of age, finishing primary school in a center for the deaf in Cotonou. He was prelingually deaf and very expressive and fluent in signing in a logic and structure that comes naturally to the born deaf (Kusters, 2015, p. 7; Sacks, 1989, p. 77f). As he had little grasp of French grammar, which is the basis for the general way of signing in Benin (Kamei, 2006), formal interviews were a complicated undertaking. Some questions and reflections on his life course and personal history were not understandable to him or I could not make myself understood. Instead, I got to know him through conversations during walks in the neighborhood, going for runs together and chatting at the beach, and a lot of participant observation in the deaf center where I lived for a few months in 2016. In 2018, while he was an apprentice at the tailor workshop on the same premises, I went there almost every second day to chat, interview, participate, and observe life and work in the center. We did not stay in touch between my two field trips as he had neither phone nor internet.

Élie was born in northern Benin; his date of birth is unknown, and he did not have a birth certificate or any legal documents. It is not even clear if he was born as Beninese or Nigerien. His name was not given to him by his parents, but by Catholic nuns who found him after his parents abandoned him at the age of about two. There is no reliable information on whether Élie was born deaf or deafened shortly after birth, nor on details of the first years of his life. The nuns placed him in a deaf school in Parakou, run by an evangelical church, directed and taught by hearing people. Joachim, the deaf director of the center in Cotonou, met Élie in Parakou at a sports event, took him south, and enrolled him into his school. I do not know what the nuns thought of this, but from other comparable situations (see Omolayo later in this story), I know that hearing people often think that the deaf should be with "their" people, with "their brothers and sisters," so Joachim's initiative was probably welcomed.

Élie was the only deaf child who stayed in Joachim's boarding school in Cotonou during the vacation, as he was practically an orphan with no connections whatsoever to his biological family. He became the foster son of Cathérine, Joachim's second deaf wife, who took care of the boarding school children's hygiene and canteen. Cathérine stated that he was now her son, whether she wanted it or not, because he had no one else. Although there was no formal adoption, he found food and shelter with the family and was regularly sent to complete different chores: buying small things, delivering messages, helping in the household, and surveilling the boarding school children during the school year. It is quite common in Benin to take distantly related or unrelated children into a household in exchange for support, sometimes leading to the children actually becoming part of the family (Alber, 2018). Nonetheless, Cathérine treated Élie differently than her own three hearing children regarding affection, attention, and care. For example, he would be sent to do chores more often, would receive worse food than her biological children, or would not be taken along with them to church or other festivities involving transport and other costs. Joachim would not call Élie his son, denying a kinned relationship (cf. Howell, 2003). Yet he felt responsibility and had the authority to make decisions over Élie's life course.

Élie had been in the center already for a few years before I met him in 2016. Due to the lack of a last name and a birth certificate, he could not take the final primary school exams (*certificat des études primaires*, or CEP) and hence was not admitted to secondary school. He wanted to become a teacher for the deaf, which was not possible without further education. After some time of reflection about what to do, Joachim finally made him an apprentice in the tailor's workshop in the center.

Élie continued to sleep in the center all year, being the oldest "son" and learning in the workshop. On the side, he helped an elderly hearing woman in the neighborhood set up her stall in the streets, where she sold deep fried yams, breadfruit, aloko, sweet potatoes, and mashed bean beignets. In return he would eat or occasionally get a little money from her. She had already supported other deaf persons in the past years and was consequently known among the deaf as Maman Vadim. In Benin and other African societies, mothers are often referred to as the mother of their first born. Vadim, a deaf painter, was not actually Maman Vadim's son but her son-in-law. Among the deaf, she became his mother through the care she gave to him (see Goody, 1982; Howell, 2003). Also in Élie's case, she cared for him beyond food by arguing with Simon, the deaf tailor and instructor, about getting Élie more involved in the actual work. Apprenticeships in Benin usually start with the apprentice watching the patron's work for several months while doing small chores, before touching the actual work for the first time. When Élie had only attached buttons for almost a year in 2018, Maman Vadim approached Simon, quite expressively, to stop wasting Élie's time and really start teaching him.

As the only permanent resident of the center who was not part of Cathérine and Joachim's family, Élie took over a particular role. He knew the place and the people. He must have felt very much at home. At the same time, he was always excited about people dropping by—other deaf people, hearing and deaf French volunteers, me as a permanent visitor, or also my mother who visited me in the field in September 2016. He insisted on sending her a video of him greeting her for her birthday in July 2018. Often when we hung out in front of the workshop, watching people walk by, or when getting food, taking a stroll in the neighborhood, or running to the beach, he would just ask random things about the French volunteers he had met in the center, my mother, or the elderly lady I was staying with for some time in Cotonou. It seems to me that this listing of names and acquaintances is a kind of outreach into the world, throwing out anchors to fix him in a virtual network. Acquaintances in Cotonou, Benin, and beyond seemed to be an orientation, maybe a status, or fixed stars for social navigation. One might say that he could not make much use of these landmarks at the time, but part of social navigation is keeping open potentialities. For example, he kept collecting telephone numbers of people he met, as well as friends of mine who came over to visit the center. He did not have a telephone. But, you never know.

Despite working his way through two deaf schools and his apprenticeship at a deaf space, Élie's access to the wider deaf community is relatively limited. In the family, just as in the workshop, he was treated as an inferior and did not receive a lot of respect or recognition. His lack of any financial means or real income kept him from getting to the deaf church in another part of town or coming often to deaf football training. The deaf church has no means to support the cost of transportation of any member but the priests, who also preach to the deaf in other cities.[4] The majority of the deaf footballers either were some years older than Élie or had formed another peer group of secondary school students. He was inferior in both age and education. He got some recognition, however, for being a good runner and taking part in different charity runs, winning a marathon in

---

[4] It is often said in West Africa that the best way to become rich is to found a church. From my experience, I suggest not to found a church for people with disabilities. There is not much money to be made from them.

Parakou in February 2018. The fact that he was mastering an individual sport instead of a team game seems quite characteristic.

His position changed slightly in July 2018 when a new deaf boy, Omolayo, around 16 years of age, arrived in the center. His Nigerian parents were concerned that he was roaming the streets all day and all night, afraid of him becoming a criminal. His parents paid Cathérine for food so that he could stay in the center. He started an apprenticeship in the tailor's workshop, based on the hope that living with other deaf people, "his brothers," as Omolayo's father said, would calm him down. Given that he was a lot harder to handle than Élie, Cathérine remarked appreciatively that Élie was too calm and confident to be provoked by Omolayo's offenses. Good for Omolayo, she said; if Élie one day would fight back, he might kill him. This was also, weirdly, an appreciative comment, as she acknowledged him as a strong young man.

From an abandoned disabled child to an apprentice with a small but diverse social network, Élie came a long way, going through different spaces of deaf sociality. In that deaf sociality, he found deaf adults who would take over care obligations. He did not become a member of the core community around the deaf church. After his apprenticeship, new contacts and support will be necessary to find a job, to found his own workshop, and to start a family. But with his 18 years of age, youth is still long.

Into the Deaf Family: Kiva

I got to know Kiva in the deaf church in Vêdoko, a neighborhood in Cotonou, when she was 26 years old. She and her deaf husband were very active members of the congregation. Although the church did not have official positions for women of importance—unlike the male priests, the precentor, the prayer instructors, custodians, even cleaners—she was close to a "soft power" of the congregation. While Nicéphore, her husband, served as the precentor and thereby was a confidant of the head priest, Homère, Kiva was close to Homère's wife, Wilhelmine, who ran a boutique in the church's building where pupils from the deaf school around the corner would come during the day to purchase candy. Kiva cleaned the boutique and ran it when Wilhelmine could not be there. I often met her there to chat; we did a video-taped interview, and we often talked after church on Sundays. I also visited Kiva and Nicéphore in their home in the inner-city swamps in the Ahogbou neighborhood.

Born deaf in Togo, the only child to her father's second wife, Kiva and her parents fled during the reign of Gnassingbé Eyadéma (president after the 1967 military takeover and until his death in 2005), which she described as a time of war. Her father was killed on the getaway. She and her mother settled in Porto Novo, Benin, where they had relatives. There her mother sent her to a private deaf school that had opened in the 1990s. She stayed until *quatrième* (equaling the eighth year in school). At some point, her mother and her family could not pay the tuition anymore, so around the age of 15, she started an apprenticeship as a hairdresser with a hearing patronne. Halfway into her apprenticeship, her mother moved to Womey, a village-like neighborhood on the outskirts of Cotonou. It was then that she started frequenting the deaf church, even though it was a long ride from Womey. Before that she had accompanied her mother to a Catholic church where she never understood anything. Her mother supported her participation in the evangelical deaf church, believing that it was good to attend any church at least. It was in church that she met Nicéphore.

They both realized, after praying a long time for advice, that God wanted them to marry. Their mothers—Nicéphore's father had died as well—hesitantly agreed. Nicéphore's mother told me in an interview that she was worried they would have deaf children. For Kiva's mother, the deafness was not as big a problem as the fact he was from Ouidah, the capital of Vodun in Benin (see Rush, 2013). Not only was she suspicious of the "heathen" culture, but she was also afraid because of prejudices against people from Ouidah in general. The interethnic incompatibilities were more relevant for her than the deafness. Eventually it was the priest of the deaf church who went to see both mothers and convinced them, arguing that Nicéphore was a good Christian, a good man, and telling them that their grandchildren would not be deaf—using his own hearing children as proof. His son would come along to those kinds of meetings to interpret. The only condition was that they shall both finish their apprenticeships before marrying.

Thus, in 2013, Kiva and Nicéphore were the first couple to marry in the newly built deaf church. The event took place at the same time as the opening of the new church building. Photographs of the ceremony and party contribute to the collective memory of the congregation.

In 2014, at age 24, Kiva gave birth to her first son. After he turned 2, Kiva and her husband gave him to her mother and her family, so he could learn to speak. This is a common practice among deaf couples, as they would not be able to teach their children language. Sign language does not get the same mother tongue recognition in Benin as it gets in other deaf communities (see, e.g., Lane, 2010, p. 83; Nakamura, 2006, pp. 1–2). As mentioned above, the practice of giving children to be raised by other family members for various reasons and to varying degrees is known among hearing Beninese as well (Alber, Martin, & Notermans, 2013). Kiva's second son was born in 2016 and was always by her side during my research in 2018. He did not speak a word but understood the sounds his parents uttered—they did not sign to him—better than words other people spoke to him. At some point, she told me, she would also give him to her mother or an aunt so that he could learn to speak.

Although Nicéphore's mother lived right around the corner from the deaf church, a lot closer than Kiva's mother, she was not involved in the children's education and barely saw Kiva at all. Instead, Kiva spent all day from Monday to Saturday in the boutique of Wilhelmine. She cleaned, sold, stocked up, and took care of her son. The boutique was very much a deaf space as Kusters sees them: many deaf people dropped by for a chat and a lemonade during the day. As a deaf school was right behind the building, the boutique also offered a contact zone for the deaf children. Most of all, though, people came by to see and consult Wilhelmine, who appeared to take over a mother's role for the entire congregation. She became a mother figure for Kiva, giving advice on how to raise her sons, giving her a job opportunity, wondering with her how to contribute to the family income—Nicéphore's work as a carpenter on different construction sites does not provide for more than a very basic budget.

Kiva told me that she had no contact with any hearing people whatsoever—overlooking the contacts with her maternal family. Her uncles sometimes gave them some money, but she did not recognize that as being enough. From her family, she expected nothing but financial support it seemed. From the deaf, she did not receive any financial support, instead a position among them and recognition. Always being around Wilhelmine, she slipped into a position of passive importance that she shares with only a handful of other members of the congregation of about 80 frequent members.

Having left her geographic place of origin, it seems that Kiva also cut ties with her hearing social origins. As soon as she accessed the deaf world around the church, she dived in and enjoyed the acceptance, recognition, and belonging that she never experienced in the hearing contexts of family, the Catholic church, or the apprenticeship with hearing patronnes. She found familiarity and belonging in church, but even more so in the deaf space it constitutes than in the spiritual message. Among the deaf, the community around the church was one of the most acknowledged ones, and through being there, through participating and receiving care from the church's mother figure Wilhelmine, Kiva's integration into church must have been a very "kinning" experience.

Achieving Through and Beyond the Deaf Community: Isaïe

In Nikki near Parakou in north eastern Benin, Isaïe was born the son of a Baptist priest in 1988. He went to a public school until he deafened from meningitis at the age of 12. He switched to the deaf school in Parakou at first, before getting into the private *lycée* in Porto Novo with the help of Swiss donors. It was the only school in Benin where deaf people could get a higher education entry qualification (*baccalauréat*). He went on to study educational science and psychology at the Université Abomey-Calavi in Cotonou; in 2018 he was still waiting for his final certificates for his license (undergraduate degree). During his school and studies, he was financially supported by international donors, organized and channeled through Joachim, and assisted by Homère, the priest. Education in both the private school in Porto Novo and the public university cost far more than a low-income family could afford for their child. It was in the yard of Joachim's center in Cotonou that I met Isaïe for the first time. As a post-lingually deaf person, he speaks almost flawless French and his mother tongue Bariba. He can read lips, and sometimes people would not even notice that he has 100% hearing loss. I conducted several interviews with him, sometimes on video tape, sometimes on audio tape (I would then sign and speak at the same time so that I could hear my parts of the informal interviews on tape as well), as the tape recorder was more easily set up than a camera. I also lived at his place in Natitingou for some time, accompanied him to the Catholic school for the deaf where he works in Pèporiyakou near Natitingou, and spent a lot of time with him when he would visit Cotonou. Furthermore, we stayed in touch through Facebook and WhatsApp when I was not in Benin.

When he came to Porto Novo, Isaïe was about 280 miles from his family and integrated well into his deaf peer group in the boarding school. He did very well in school, as he said, but often got into trouble with teachers and the directorate due to his recalcitrant nature. When in Cotonou, he lived with Homère and Wilhelmine—just like their own children, as

Wilhelmine would say. Even though he had no family ties or contacts in Porto Novo nor in Cotounou, he immediately found support—regarding both financial help and kin care—through the deaf community, just as Élie and Kiva did.

During and after school, however, Isaïe took a different turn. Instead of adhering to the smaller (Élie) or bigger (Kiva) deaf community, he questioned the discourses and practices of those communities in general. He was one of the few deaf Beninese—all in all less than ten individuals—who went to university. The education he received was much more advanced than what was available to the older authorities at their time of youth, taking into account that the first deaf class to receive a baccalauréat graduated in Porto Novo in 2009.[5] Isaïe's experience and performance of youth can then rather be seen in the light of recent discussions of African (and global) youth that present young people simultaneously as hope for and as a threat to their societies. People invest their hopes and resources into the young to provide for a better future, while at the same time they tend to complain about the lack of morals and the threat to the existent order of society or community (see Diouf, 2003; Martin et al., 2016). Youth can be described as a "fantasized or real factor of disorder or renewal" (Le Meur, 2008, p. 211). This seems quite the role that Isaïe took over in the Beninese deaf community. The older authorities invested in him, but they were displeased to discover that he would not envision the future in the way they expected he would and should (Diouf, 2003, p. 4). Rather, he spoke out against them publicly on Facebook—a central medium for many discussions within the deaf community. His criticism was directed against certain conservative evangelical positions that Homère took against the allegedly immoral behavior of Isaïe and other young deaf (cf. Diouf, 2003, p. 9), but also against some corrupt ways of leading deaf organizations and associations by Joachim and others of his generation. On the one hand, he proclaimed the need for young people's self-organization in opposition to "the old," while at the same time wanting to become a patron himself, wanting to take over responsibility for his "deaf brothers and sisters" who did not (yet) have the chances he had, thereby directing himself to the

---

[5] There are some other deaf people who studied in public or private universities. Those, however, received their baccalauréat in schools for the hearing and usually deafened so late that they saw themselves as members of the hearing world who just happen not to hear—I mentioned this in the physiological dimension above. To my knowledge, these non-hearing, rather than deaf, academics never showed up in church, deaf sports, or deaf community events.

ones younger than him. That seems to be in line with Martin et al.'s (2016) insight that "the young people who are receivers today wish to become givers in the future" (p. 9). Becoming a giver then means becoming a patron, and thereby challenging the authority of the current patron. The authority of figures like Homère and Joachim was, however, solidified by the somewhat clientelist (cf. Le Meur, 2008, p. 229) networks of support and care they assemble around them—as can be seen in the stories of Kiva and Élie. Up until now, Isaïe has not been able to realize any of his endeavors. Following a scandal involving his alleged affair with a student at a rural school where he was teaching in 2015, he had to get a new job. He found it at the Catholic school for the deaf up north near Natitingou. The geographic distance from the deaf communities, whose centers were mostly in Cotonou, left him no other channel but publishing reproachful messages on Facebook. He claimed that he got a lot of support from other young deaf people there, but the ones who supported him publicly by "liking" or commenting on his posts were mostly young deaf activists from other West African countries. The value of his messages to the Beninese deaf was being discussed in conversations and gossip in face-to-face interactions in the communities—also because many deaf did not read well enough for his elaborate discourses. These renegotiations of his claims were literally beyond his reach. Ironically, or maybe even purposefully, the job in the north was mediated to him through Joachim's support.

Conclusions: Making a Life in Deaf Communities

The three people I introduced represent different pathways young deaf Beninese can take toward adulthood. Similar dynamics are at stake in each story—only to play out quite differently. In these conclusions I wish to focus on the question of belonging and affiliation on the one hand and the position within the youth discourses on the other. The question of belonging is particularly relevant for the deaf youth as their double bind condition means that affiliation to family, society or culture does not come naturally. Oliver Sacks (1989) stated that "deafness as such is not the affliction; affliction enters with the breakdown of communication and language" (p. 117). As communication with hearing families is difficult and deficient for the deaf, they need to find or create spaces where it is possible.

I have shown how Élie, Kiva, and Isaïe all sought new affiliations when family did not provide the belonging and orientation needed. Élie was simply cut off from any birth family ties and kept at a distance by his informal foster family. Isaïe seemed to gradually drift away from the hearing world in which he no longer felt comfortable. He once told me that he considered deafness as one of the gravest disabilities as it prevented him from fully participating in any given situation in the dominant hearing world. Although he was very competent in spoken communication, his communicative impairment felt like a hidden stigma (Goffman, 1963, p. 41f). Among the other deaf—in school, in church—he was standing out in a positive way, being among those who were better able to participate in the hearing world. Thus, compensating for the stigma with a superior role among the deaf gave him a position that he would not find among the hearing, among his family.

Kiva's situation seems similar. It was not until she embraced the community of the deaf church that she realized how excluded she had been from the hearing community, even though she attended church services and worked among the hearing. But Kiva's and Isaïe's respective affiliations to the deaf communities played out quite differently. Kiva was included in the community in and around the deaf church. She married and introduced her children into the community, and she affiliated intensively with other deaf members of the congregation and did not even have contact with the hearing society anymore.

Élie might have had that chance, but the community he entered was not as inclusive as hers. The thicket of belonging seemed more filigree and less permeable; different categories of belonging—deaf/kin/age/experience—were at stake, whereas it seems that in church, it sufficed to be "a good Christian" and adhere to the rules and hierarchies to get to its core. Maybe that was why Élie was reaching out for hearing outsiders like Mama Vadim, French volunteers, or me more than others did.

Isaïe then became part of the broader deaf community, having his feet in many doors: the private school in Porto Novo, the deaf church, Joachim's center, and having access to the local and international deaf online communities. Mere affiliation and subsequent subordination were not enough for him though. With his rebellious behavior, he felt excluded based on his youth when trying to partake in the deaf community discourse. At the time of the publication of this chapter, his mission was still going on. After conflicts and confrontations, he had cut ties with the established communities and their authorities, while he had not yet become an authority himself among the young, which was absolutely his plan.

The three individuals each represent a different shade of youth discourses briefly discussed above. Kiva adhered to the expectations and moral codes of the community authorities. Thereby she personified the above-mentioned hope of the elders to shape and reproduce the future in their own imagination. Élie, quite on the contrary, served as the prime example of the young who are a disappointment to the elders' hopes. He wanted to become a teacher, turn from receiver to giver so to speak, but the circumstances did not allow him to—yet, at least. Isaïe represented both the hopes for the future and the threat of change. His commitment to political participation in the community and his far from coy rhetoric made him the target of long lists of accusation along the lines of depicting the young "as dangerous, criminal, decadent, and given to a sexuality that is unrestrained and threatening the whole of society" (Diouf, 2003, p. 4).

And yet, through passive or active engagement with society, Kiva, Élie, and Isaïe partook in the structural reproduction and transformation of the deaf communities. Their experiences suggest some of the ways in which the experiences of deaf youth in Benin confirm or scrutinize, and reproduce or reshape, their communities, thus constructing the frames within which their individual futures unfold. Regarding people's narratives, anthropologist Michael Jackson (2010) stated that "our lives belong to others as they belong to ourselves" (p. 137). When deafness is first and foremost seen as a social role instead of a medical or physical condition, it becomes clear that young deaf people's future lives are inevitably interconnected with the hearing world, but also with their deaf peers—older and younger. As double bind deaf youth, they are potentially excluded from their deaf communities as well as the hearing youth. The young deaf need to handle that social role of deaf youth which is "a position which is internally and externally shaped and constructed" (Christiansen et al., 2006, p. 11). But, however contentious the deaf communities might be—or might be portrayed by Isaïe—the three case studies also show that the communities are there to take care of the young deaf when other networks fail.

In this contribution, I did not discuss the ways young deaf people grow up where deaf spaces or communities are not available, which is mostly the case in rural settings. Also, further exploration should look into the gender disparities regarding which pathways are open to whom. Additional research and analysis should be undertaken on the intergenerational dynamics among the deaf as well. Deaf communities and cultures around the world have their mythologies and ancestries. A simplistic denial of the elders' contributions will help the deaf cause as little as rejecting the new ideas of the young. I see the crucial challenge for the deaf communities in Benin in the lack of clear representation, the lack of a collective agency to discuss their identity and language issues, as well as to claim their rights toward the hearing society or the government. Despite and because of their interstitial positioning, Beninese deaf youth, as "a constant source of creativity, ingenuity, possibility, empowerment, a source of alternative, yet-to-be-imagined futures" (Comaroff & Comaroff, 2005, p. 29), might be the ones to initiate deaf collective agency. After all, it is the future of the deaf communities that will be the future of the deaf youth in Benin.

References

Abbink, J. (2005). Being young in Africa: The politics of despair and renewal. In J. Abbink & I. van Kessel (Eds.), *Vanguards or vandals. Youth, politics and conflict in Africa* (pp. 1–34). Leiden, Netherlands: Brill.

African Union. (2006). *African youth charter.* Retrieved February 25, 2019, from https://au.int/sites/default/files/treaties/7789-treaty-0033_-_african_youth_charter_e.pdf

Alber, E. (2018). *Transfers of belonging: Child fostering in West Africa in the 20th century.* Leiden, Netherlands: Brill.

Alber, E., Martin, J., & Notermans, C. (Eds.). (2013). *Child fostering in West Africa. New perspectives on theory and practices.* Leiden, Netherlands: Brill.

Aoki, K., & Feldman, M. W. (1991). Recessive hereditary deafness, assortative mating, and persistence of a sign language. *Theoretical Population Biology, 39*(3), 358–372.

Christiansen, C., Utas, M., & Vigh, H. E. (2006). Introduction. In C. Christiansen, M. Utas, & H. E. Vigh (Eds.), *Navigating youth, generating adulthood: Social becoming in an African context* (pp. 9–28). Uppsala, Sweden: The Nordic Africa Institute.

Comaroff, J., & Comaroff, J. (2005). Reflections on youth from the past to the postcolony. In A. Honwana & F. de Boeck (Eds.), *Makers & breakers. Children and youth in postcolonial Africa* (pp. 19–30). Trenton, NJ: Africa World Press.

Davis, L. J. (1995). *Enforcing normalcy: Disability, deafness, and the body.* New York, NY: Verso.

Devlieger, P. (1999). Developing local concepts of disability: Cultural theory and research prospects. In B. Holzer, A. Vreede, & G. Weigt (Eds.), *Disability in different cultures: Reflections on local concepts* (pp. 297–302). Piscataway, NJ: Transaction.

Diouf, M. (2003). Engaging postcolonial cultures: African youth and public space. *African Studies Review, 46*(2), 1–12.

Erting, C. J., Johnson, R., Smith, D., & Snider, B. (Eds.). (1994). *The deaf way. Perspective from the international conference on deaf culture*. Washington, DC: Gallaudet University Press.

Ette-Akre, E. (2012). Approche scientifique de la surdité [Scientific approach to deafness]. In Y. A. Sanogo (Ed.), *Écoute mes mains – Dictionnaire de la langue des signes d'Afrique Francophone [Dictionary of the sign language of Francophone Africa]* (pp. 17–34). Abidjan, Ivory Coast: Edilis.

Friedner, M. (2015). *Valuing deaf worlds in urban India*. New Brunswick, NJ: Rutgers University Press.

Friedner, M., & Kusters, A. (Eds.). (2016). *It's a small world. International deaf spaces and encounters*. Washington, DC: Gallaudet University Press.

Ginsberg, F., & Rapp, R. (2013). Disability worlds. *Annual Review of Anthropology, 42*, 53–68.

Goffman, E. (1963). *Stigma – Notes on the management of spoiled identity*. New York, NY: Simon and Schuster.

Goody, E. (1982). *Parenthood and social reproduction. Fostering and occupational roles in West Africa*. Cambridge, UK: Cambridge University Press.

Hacking, I. (2002). *Historical ontology*. Cambridge, MA: Harvard University Press.

Hacking, I. (2011). Between Michel Foucault and Erving Goffman. Between discourse in the abstract and face-to-face interaction. *Economy and Society, 33*(3), 277–302.

Honwana, A., & de Boeck, F. (Eds.). (2005). *Makers & breakers. Children and youth in postcolonial Africa*. Trenton, NJ: Africa World Press.

Howell, S. (2003). Kinning: The creation of life trajectories in transnational adoptive families. *Journal of the Royal Anthropological Institute, 9*(3), 465–484.

Igwe, L. (2016). *The witch is not a witch: The dynamics and contestations of witchcraft accusations in Northern Ghana* (Doctoral dissertation). Retrieved October 23, 2018, from https://epub.uni-bayreuth.de/3377/

Jackson, M. (1995). *At home in the world*. Durham, NC: Duke University Press.

Jackson, M. (2010). Myths/stories/lives. In B. J. Good, M. M. J. Fischer, S. S. Willen, & M. D. Good (Eds.), *A reader in medical anthropology: Theoretical trajectories, emergent realities* (pp. 137–142). Chichester, UK: Wiley-Blackwell.

Jenkins, R. (1996). *Social identity*. London, UK: Routledge.

Kamei, N. (2006). The birth of langue des signes Franco-Africaine: Creole ASL in West and Central French-speaking Africa. *Sign Language Communication Studies, 59*(3), 67–68.

Kiyaga, N., & Moores, D. (2003). Deafness in sub-Saharan Africa. *American Annals of the Deaf, 148*(1), 18–24.

Kusters, A. (2015). *Deaf space in Adamorobe. An ethnographic study in a village in Ghana*. Washington, DC: Gallaudet University Press.

Lane, H. L. (2010). Construction of deafness. In L. J. Davis (Ed.), *The disability studies reader* (pp. 77–93). New York, NY: Routledge.

Le Meur, P.-Y. (2008). Between emancipation and patronage: Changing intergenerational relationships in central Benin. In E. Alber, S. van der Geest, & S. Reynolds Whyte (Eds.), *Generations in Africa. Connections and conflicts* (pp. 209–235). Berlin, Münster, Germany: LIT.

Martin, J., Ungruhe, C., & Häberlein, T. (2016). Young future Africa – Images, imagination and its making. *AnthropoChildren*, Special Issue 6, 1–18.

McIlroy, G. (2010). *Discovering deaf identities: A narrative exploration of school experiences on deaf identities.* Saarbrücken, Germany: Lambert Academics.

McIlroy, G., & Storbeck, C. (2011). Development of deaf identity: An ethnographic study. *Journal of Deaf Studies and Deaf Education, 16*(4), 494–511.

Monaghan, L. (2003). A world's eye view: Deaf cultures in global perspective. In L. F. Monaghan, C. Schmaling, K. Nakamura, & G. H. Turner (Eds.), *Many ways to be deaf. International variation in deaf communities* (pp. 1–24). Washington, DC: Gallaudet University Press.

Nakamura, K. (2006). *Deaf in Japan: Signing and the politics of identity.* Ithaca, NY: Cornell University Press.

Neubert, D., & Cloerkes, G. (2001). *Behinderung und Behinderte in verschiedenen Kulturen. Eine vergleichende Analyse ethnologischer Studien [Disability and disabled people in different cultures. A comparative analysis of anthropological studies].* Heidelberg, Germany: Universitätsverlag Winter.

Nyst, V. (2010). Sign languages in West Africa. In D. Brentari (Ed.), *Sign languages* (pp. 405–432). Cambridge, UK: Cambridge University Press.

Padden, C. (1980). The Deaf community and the culture of Deaf people. In C. Baker & R. Battison (Eds.), *Sign language and the Deaf community. Essays in honor of William C. Stokoe* (pp. 89–103). Washington, DC: National Association of the Deaf.

Philipps, J. (2018). A global generation? Youth studies in a postcolonial world. *Societies, 8,* 14.

Rush, D. (2013). *Vodun in coastal Benin. Unfinished, open-ended, global.* Nashville, TN: Vanderbilt University Press.

Sacks, O. (1989). *Seeing voices: A journey into the world of the deaf.* Berkeley/Los Angeles, CA: University of California Press.

Scheper-Hughes, N., & Lock, M. (1987). The mindful body: A prolegomenon to future work in medical anthropology. *Medical Anthropology Quarterly, 1*(1), 6–41.

Shakespeare, T. (2010). The social model of disability. In L. Davis (Ed.), *The disability studies reader* (pp. 266–273). New York, NY: Routledge.

Spittler, G. (2001). Teilnehmende Beobachtung als dichte Teilnahme [Participant observation as thick participation]. *Zeitschrift für Ethnologie, 126,* 1–25.

United Nations Educational, Scientific and Cultural Organization (UNESCO). (2017). *What do we mean by 'youth'?* Retrieved October 22, 2018, from http://

www.unesco.org/new/en/social-and-human-sciences/themes/youth/youth-definition

VanGilder, K. (2016). Exploring the contours of DEAF-SAME kinship bonds and mutuality in United Methodist short-term missions. In M. Friedner & A. Kusters (Eds.), *It's a small world. International deaf spaces and encounters* (pp. 140–149). Washington, DC: Gallaudet University Press.

Vigh, H. E. (2006). *Navigating terrains of war. Youth and soldiering in Guinea-Bissau.* New York, NY: Berghahn Books.

Vigh, H. E. (2010). Youth mobilisation as social navigation: Reflections on the concept of *dubriagem. Cadernos de Estudos Africanos, 18*(19), 139–164.

Vodounou, V. (2008). *The incredible journeys of Victor Vodounou: Africa, deafness, and Christianity.* El Cajon, CA: CSN Books.

World Health Organization. (2018, March). *10 facts about deafness.* Retrieved February 25, 2019, from https://www.who.int/features/factfiles/deafness/en/

CHAPTER 7

Someone Has to Tell These Children: "You Can Be As Good As Anybody!"

Cecilia Fiaka

INTRODUCTION

I hail from Ve-Agbome in the Volta Region of Ghana. I grew up in the 1960s in a farming community and completed Elementary School Form Four there. At age 15, I was sent off to Accra to work as a house help to save some money to support my mother and continue my education.

COMING TO ACCRA

When I was ten years old, a lady moved into our house with her son, who happened to be my father's child. This lady became a permanent member of our household and a second wife to my father, which was very uncomfortable for my mother and my siblings. This led to the marriage between my parents hitting the rocks, and my mother had to move to her parents' home with four of my younger siblings, leaving my elder brother and I to stay behind with my father and his new wife. My brother and I were left

C. Fiaka (✉)
Nneka Youth Foundation, Tema, Ghana
e-mail: cecilia@nnekafoundation.org

© The Author(s) 2020
M. L. McLean (ed.), *West African Youth Challenges and Opportunity Pathways*, Gender and Cultural Studies in Africa and the Diaspora, https://doi.org/10.1007/978-3-030-21092-2_7

behind because my mother felt the two of us could manage ourselves, as we were a bit older. I was ten years old at that time.

My brother and I were maltreated and most of the time slept with an empty stomach because my stepmother would not feed us. My father, even though he was a teacher, had taken to drinking and could not see what was happening to us. As a result of the conditions under which we were living, my brother was sent to boarding school, and immediately after I finished elementary Form Four, when I was 14 years old, my mother sent for me to come back to her. Knowing what my mum was going through to pay for my elder brother's secondary school—she had to pay his school fees all by herself—I did not have any hope of continuing my education any time soon. My mum felt bad about keeping me at home for so long while my brother completed school, so she decided to send me away to work as a house help.

One early Tuesday morning, she woke up and called me to her side, as we were all sleeping in the same room. She said she had discussed with a cousin of hers a plan to take me to Accra to work as a maidservant—a "baby nurse," as it was called in those days. I thought I was having a bad dream. All that came to my mind was that I was finished. I was young and immature, but I knew a few people from my area who grew up in that job, or did it for a long time, and none of them was able to achieve much as adults. I could not imagine how my dream of becoming somebody was going to be fulfilled as a baby nurse.

Hearing that message from my mother that fateful morning, I broke down in tears. Seeing me in that state, my mother also broke down. "Ceci," she called over and over again before I could respond. She tried to comfort me by saying that she would ensure that I would be able to continue my education after one year of employment. "Child," she said, "I trust you. I know you are a good girl. But staying in the village for such a long time without doing anything meaningful would be frustrating. You might end up getting pregnant, for the devil finds jobs for the idle hand and mind." I quickly sat up, wiped my face, and became interested in what she was saying, as I did not want to become a mother at the age of 15.

My mum told me that an auntie was in town for a funeral and was going to go back to Accra on the following Monday morning, so I should prepare to go with her. The day came for me to leave home. With my auntie and my mother walking beside me, tears flowing, I carried my small woven rubber bag to the roadside to look for a *trotro* to go to Accra. Standing there on the roadside, it dawned on me that a new life had begun for me, a new chapter had been opened, and the sooner I stopped thinking negatively and started living that chapter, the better it would be for me.

It was not a journey of no return. It was going to be for just one year. I trusted my mother to fulfill her promise to me. With these new thoughts, I started enjoying the journey—admiring the various towns and countryside along the way. It was my first time traveling that kind of long distance. My auntie would ask once in a while, "Are you sleepy?" or "Are you tired?", and I would answer, "No." So she said, "Keep watching things on the road." She pointed out places of interest like the Adome Bridge, which I had read about it in a textbook but was now actually seeing for the first time. It took us more than six hours to get to Accra.

I stayed in my aunt's house for just one week before she made arrangements for me to move in with the family I was to work for. I was told that, due to the stubbornness of the children—two boys, 5 and 7 years old—no maid had survived more than three months with that family without either leaving or being sacked. The madam I was to serve was a white lady, and the husband was a black Ghanaian. I counted myself lucky because it was a prestigious thing to have whites as your employers. After agreeing on how much I would be paid, my auntie left me alone with the family. I was shown my small room—the storeroom to the main house that was not being used for that purpose. Although the room was small, it was more than enough for me. But I had mixed feelings because it was my first time being alone in a bedroom.

I quickly adjusted my thoughts and told myself that I would try, no matter how difficult, to stay with this family for the one year I was there to work, and nothing was going to make me fail. To encourage myself, I recited my mother's words to me: "I gave birth to you, and I know that you, Cecilia—even if they put you in the lions' den, you could cohabit with the lions and they would not hurt you." I became stronger by the day when I remembered my mother's words, such as "I trust you, you are a good girl, and I do not want you to become a spoiled child," and the like. This experience taught me what a potentially powerful impact parental encouragement can have on children.

The boys became my kid brothers as I was only 15 years old myself. I was put in charge of all the household chores, including cooking, washing, and ironing. Chaamber, the garden man, only came to weed and tidy up the garden in the afternoon. He was a good man. He would sometimes help me with the ironing. The boys were very strong, and one really needed to be tough to manage to stay with them. My madam, Mrs. White, liked me very much because she realized I loved the boys so much. I was treated very well by the family, though there were times I felt I was truly a maidservant. For example, I was not allowed to eat at the table with them, and I only ate after they finished their meal. There was no way I could sit to watch television with them in the living room. Also, I now realize that the workload given to me was too much for a child my age.

The reality of having to learn how to cook the white man's food hit me when, barely a week into the job, I was asked to prepare lunch for the family. I had no option but to prove myself. However, I really did fail. I opened a full 600 grams of tomato paste for a small meal. My madam, who was a designer—she designed clothes for the former First Lady, Mrs. Faustina Kutu Acheampong—had a lady apprentice who was learning how to sew with her, and that lady came to rescue me. She taught me what to do next time when preparing such a meal. Another time, when I was washing the dishes, due to a little carelessness the whole rack fell and I broke all the glasses, plates, and bowls. I broke down weeping thinking that was going to be my end in that house, as I thought there were no other bowls to be used. My madam came out from her room to console me and later brought a new set of plates and bowls to replace the broken ones.

My master drove past El Wak Stadium every day to work and could buy newspapers for himself on the way, but I had to wake up early in the morning and walk almost two kilometers to El Wak Stadium to buy newspapers for him. That was how I started every day. One morning, something happened that I never forgot. That day the newspaper vendor was delayed, so all of us, especially the regular customers, decided to form a queue while waiting. Just as he arrived, the queue jammed up as everybody was in a hurry to go to work. As we struggled to get the papers, I felt a stinging slap on my ear that stretched to my eye. It came from a navy man who claimed I had crossed him. I could not believe such a thing could happen to a poor girl like me. Onlookers just shouted, "Oh!" And that was all they could say, because who were they to challenge a navy man? I left the place without the paper, and by the time I got home my eye was red and swollen. By the time my master drove me in his blue Datsun 120Y to the spot, the gentleman had left. To this day, the sight of a navy man in white drives me mad.

Despite the self-pity I felt about working as a maidservant rather than attending school, which I now realize there should not have been the need for, I also had good moments with the family. I was exposed to several beautiful things, I learned so much, and my desire to make it in life became stronger. They took me everywhere with them, and when the boys enjoyed popcorn or ice cream, I enjoyed it too. At the Russia Cultural Centre, for the first time in my life, I watched a movie on a large screen. We did this almost every weekend, and we had this opportunity, which existed only for Russians, because my madam was Russian. I had a lot of fun with the boys, from climbing trees to riding a bicycle. I once fell from a mango tree and still have the scars on my belly to date. I could not complete my bicycle riding lessons because I fell once during the exercise. Despite these activities, my skin color still made me feel I was a maidservant most of the time.

The children would confide in me as a true sister even though they infuriated me sometimes. They sometimes soaked their pillows, jeans, shorts, and towels in their bathtub, which I had to take care of. They dropped toys and many things in their toilets, which I had to remove with my hands. They were very daring, and some of their plans I could not keep secret—I had to tell their parents in confidence for guidance. But no matter how troublesome they were, I was able to manage that which most people could not.

Most evenings I had to walk back to El Wak Stadium to buy *kenkey* (a local food made from corn dough) for the family and the dogs. I really developed a love for dogs while in the house of the Whites and nurtured the desire to own and keep them when I became somebody. Strong desires that are not relented yield success. I currently own many dogs, and I can proudly say that being a maidservant taught me many lessons in life and made me a stronger person. I named my first dog after their dog, Skippy.

After about eight months of my stay with the family, the unexpected happened. The marriage between the couple hit the rocks, and my madam had to return to Russia, her home country. She wished I could go with her, but that was not possible. She gave me wonderful gifts, like a Pronto wristwatch, a ring, and clothes, among others, and asked me not to leave her children alone. At that point in time, I became like a mother to the boys. The White family became my family and remain so to this day.

As the days went by, I was counting when the one year was going to be up so I could continue my education. The time finally came for me to leave. I collected the little savings I had made during the year and went to the market to buy a few things for school. The rest I reserved for my mum to supplement my school fees. I finally bid the White family goodbye and returned home. They were sad to see me off. My master assured me that they would always receive me as part of the family should I return to Accra anytime in the future.

RETURNING TO THE VILLAGE

After I got back home to the village, my father sent for me. "I have heard that you returned from Accra, and I hope this is the best time for us to discuss your going back to school." This was my father's welcoming address when he saw me for the first time in close to two years. He had just been transferred to our village to continue his teaching career, which was nearing retirement.

I was excited, and I thanked him because I thought I saw repentance on his face. I thought he really regretted what he had done to me before I left for Accra. He always told me, "Cecilia, you are a very determined girl, and I know you would go places if you do not relent." We discussed which school I could possibly go to at the time, since my last Common Entrance results had expired and could not be used. He had agreed on the date we should travel to Kpando in the company of his wife and the children to look for the school. I bade them good day and left for my mother's house.

"Ceci, Ceci!" I heard someone calling from behind. I turned only to see my aunt, my father's sister, on the main road on which I was walking back home. She had come out from my grandfather's house by the roadside. "I would like to have a word with you," she said. "I heard your father says he is planning to send you to school; but you know what, he just returned home with so many children, and he has no farm to start feeding them yet. Your going to school under your father's care is not going to be possible. Why don't you go back home to tell your mother to enroll you to learn how to sew? Your mother has a sewing machine and is better able to take care of you than your father."

Again, I thought I was having a bad dream. My father and I had discussed going back to school not quite ten minutes earlier. The only people present were my stepmother and her children. How did the news get to my father's immediate younger sister?

"I knew it! I knew it" my mother exclaimed when I told her. But I retorted, "Since it is not my father who said this, let us give him the benefit of the doubt."

A few days later, my father called me and said I should prepare so that we could go and look for a school. I prepared, and one early morning we took off to Kpando. We went to the Secondary, the Technical, and the Commercial schools that were there, but as I could not use my previous Common Entrance results to enter the Secondary and the Technical, we had to settle for the Commercial school, which was a private school. I told myself that, wherever I find myself, I can make it with all my determination. I was granted admission to the school after a partial payment of the school fees. But we did not have enough to pay for the hostel facilities.

I had dreamt of going to a very good secondary school, living in a boarding house, and enjoying being a student. But I got it all wrong. It was not meant to be. I knew nothing of a boarding house, chop box (the trunks students took to boarding school) with provisions, or even pocket money. For us growing up, pocket money never existed, not that it was ever expected.

After staying in Accra and watching children being driven to and from school, with all the pocket monies and all the pampering, I felt there was something fundamentally wrong. There were children who have never worked for five minutes in their lives insisting on their rights to have all their expectations fulfilled by their fathers, demanding Victoria's Secret underwear and Jimmy Choo's (designer shoes), fully paid for by their "loving" parents. Meanwhile, I often saw anxious parents, desperately looking for ways to make life better for their pampered son who graduated two years earlier and was still looking for a job!

"Ceci," my father called. "You know what," he said, "my cousin Caroline lives near the school. Let us go and talk to her to see if she could find a space for you in her house where you could reside as a day student." I had no option but to follow him. Auntie Caroline and the husband agreed to take me in. We were so thankful and returned home with the good news. I had a little savings from the baby nursing I had done in Accra. My mum added some money to it for me to prepare for school. After a tug-of-war and a long deliberation with his family as to whether I could have it, my father released an old chop box for me to use for school. I appreciated it so much! At that time, there was nothing like a metal trunk in our vocabulary.

Pursuing My Dream of Getting an Education

On arrival at my Auntie Caroline's house, I found that two other young ladies were already staying with the family. I became the third. They were seniors in the same school I was to attend. Whenever the taps were closed—which was often, especially during dry season or when the village water pressure was low—we had to wake up very early between 3:30 a.m.

and 4:00 a.m. to go out to look for water before going to school. The closest location where one could get water was over three kilometers away.

We also had to find and fetch firewood for the house. Woe betide us should my Auntie Caroline have to use her money to buy firewood for the house. She would insult me especially, as well as my father, saying how useless he was, how his own family could not even get three square meals a day, and how my poor mother had to fend for my brother and me by herself. It was only my mother who brought foodstuff like yams, cassava dough, and the like to the house on every market day. We went fetching firewood one day in somebody's farm; you can imagine what happened. Our bowls and cutlasses were seized, and we were threatened with the chief's sanction. We pleaded and explained who we were, and as our story was touching, we were released—but without our bowls and cutlasses. Firewood had to be fetched anyway, and so we needed to find another field. We discovered Blue Army Centre, a religious land, a grotto, a special prayer ground for Catholics and non-Catholics alike. We were chased out from that place too. Going out at dawn to fetch firewood became a nightmare, but we had to go. We had to do this at least once a week, and it had to be a weekday, not weekends when farm and landowners would be on their farms and could spot us carrying off their firewood.

Any time we had to go fetching firewood or water, we went to school very late and tired. This coupled with my auntie's insults was not going to help my course, so I discussed the matter with my mother. We thought and deliberated on it, but a hostel could not be an option. The means to afford a hostel or boarding house was out of our league. One good thing was that my desire grew very strong to change my school from the Commercial School to a Technical School, which was one of the choices I had when I passed my Common Entrance examination at elementary Form Four. I succeeded in getting admission into the part-time stream, which meant I could only go to school in the afternoon.

I realized progress had been made at age 17. I saw the method of lecturing was better in the Technical school compared to the Commercial school and made up my mind to attain the highest level of education available for me at the time. I discovered that some subjects that I needed to achieve my aim were not available to part-time students. So once in the school, I started finding ways to get into the full-time stream, which I succeeded in doing after doing one year part-time. This taught me that determination always brings results. I finally became a full-time student of Kpando Technical Institute, a government school. The feeling of achievement and satisfaction was even better than when I had to settle for the private Commercial school.

MOVING BACK TO ACCRA

Immediately after I completed school, I packed my bags and returned home. My mum was happy because the first hurdle was crossed without any casualty. My next line of action was to find work in Accra. I told myself that my lot should be better than my mum's, and I believed at the time that whatever I asked from God, I received. So, with my mother's blessing, I set off for Accra, this time to go live with my mother's elder sister. My auntie and the husband became my parents. But soon after I realized I was an extra mouth in their house to feed, which was not a pleasant thing for them.

Considering the situation, I was torn between staying in Accra to weather the storm and returning home to help my mother farm and support my siblings—just as my father's sister had urged me a year earlier. With all that had happened up to that point, the decision became clear: I stayed on and decided to go to Accra Polytechnic. It was not too difficult for me to get admission into the school, and at the same time I got admission into the School of Languages to study French on a part-time basis. I was determined to occupy myself such that no idle thoughts could disturb me.

STARTING ON A NEW PATH

Immediately after earning a diploma certificate, I hit the ground running. I would wake up early in the morning, finish my household chores, and move from office to office looking for a job. After about three months, I got my first job at the West African Examination Council. I counted myself truly blessed when, after an interview, I was informed that I got the job! I started work as the personal assistant to the head of one of the departments. Real life had begun for me—I considered myself an adult worker. I had worked there for one year exactly when I received a letter inviting me for an interview at Standard Chartered Bank. Once again, I was favored by God to be employed after a successful interview. I joined Standard Chartered as a personal assistant to the head of the agriculture department of the bank.

Determined to keep moving forward, I decided to register for the Chartered Institute of Bankers course, which was the only thing I could consider at that time, as it was a professional course which related to my banking job. My experiences with "The Bank" were indescribable. I call it The Bank because it gave me my most memorable work experiences. After working at the head office for three years, I applied to join the banking stream. This was not difficult to achieve as I did well in the banking course. I worked in various departments at various levels, some very pleasant and some not, especially when I had to work through the night only to come home in the morning to go back the same morning. My work became very tedious at that time because there were technological system upgrades and I needed to make sure things were done appropriately as the manager of the department.

There were good times when I felt I was assured a sustaining and secured job. I could take a loan to do things I could never have done without The Bank, and I made very good friends. My greatest joy was when I received the best Sales and Services Award for the year. The award was presented in cash and presents, like a set of briefcases, which I still keep and am proud of. I suspect the first place Edem, my husband, ever saw me was at the Bank. He was an employee of the Central Bank of Ghana, which was located close to my bank. In 2006, I rose to the level of bank manager. I felt very humbled and fulfilled. My family, mum, and everybody were so proud, happy, and thankful to God.

Nneka Youth Foundation Is Born

One day in January 2012, while I was on a visit to my small village for an aunt's funeral, I was out and about when more than five girls, aged 12 to 16 years, carrying their babies approached me asking for money. In the evening of the same day, I walked out of my house at around six o'clock and saw boys of the same age openly smoking marijuana. I was upset; I could not sleep the whole of that night. I asked myself, if the situation in my small village could be this chaotic, what could be the situation in the whole district, and in all the rural and deprived communities in my country? I immediately pulled statistics from the Municipal Education Directorate to see what effect these vices were having on education, and I found that of the 3200 youth enrolled in junior high school in the 2010–2012 academic period, 1142 youth had dropped out of school and over 84% of these dropouts were a result of these vices. I broke down!

I had also noticed that young women in their early 40s already had great grandchildren! All of this was very distressing to me. Over the years, there has been a disastrous cycle of teenage pregnancy that has set a huge stumbling block in the path of any worthwhile achievement by the rural folk. This is because they never get the opportunity to fully develop themselves before they begin to have children, which often leads them into child marriages/parenthood. I told myself I had no business sitting behind my desk, calling myself a bank manager, when the human resource base of my community had eroded and was becoming almost nonexistent. I had to do something to break the cycle of teen motherhood.

I started out by supporting orphans in an orphanage by providing food items, toiletries, and medical needs. This I did because I was touched by their plight and the inability of the orphanage to adequately provide for the needs of these children. Eventually, I had to call on Social Welfare to intervene when I realized my support was not going to be sustainable. I was providing support for out-of-school youth by supplying basic school needs for girls, especially to return to school or learn a trade to become self-sufficient.

As a young girl, I strove on my own and left the village for school, and my dreams of becoming a responsible person, of not being a burden on society, became realities. Growing up in a typical rural setting came with many challenges. We were confined to a rustic limiting environment, lacking amenities like electricity and water, not to mention libraries and recreational centers. As an adult, I could see that teenage pregnancy and drug abuse were becoming the norm, and the possibility of a good education was almost nonexistent. My peers in urban communities seemed to have a clearer educational pathway, with learning materials and quality teachers. I observed that the potential of children in rural areas could not be translated into achievement due to very minimal exposure and many more problems. I saw, and continue to see, a major gap between rural and urban communities, and this is the gap I am vigorously seeking to bridge.

In 2012, I went from being a banker to a full-time youth activist. I formed Nneka Youth Foundation to change the mindset of these vulnerable youth, so that they could believe in themselves. They needed to learn that though they came from such deprived communities, they can still become somebody in life; they could become world changers and future leaders if they focused on their education. We have reached over 11,000 children from 200 communities since our inception in 2012, and we have made an incredible impact through the interventions we put in place.

"Nneka" is an Igbo word meaning, "Mother is Supreme." The name Nneka was discovered in Chinua Achebe's award-winning classic, *Things Fall Apart*. One character, Okwonkwo, was sent into exile and decided to run to his mother's land. When he was received and welcomed as if there was not any problem, he exclaimed, "Nneka!" The expression is meant to capture the encouragement and security that is available to children in vibrant and united communities. Sadly, this reality remains elusive in underserved regions in Ghana.

Nneka Youth Foundation has made giant strides in changing the lives and mindset of children in 200 rural communities. My passion and experience have come in very handy. When I talk to young people in the communities I work with, they most often express concern about the level of poverty; they lack clothing, food, and, in some cases, shelter; this usually makes them susceptible to all forms of vices, becoming victims of teenage pregnancy, child marriage, and child trafficking. Teenage mothers and vulnerable girls are stigmatized, excluded from school and other social settings, and are subject to abuse and violence by their parents and the men who impregnate them. They lack information on their rights and are unable to engage in any meaningful employment to fend for themselves. Just about all the young people worry about not having educational and employment opportunities. Most young people just want the things that those who are more fortunate have but take for granted: they want to be safe, go to school, have a comfortable life, and build a lasting career. Our biggest challenge is to get the young people we work with to believe in themselves. Someone has to tell these vulnerable children that, Yes! They too can make it, despite the challenges. They too can be as good as anybody in the world and can be the world changers!

CHAPTER 8

The Limits of Individual-Level Factors for Ghanaian and South African Girls' Learning

Sally A. Nuamah

THE BARRIERS TO LETTING GIRLS LEARN

While girls struggle to enter school, many also struggle to stay in school (Glick & Sahn, 2000). Research on African girls consistently shows that girls miss several days of school per month for a plethora of gender-based responsibilities related to domestic work (United Nations Educational Scientific Cultural Organization [UNESCO], 2014). These are the same responsibilities that make them vulnerable to never returning to school once they are forced to take a gap year due to lack of enrollment spaces. With the re-emergence of three-year education in Ghana, for example, a typical girl must wait one to two years before entering the next stage of her education. During this wait, girls often veer off course in irreparable ways.

In particular, girls get discouraged from applying and often fall victim to early marriage and pregnancy. Their families, many of which are already

S. A. Nuamah (✉)
School of Education and Social Policy, Northwestern University,
Evanston, IL, USA
e-mail: sally.nuamah@northwestern.edu

© The Author(s) 2020
M. L. McLean (ed.), *West African Youth Challenges and Opportunity Pathways*, Gender and Cultural Studies in Africa and the Diaspora, https://doi.org/10.1007/978-3-030-21092-2_8

uncertain about the value of education, lose sight of the end goal as the girl student may begin to contribute to the family full time as a petty trader. Once families get used to her contribution, they do not want to revert to a period when she did not contribute in lieu of the delayed gratification associated with a four-year college degree, for a girl who will likely get married off anyway. Thus, a girl may have the choice of either getting married so that she is no longer a resource drain on her already poor family or directly contributing to their survival by not going to college but rolling up her sleeves and working. Many guardians discourage college or completion with reasoning such as "you have had enough education" and "you have to come back home and help the family now." Furthermore, when they seek to return, girls suffer from lower exam scores, making admission into the next level of education more difficult when compared to boys.

Confidence as a Potential Solution?

One critical effect of negative experiences with school and community is that it lowers girls' confidence. In the United States, there is significant research on the role of individual-level factors such as confidence in shaping educational and career outcomes for girls, despite the above barriers (American Association of University Women [AAUW], 1995; Kay & Shipman, 2014). Similarly, in Ghana, country-level analysis reveals that as girls enter high school they experience a decline in their confidence and subsequently their mathematics performance, despite demonstrating equally positive attitudes toward math as boys during junior high school (Asante, 2010; Nyala, 2008). Furthermore, results from another study of 500 ninth grade (high school) students from the central region of Ghana found that students expressed high interest and value for math but shared a need for more confidence from their teachers in their mathematics ability and more encouragement for them to develop interest (Ampadu, 2012). The multiple studies on the impact of confidence have spurred initiatives to increase the confidence of girls across the Global North and South as a solution to achievement.

At the same time, Black girls display a high level of confidence in math and science, compared with their majority counterparts, but they struggle to achieve at the same level as these groups (Riegle-Crumb, Moore, & Ramos-Wada, 2011). In addition, although confidence narrows gender gaps for girls in Ghana, they still fail to close them (Mullis, Martin, Foy, & Arora, 2012). This suggests that there is a need to look beyond individual-level factors such as confidence for improving the educational outcomes of girls. I argue that confidence, and likely any other single factor alone, is not enough to enable the collective achievement of girls. Rather, female students need self-belief (which confidence feeds into) and strategies to respond to challenges. However, most importantly, they need institutions that intentionally create environments that eliminate the gendered barriers that students face.

In this chapter, I analyze data from 30 interviews and a targeted survey in Ghana and South Africa. These are African countries with a clear, legal commitment to gender equality. Still, they both struggle to ensure their girls (1) are performing well academically (Mullis et al., 2012; Reddy et al., 2016), (2) have the resources they need in schools, such as toilets and clean water (UNESCO, 2015), and (3) have the quality of education they deserve. While I acknowledge that making direct comparisons remain difficult given the middle-income status of South Africa and the lower-income status of Ghana, I examine the role of confidence in shaping learning in South Africa, before using the findings to evaluate an intervention in the case of Ghana. In doing so, I highlight the factors needed to let girls learn across these contexts.

A Case Study of Limpopo in South Africa

In 2014, in collaboration with members of the Human Sciences Research Council, I investigated secondary schools in South Africa that serve mostly disadvantaged students (K-12) and yet are successful in transforming them into academically successful learners. The study found that, despite the challenging conditions experienced by students at these particular schools, 88% of students reported liking school (12% higher than the population average), 63% indicated that they felt safe at school, and 60% felt a sense of belonging at their specific school. The research placed particular focus on the schools in one of South Africa's nine provinces, Limpopo. Limpopo is a largely rural area in the northernmost part of the country. It is one of South Africa's poorest provinces, with nearly 80% of its population living below the poverty line. It is also home to the largest Black population in the entire country, with them making up 97% of the population.

Out of South Africa's 11.4 million students, 2 million are in Limpopo. In 2015, students in the province scored among the lowest, with 76% of its learners scoring below the low benchmark of 400, compared to 60% for the country. Overall, the passing rate of all Limpopo students is below the national average across grade levels, and girls' passing rates in Limpopo are even lower than the national girls' average (National Department of Basic Education, 2016). Similar to national patterns, a higher percentage of girls in Limpopo sit to take the college matriculation exam than boys (53% versus 47%). Yet, fewer girls than boys pass (70% versus 77%). As illustrated by the cases discussed in this chapter, fewer girls than boys qualify for higher degree programs, likely due to a number of gender-based barriers.

To overcome these challenges, quality schools in Limpopo strive to create environments that offer creative solutions and are dedicated to their students' achievement. These schools often offer girls a high number of additional classes and course work before and after school. Educators in these Limpopo schools try to make complex courses such as math practical, share resources with teachers at other schools, work with students on homework before they go home, and attempt multiple techniques to encourage parents and grandparents to be involved by sharing their children's successes and challenges. These additional efforts have enabled schools in Limpopo in 2015 to experience immense growth, particularly in mathematics and science, relative to every other province (Reddy et al., 2015). Although in 2015 Limpopo scored 361st in math and thus ranked as the fourth lowest province, it has achieved the highest gains, compared with other provinces, in math and science since 2003. These services are provided to both boys and girls and positively impact both groups.

A Safe School

One particular secondary school in Limpopo stood out in my study for its ability to improve both overall academics and the experiences of girl learners, in turn creating a safe space to learn. From the onset of the study, it was clear that Mapate Elementary represented the surest sign of Limpopo's progress. The school benefited from a principal that engaged the community to view Mapate as an asset that they were all responsible for protecting. Principal Matthew Bokamaso used this approach to make the broader community, rather than just the school staff, responsible for the success of the students at the school. The result was a community that took ownership and created the conditions that ensured learners had a safe environment in which they could achieve.

To facilitate a safe space, Principal Bokamaso emphasized to his teachers the importance of treating the students with the same level of urgency they would their own kids. As he stated:

I am a parent. I have a child and you also have a child ... and our responsibility here is to make sure that each learner here gets everything our children get ... And if you find me doing something that is contrary, don't do that. If you see me do it, you tell me straight that, "Sir, this is not what we are supposed to do."

Principal Bokamaso stresses this point to teachers, staff, and parents in order to promote a more community-based approach to caring for the students, to emphasize the level of responsibility this requires, and to institute accountability in achieving this approach. This supportive learning environment becomes critical for ensuring the students at the school can develop the achievement-oriented identities—confidence, strategy, transgression—necessary for confronting and overcoming personal and academic challenges (Nuamah, 2019).

Achievement-oriented identities are not created easily in Limpopo or in, Mapate, specifically. Because of Limpopo's economic status, its schools lack basic resources such as books and paper. Principals often report teaching a full load of courses in addition to their administrative responsibilities. School cancellations are commonplace when it rains because it is too hard to access the entrance through muddy, unpaved roads. The schools are also filled with students who are just as impoverished.

Another challenge is the low education level of many of the students' parents or household guardians, which directly shapes the children's preparation level and the parents' or guardians' ability to help children with their schoolwork. In fact, many students' parents or grandparents were products of the Bantu Education Act and lack the formal education they are seeking to give to their kids and grandkids. As one teacher stated in response to the question of challenges facing her school, "The challenges for the learners is that they stay alone or with grandparents, and most of the adults in the families are illiterate so they can't help students complete their homework." When parents or guardians are unable to help at home, teachers make up for this by offering extra classes and encouraging students to complete their homework before they head home. This results in improved academics, as one first-grade teacher, on the job for 23 years, noted, "When learners come here, they are unable to read and write. Counting for students is a challenge, even simple numbers. I deal with this by giving extra classes ... before they go home."

Beyond providing extra courses and encouraging students to come early or stay late after classes, teachers work to engage parents as well. The head of the math department at Mapate, for example, shared that he encourages parents to get involved by calling them if students do well as a mechanism to build rapport and trust. Furthermore, he prioritizes finding ways for parents to directly contribute to improving the educational practices of their children, even if they themselves are not educated. Accordingly, he provides parents with tangible tools for helping their kids. In the words of this teacher, "At the beginning when parents collect books, each parent will be carrying a packet of books and an assessment plan for the whole year for the child."

The rest of this chapter will detail Mapate's efforts using data derived from 30 interviews conducted between 2013 and 2014 in English. In the interviews, there were constant references to the multiple stakeholders involved in ensuring that disadvantaged students succeed. As stated by one of Mapate's school leaders, "There are three parties involved in education: the learners, the parents, and the educators ... the school has a uniting role. Each party puts on the table their level of commitment to ensure they will perform well." Schools recognize that they cannot ensure the achievement of their students without the support of the broader community, and, thus, their ability to bring these multiple partners together becomes an essential starting point for building academically successful students. Once stakeholders are convened, the school works to identify its students academic challenges.

To gauge the students' specific academic challenges, Mapate first meticulously documents their progress:

> On weekly basis, there is a report that must be submitted by the [head of department]. I must see how we are doing. It contains what the learners are [doing] in math and all those things ... and that works.

Second, each week teachers are updated on the learning outcomes of their students, and strategies to help those students are discussed and shared. These small actions keep everyone accountable for the academic fate of each student and encourage teachers to become invested in helping each other as well as the students. Principal Bokamaso then conducts class visits to provide feedback on teaching practices.

The most veteran teacher in the study is Ms. Magda, who had been working in Limpopo schools teaching math and a local language for 26 years. She specified other important factors for helping students from poor backgrounds achieve, despite low resources and education at the school.

In addition to emphasizing extra classes, she stressed the importance of making herself available for students to "approach her about everything," "coming down to their level and making sure that learners are not afraid" of her, "making them believe that math is easy and all a student has to do is believe that," and being committed to using "practical examples to illustrate the problem." Her methods epitomize the type of environment necessary for facilitating achievement-oriented identities among students, as they enable students, especially girls, to feel confident in their abilities to both tackle the hardest subjects, such as math, and present concerns that are important to them in order to develop solutions to address them.

REFRAMING FAILURE TO HELP GIRLS LEARN

Girls that attend school at Mapate struggle initially to make substantial progress, even under the guidance of teachers like Ms. Magda. While some girls overcome both personal and academic struggles to become model students for the school, other girls struggle to achieve as easily, particularly in math and science. To improve achievement in math, Principal Bokamaso and teachers at the Mapate school decided to teach students to apply math to their real-world experiences, in the process also teaching them how to become achievement oriented. Principal Bokamaso had noticed a disconnect between how math is used in the classroom and how it is used practically in the real world:

> If [a girl student] goes to the market with 100 rand and buys something that costs 27 rand, that learner will know that [her] change is 73 rand, but if you ask the same question in the classroom, [she] does not get it right. It seems what we are teaching is removed from reality.

Principal Bokamaso did not view students' inability to connect math in the real world to math in the classroom as an incompetency due to gender or innate ability; instead, he viewed it as an area where educators could improve their curriculum and teaching. Principal Bokamaso also wanted students to understand that failure in the classroom can be beneficial. As he tells his students, "People who struggle in the classroom become more successful because they are used to the wrongs. A guy who fails every class will repeat until he finds another strategy. Once you fail, you don't give up." Framing failure as an asset essential for success becomes fundamental for enabling girl students' self-belief, a critical factor for developing achievement-oriented identities. Instead of viewing their challenges as ones they cannot overcome, girls at Mapate are encouraged to believe that there is always another strategy they can engage in and utilize to succeed the next time around. For girl students who are vulnerable in a number of ways, this message acts as a powerful tool for helping them find proactive ways to confront their barriers.

Being intentional about gender dynamics within the classroom is especially important for ensuring the achievement of girls. In fact, studies show that girls in co-ed schools may struggle with subjects such as science due to fear of answering questions incorrectly, while boys may not hold this fear at all (Sadker & Sadker, 2010; Shapka & Keating, 2003). Girls often need to be assured that it is okay to be wrong. It is unsurprising then that one teacher at Mapate says, "There is no wrong answer in science. We only make mistakes and then we correct the mistake. [Students] have told [me] that science is difficult, but I tell my learners, it is practical." Undoubtedly, schools must create environments where all students feel comfortable participating, even if they are wrong, as a central mechanism for achieving gender equality. Once students remove the fear of failure, they more easily find a pathway to confidence, a fundamental aspect of building achievement-oriented identities.

BUILDING ACHIEVEMENT-ORIENTED IDENTITIES IN GHANA

In another study, I evaluated a gap-year program in a poor slum in Accra, Ghana, that sought to prepare girls who were not admitted into college to reapply between 2016 and 2018. A total of 33 girls were included in the program, 7 of whom participated in the gap-year program. The age of the girls ranged from 16 to 22. Each of the girls attended a government subsidized school located in Accra. Each of the girls was selected through an application process. Those that were admitted into college were provided with college scholarships and mentorship workshops. Those who were not admitted were provided with remedial test prep (the gap-year program) and mentorship workshops. The girls were surveyed throughout the year. The program was developed to try to support girls' college entry and to institute identities that would enable first generation girls to become confident based, in part, on what was learned in the case of Limpopo. The program was funded through resources provided through a small grant by the Ford Foundation and the International Education Program.

Overall, the findings reveal that girls need not only confidence in a subject area, but also the resources necessary for the test and strategies to study for it. Several girls reported that they felt they "did not have enough time to study," or that "teachers were moving too quickly." In addition, girls who had "unlimited access to wifi … [and] free 24-hour libraries" reported more confidence in their ability to go over difficult homework problems, while those who did not professed their desire to have more time in small groups outside of class to go over work problems. Many girls commended the long period of time provided to prep for an exam, as it made them feel they had time to prepare; however, for those who had to work due to needed finances at home, there were diminishing returns as the class demand increased. These students also reported the challenge of "not having a personal laptop as a non-resident [and] not being able to access internet facilities" or afford books. In one case, a student fell sick and missed multiple classes, thereby disrupting the progress she had made right before taking the exam. It was a challenge to get her back on track before the scheduled exam. In the future, it is important to be able to better schedule make-up opportunities to account for these types of unexpected events.

Generally, there were strong reasons to suspect that conducting independent classes would produce stronger outcomes, as it would facilitate better regulation of the program quality. However, with populations that are already so vulnerable, this would likely be very expensive. It is clear that the students who were in remedial courses were academically lower than the other girls in the program and faced an additional set of challenges at home. Thus, it became clear that it was also important to consider how organizations may be able to supplement the incomes of these students over the long term to allow them to focus on their studies.

Given these constraints, the goal of keeping students in the college pathway was met. Each of the students expressed a continued desire to go to a four-year college and had increased grit scores. Many of the students also realized the different tools they would need before entering college and how those tools were in some ways different than what they needed in high school. As one student reported, "It's all about time management and confidence in yourself to undertake certain things." Additional positives of the program include being able to keep girls who were most at risk of never attending college still on track to their college dreams. Each of the girls who participated in the program is writing the college entry exam and maintaining an interest in attending college. Not a single girl dropped out of the program, and attendance was high from start to finish for 90% of the participants. The confidence-building mentorship workshops were an even bigger success. Girls spent their entire Saturday learning from established women and their peers who are already in college about important issues related to their future. At these meetings, they were encouraged to continue to strive for their goals. When they were surveyed at the end of the program, each girl noted an increased confidence in their capacity to enter college. Nonetheless, their objective conditions had not changed. These conditions limited their ability to attend college, despite their heightened confidence levels.

Letting All Students Learn

Across the data collected for this research, it appears that the most successful tools for all students centered on the following themes in their everyday practices: passionate teachers, community, love, self-belief, and academic excellence.

- *Passionate Teachers*

    Teachers serving some of the poorest students in the nation must go well above their normal load in order to help their students catch up and achieve. Thus, a stand-out quality among those who are able to help poor learners excel is a sense of urgency about their role in the lives of their students. Teachers must have important internal justifications to rationalize what may seem like a tireless effort. It requires a fundamental belief that the students see education as their pathway to a better future. Even so, teachers recognize that they are not able to simply help students out of mere passion alone. Instead, they need to bring together various members of the community to invest in the success of the student.

- *Community*

    There were constant references across the data to the multiple stakeholders involved in ensuring that disadvantaged students succeed. School leaders commonly referenced the importance of uniting students, educators, and families for the sake of the educational success of the student. Schools recognize that they cannot ensure the achievement of their students without the support of the broader community, and, thus, their ability to bring these multiple partners together becomes an essential starting point for building academically successful students.

- *Love and Self-love*

  Two important parts of building community for students at school is infusing love and self-love within them. Students who are successful often expressed feeling loved by their educational communities, and part of how they make that determination is through examples of how that educator helped them believe in themselves. This notion of love being intentionally espoused by school teachers and directly felt by students and their parents plays a critical role in building achievement-oriented identities among the student population. When students experience these actions from their teachers, they are also being taught how to treat others, which introduces an important opportunity for practicing gender equality in the classroom.

- *Academic Excellence*

  There is no clear, single way to help girl students achieve academic excellence, but it is clear that at a basic level there are two main values: hard work and discipline. Many schools pitch these pillars to students as the magic solution to changing their situation. And, indeed, students take on these tropes and come to associate them with everything they do. To ensure that girl students remain encouraged through the various setbacks they are likely to endure, even if they work hard, these schools emphasize the importance of not comparing themselves to one another but rather helping each other and competing only with oneself.

Each of these tactics plays a critical role in developing girl students who have a strong sense of self-belief and self-efficacy as well as the tools to think and respond to their challenges.

Yet, none of these factors removes the structural barriers that impede girls' ability to experience equitable academic experiences and life outcomes: In South Africa, 14-year-old Amahle is leaving school for the day when a man approaches her. He tells her to come with him, that her aunt has arranged for her to marry him. As Amahle notes in her own words:

> I tr[ied] to tell him that I must go and get my things, because I was thinking it would give me time to run away, but he said no and forced me into the car. I was afraid and knew I had my rights. (Wilson, 2006, p. 10)

This is not something that happened decades ago. Rather, this is a recent, true story of a schoolgirl being forced into an arranged marriage with a 43-year-old man by her own aunt without her consent. Indeed, Amahle did know her rights, thanks to the Girls Education Movement (GEM), a program formed in 2003 by the Ministry of Education in South Africa to build knowledge and self-esteem among girls, but in that moment, there was nothing she could do.

Amahle's story is important for several reasons. First, it demonstrates how gender-based violence in South Africa can, and often does, occur in and around the schoolhouse. Second, it highlights how important it is for girls to be informed of their rights and be empowered to speak up. For Amahle, her involvement in GEM played a critical role in providing her with the tools to at the very least attempt to defend herself, but structural changes are necessary for her to not have to deal with these issues to start.

Conclusion

Across both countries, confidence matters (as do other factors). Still, as expected, it is conditional on various aspects of structural inequality, whether related to parental education, individual- or school-level economic status, or school experience (Nuamah, 2018). Most importantly, girls across these contexts are dealing with unequal gender relations that actively chip away at confidence rather than build it. Given the various factors affecting girls' educational achievement, the analysis of the data raises more questions than it answers. Yet, a clear takeaway is that a singular effort focused on building confidence to close the achievement gap by race and/or gender is not enough. Improving individual achievement through confidence, or any other similar factor, cannot save every girl student (Nuamah, 2019).

References

American Association of University Women (AAUW). (1995). *How schools short-change girls: The AAUW report.* New York, NY: Marlowe.

Ampadu, E. (2012). Students' perceptions of their teachers' teaching of mathematics: The case of Ghana. *International Online Journal of Educational Sciences, 4*(2), 351–358.

Asante, K. O. (2010). Sex differences in mathematics performance among senior high students in Ghana. *Gender and Behaviour, 8*(2), 3279–3289.

Glick, P., & Sahn, D. E. (2000). Schooling of girls and boys in a West African country: The effects of parental education, income, and household structure. *Economics of Education Review, 19*(1), 63–87.

Kay, K., & Shipman, C. (2014). The confidence gap. *The Atlantic, 14*(1), 1–18.

Mullis, I. V., Martin, M. O., Foy, P., & Arora, A. (2012). *TIMSS 2011 international results in mathematics.* Amsterdam: International Association for the Evaluation of Educational Achievement.

National Department of Basic Education. (2016). *Education statistics in South Africa 2014.* Pretoria: Department of Education. Retrieved July 21, 2018, from www.education.gov.za/EMIS/StatisticalPublications/tabid/462/Default.aspx

Nuamah, S. A. (2018). Achievement oriented: Developing positive academic identities for girl students at an urban school. *American Educational Research Journal, 55*(6), 1307–1338. https://doi.org/10.3102/0002831218782670

Nuamah, S. A. (2019). *How girls achieve.* Cambridge, MA: Harvard University Press.

Nyala, J. I. (2008). Sex-differences in attitude towards mathematics of junior high school students in Ghana. *Edo Journal of Counselling, 1*(1), 137–161.

Reddy, V., Visser, M., Winnaar, L., Arends, F., Juan, A. L., Prinsloo, C., et al. (2016). *TIMSS 2015: Highlights of mathematics and science achievement of grade 9 South African learners.* Pretoria: Human Sciences Research Council.

Reddy, V., Zuze, T. L., Visser, M., Winnaar, L., Juan, A., Prinsloo, C. H., et al. (2015). *Beyond benchmarks: What twenty years of TIMSS data tell us about South African education.* Pretoria: Human Sciences Research Council Press.

Riegle-Crumb, C., Moore, C., & Ramos-Wada, A. (2011). Who wants to have a career in science or math? Exploring adolescents' future aspirations by gender and race/ethnicity. *Science Education, 95*(3), 458–476.

Sadker, M., & Sadker, D. (2010). *Failing at fairness: How America's schools cheat girls.* New York, NY: Simon and Schuster.

Shapka, J. D., & Keating, D. P. (2003). Effects of a girls-only curriculum during adolescence: Performance, persistence, and engagement in mathematics and science. *American Educational Research Journal, 40*(4), 929–960.

United Nations Educational Scientific Cultural Organization (UNESCO). (2014). *Puberty education & menstrual hygiene management.* Retrieved October 21, 2018, from http://unesdoc.unesco.org/images/0022/002267/226792e.pdf

United Nations Educational Scientific Cultural Organization (UNESCO). (2015). *Education for all 2000–2015: Achievements and challenges* (Global Monitoring Report 2015). Retrieved October 21, 2018, from http://unesdoc.unesco.org/images/0023/002322/232205e.pdf

Wilson, F. (2006). *Gender based violence in South African schools.* Paris: International Institute for Educational Planning.

PART III

Vulnerability and Well-Being

CHAPTER 9

Youth Employment and Labor Market Vulnerability in Ghana: Aggregate Trends and Determinants

Adedeji Adeniran, Joseph Ishaku, and Adekunle Yusuf

INTRODUCTION

Because youth account for nearly a third, and an increasing percentage, of Africa's population, many scholarly and policy efforts aim to increase youth employment on the continent. Among recent such efforts, the African Union's ambitious Agenda 2063 development plan gives high priority to investing in youth as the driving force for achieving socioeconomic development in Africa (African Union Commission, 2015, p. 37). However, recent studies suggest that, unless proposed solutions are based on a thorough understanding of youth livelihood and employment realities, they are at risk of not achieving adequate impact and scale (Williams & Pompa, 2017).

In order to contribute to this understanding, our study analyzed the circumstances of already employed youth in Ghana in order to assess their ability to enter and remain connected to the labor market across the dura-

A. Adeniran (✉) • J. Ishaku • A. Yusuf
Centre for the Study of Economies of Africa (CSEA), Abuja, Nigeria
e-mail: aadedeji@cseaafrica.org; jishaku@cseaafrica.org

© The Author(s) 2020
M. L. McLean (ed.), *West African Youth Challenges and Opportunity Pathways*, Gender and Cultural Studies in Africa and the Diaspora, https://doi.org/10.1007/978-3-030-21092-2_9

tion of active life. Based on the assumption that any larger effort to bring about full employment depends partly on the durability of new employment opportunities as well as access to them, our goal was to understand the extent and determinants of youth labor market vulnerability. The study illuminated key variables that shape labor market conditions faced by youth, as compared to middle-aged (25 to 54 years) and older adults (55 to 64 years), somehow employed in Ghana. We found that these variables, which include gender, level of education, and geographical area as well as sector of employment, signal the trajectory of Ghanaian youths' work lives and the likelihood that labor market vulnerability early on will cast a shadow on their late adulthood years.

Focusing on South Africa, Bhorat, Lilenstein, Oosthuizen, and Thornton (2016) identify conditions that render workers vulnerable in the labor market, including "working in the informal sector; earning low wages relative to the cost of living; not having a written contract; working in adverse conditions; not having access to benefits; and a lack of job security" (p. 2). Approaching the issue from another angle, the World Bank (2018) World Development Indicator data project defines vulnerable employment based on employment status of workers. Basically, the World Bank considered only contributing family workers and individuals working in self-employment jobs or on their own account as being engaged in vulnerable employment. This is because contributing and own-account workers experience the vulnerable conditions enumerated by Bhorat, Lilenstein, et al. (2016). For this study, except where otherwise stated, we define vulnerability in the labor market along the World Bank approach; however, we added domestic workers and apprentices to the vulnerable employment class, given the context of Ghana's labor market. Specifically, domestic employees and apprentices in Ghana share similar conditions as contributing family and own-account workers within the labor market (see Barret et al., 2015).

Empirical studies have documented that Ghana's youth, defined as individuals aged 15 to 24 years, faces higher barriers in gaining access to, and progressing in, Ghana's labor markets than any other segment of the population (Baffour-Awuah, 2013). Several factors play into the labor market vulnerability of the youth overall and Ghanaian youth in particular. As young people seek to enter formal labor markets for the first time, employers may be reluctant to hire them on permanent contracts or on a full-time basis, and entry wages are likely to be lower. This is often the case as young people lack the previous experience that signals their productivity potential to prospective employers. Hence, youths are faced with the trade-off between taking up vulnerable employment or remaining unemployed indefinitely.

Labor market vulnerability is particularly harmful to youth: it has life-long effects on income—referred to in the literature as wage-scarring—and on employment stability. Existing research shows that these effects can have the long-term impact of diminishing young people's confidence and resilience in dealing with labor market opportunities and setbacks over the course of their working lives (see Gregg & Tominey, 2004; Mavromaras, Sloane, & Wei, 2013; Nilsen & Reiso, 2011).

This study aimed to identify the specific areas in which the circumstances of Ghanaian youth deviated from adults competing within the same labor market, that is, to understand the nuances of youth labor market vulnerability. As a first step toward gaining this understanding we juxtaposed data on the labor market conditions of youth with data on older cohorts—middle-aged (25 to 54) and older-aged (55 to 64). We then estimated the probability of labor market vulnerability for youth and older cohorts based on the significant variables of gender, sector of employment, and geographic location.

Our analysis revealed that youth have a higher likelihood of being vulnerable in the Ghanaian labor market relative to older cohorts, even after controlling for their individual characteristics. Nonetheless, we identified gender, location of residence, education, and sector of employment as significant for the likelihood of being in vulnerable employment for youth and other cohorts. For instance, not surprisingly, we found that Ghanaian women experience a higher degree of labor market vulnerability than Ghanaian men, across all age cohorts. It has been well-documented that women face comparatively more labor market barriers than men, for instance, with respect to owning productive resources and pursuing economic and entrepreneurial opportunities (World Bank, 2016).

In addition, while labor market vulnerability generally declines as individuals attain higher levels of education, educated Ghanaian youth remain more vulnerable relative to older cohorts. For instance, the results suggest that a youth with tertiary-level education credentials and a middle-aged adult with no formal education have a similar likelihood of ending up with vulnerable employment. Highly formalized sectors, such as finance, insurance, and real estate, have the least likelihood of vulnerability for youth.

However, the entry barriers to these sectors is high, and the proportion of youth employed in them is low.

A cross-cutting finding in our analysis is the U-shape phenomenon of vulnerability in the Ghanaian labor market, whereby high vulnerability is recorded in the early years, falls in middle age, and rises again as workers approach retirement. Another important contribution of this study is in our empirical approach. We estimate separately the vulnerability likelihood for different age cohorts to document the experiences for each cohort and likewise compare conditions across cohorts.

The next section of this chapter reviews the empirical literature on labor market vulnerability. This is followed by a discussion of key trends in Ghana's labor market over a ten-year period (2008–2017). The fourth section presents the theoretical framing of vulnerability in the literature, as a lens and in responding to the understanding of vulnerability. The fifth section presents the detailed methodological approach adopted in the present study. Results and analyses are presented in the sixth section, and we conclude with a summary and some policy options in the final section.

Review of Empirical Literature

The issue of relative vulnerability, which is the comparison of conditions faced by different groups of workers competing in the same labor market, has drawn wide scholarly interest.[1] Collectively, the research to date shows there is no singular experience of labor market vulnerability. Differential vulnerability in the labor market can be based on education, age, family responsibility, occupation, industry, welfare, and the absence or presence of labor market protections (Arnold & Bongiovi, 2013; Bălan, 2014; Saunders, 2003). Additionally, the structure of a labor market has consequences for participants' risk of vulnerability. For instance, the high level of informality that characterizes the economies of many countries in the Global South is linked with a higher risk of vulnerability in the labor market (International Labour Organization [ILO], 2015; Shehu & Nilsson, 2014).

In their analysis of the extent of informal employment among youths in 20 "developing" economies based on school-to-work transition surveys, Shehu and Nilsson (2014) found that for young people in these countries,

---

[1] See, for example, Bălan (2014).

the informal employment was the "standard" sector of employment. This finding supports the conclusion that, in many cases, informal employment represents the only option available to young people. The study also found that past working experience played a crucial role in determining vulnerability over a lifetime of labor market participation. At entry level, a lack of past labor market experience increased youths' risk of ending up in informal employment, and this and other inequalities in early life were likely to follow youths throughout their work lives. Sparreboom and Staneva (2014) reached a similar conclusion regarding the high vulnerability of the youths in the labor market, based on a sample of 28 low- and middle-income countries.

Studies on what makes youths more vulnerable than other cohorts have also revealed a plethora of factors that are largely country-/region-specific. For example, Bhorat, Oosthuizen, Sharp, Lilenstein, and Yu (2016) modeled the determinant of vulnerability in labor markets in selected low-income countries in Africa. They find that labor force participation rates are generally higher for men than for women and that young people aged between 15 and 24 years tend to have a substantially higher underemployment rate than all other age cohorts. Furthermore, the authors estimate an employment probability equation and earnings function to explore drivers of vulnerability within the labor market. The results revealed the most significant determinants of vulnerability in low-income countries in Africa to be age, gender, location, education, employment industry, and dependency.

Calvès and Schoumaker (2004) used retrospective data in Burkina Faso to investigate and compare the labor market outcomes of youths against the labor market outcomes of older cohorts documented during their youth. Their data allowed them to compare the labor market outcomes of three different age cohorts, drawing upon longitudinal data on the youth stage of each cohort. The authors observed that the youngest cohort found paid employment at an older age relative to the oldest cohort, especially among males. Similarly, the youngest cohorts were less likely to find their first paid employment in the formal sector relative to the oldest cohort, meaning that youths in the study were more likely to start work in the informal sector today than they were in the past.

In a study of Global South countries, Sparreboom and Staneva (2014) reported that vulnerability among youths decreased with higher levels of education. The study also concluded that the level of vulnerability was in direct proportion to the level of economic development. They estimated that vulnerability is highest for youth in low-income countries (70%), relative to their counterparts from lower middle-income countries (31%) and upper middle-income countries (23%).[2] This finding is plausibly related to the observed correlation between the size of a country's informal sector and its level of economic development.

With respect to Ghana, studies, including World Bank (2016), Porter, Blaufuss, and Acheampong (2007), Aryeetey and Baah-Boateng (2015), and Barret et al. (2015), have examined the circumstances of youths who are vulnerable within the labor market. A key conclusion from these studies is that youth labor challenges stem from the low quality of jobs, rather than unemployment. In the Ghanaian context, low-quality jobs are characterized by low pay and absence of job security, contract, or health benefits. However, how youths' conditions compare to older cohorts, and the socioeconomic factors driving their vulnerability, are questions that are not clearly understood.

The present study seeks to fill the gap in the literature in two significant respects. First, it investigates the key drivers of vulnerability among youths rather than youth employment outcomes or job status—a key departure from previous studies. Second, the study compares drivers of vulnerability among the youths to older cohorts in order to determine the extent to which the identified factors persist over time.

STYLIZED FACTS ABOUT THE GHANAIAN LABOR MARKET

This section discusses what are widely considered to be key trends within Ghana's labor market between 2008 and 2017. This period coincided with the global financial meltdown that affected productivity and labor market activities around the globe. The period was also marked by significant Ghanaian government policy interventions around youth issues, such as the introduction of the National Youth Policy of Ghana in 2010. We focus on labor market conditions (participation, unemployment rate, and vulnerability) and circumstances of youth relative to other labor market participants.

---

[2] This is based on the World Bank country classification by level of income per capita. Benin and Bangladesh are examples of low-income countries, while Zambia and Ukraine are lower middle-income countries, and Tunisia and Brazil are upper middle-income countries.

Demographic Profile of the Youth in Ghana

Table 9.1 describes the key demographic profile of youth in Ghana, as drawn from Youth Policy Factsheets (2014). Specifically, youth constitutes about 18.63% of the population, and 50.3% of the youth population are female. Youth literacy in Ghana is among the highest in Africa at 91.32% for males and 89.86% for females. In comparison, youth literacy for sub-Saharan African countries is about 77%. The demographic analysis shows that Ghana has yet to experience a youth bulge, as the majority of the population is not within the youth age bracket. However, with 38% of the population less than 14 years old and an annual population growth rate of about 2.17%, Ghana is on course to reach the stage for a youth bulge within the next 30 years. The implication of this population dynamic is that new entrants into the labor market will arrive at an increasing rate over the next 30 years. Therefore, to meet the lofty objective of Agenda 2063 in terms of providing decent jobs for all, the rate of job creation must exceed the arrival rate in the labor market.

Labor Force Participation

Labor force participation refers to the proportion of the working age population that is active within the labor market, through either being presently engaged or actively looking for work. In Ghana, labor force participation is high: according to World Bank (2018) close to 77% of the working population were recorded to be active in the labor market in

Table 9.1 A snapshot of youth demographic profile

Age distribution
0–14 years: 38.01%
15–24 years: 18.63%
25–55 years: 34.14%
56–64 years: 4.97%
65 years and over: 4.25%
Gender distribution
Male: 49.7%
Female: 50.3%
Youth literacy rate
Male: 91.32%
Female: 89.86%

Source: Compiled from World Bank (2018) and Ghana Statistical Service Database (2019)

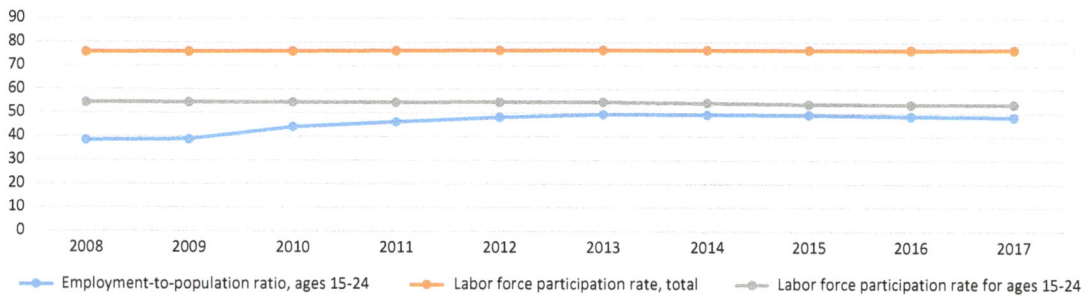

Fig. 9.1 Labor participation and employment-population in Ghana, 2008–2017 (Source: World Bank, 2018)

2017 (see Fig. 9.1). The participation rate is also stable over time, hovering around 74–77%. As expected, the labor participation rate by the youth is much lower than for the entire population, estimated at 53.7% in 2017. The main reason for the low labor participation is the large number of youths in education and training—estimated at around 49.8% according to Ghana Living Standards Survey Round Six (GLSS 6) (Ghana Statistical Service, 2014).

Another important trend within the labor market, as shown in Fig. 9.1, is the employment-to-population ratio among the youth. The employment-to-population ratio measures the proportion of the working age population in a country that are employed. Although similar to the employment rate, it provides a much more relevant indicator of the potential of the economy to create jobs. Within the Ghanaian economy, the employment-to-population ratio for the youth stood at 51.1% in 2017, an increase of 10 percentage points since 2008 (World Bank, 2018). Comparatively, the employment-to-population ratio for the entire population stood at 75% in 2017 and has remained fairly stable over time (World Bank, 2018).

However, the level of youth employment in Ghana masks a major issue around underemployment faced by youth within the labor market. According to GLSS 6 data, over 50% of the young workers in Ghana are underemployed, compared to 35% for the entire labor force (Ghana Statistical Service, 2014).

Youth Unemployment

Figure 9.2 shows the trend in unemployment rates between the youth and the total labor force in Ghana. The aggregate unemployment rate reached its peak in 2009 at 8.3%, which reflects the negative effect of the global

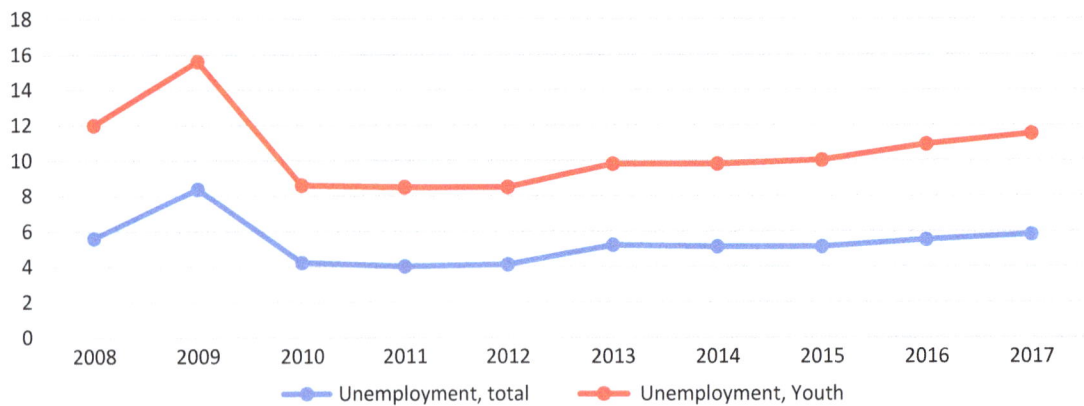

Fig. 9.2 Unemployment rate in Ghana, 2008–2017 (Source: World Bank, 2018)

financial meltdown (World Bank, 2018). Afterward, the unemployment rate stabilized at around 4–5%, but there appears to be an uptick in recent years (World Bank, 2018). The youth unemployment rate, also shown in Fig. 9.2, is a mirror image of the rate for the aggregate population over the period. However, youth unemployment is consistently higher than the total unemployment over the period. This reflects the labor market condition for youths, in which they face less absorption and more stringent conditions for employment.

Ghana's youth unemployment is also exacerbated by the low level of formal education among young people.[3] Only 7% of youth workers have attended university, vocational training, or other forms of postsecondary education. The lack of formal qualifications and skills makes it unlikely for youths to get employment in the formal sector (with high pay and more job security). The absence of formal education and the inability of the formal sector to adequately absorb the large population of job seekers have led to the informal sector becoming the only viable channel of employment for youth (Ismail, 2016).

Furthermore, the relatively high youth unemployment rate is fueled by socioeconomic circumstances such as rural-urban migration. For example, the Ashanti and Brong-Ahafo regions, the country's most urbanized areas, are home to a large portion of youths[4] that are in search of opportunities

---

[3] The point here is that lack of formal education by a majority of the youth means they have a chance in only the informal sector, whereas the older cohorts have the opportunity to draw on both formal and informal sectors.

[4] This is a global phenomenon which Ghana is not immune from. In every country of the world, urban unemployment is always higher than rural unemployment. The Haris-Todaro model captures this idea vividly.

in the formal sector. Generally, the average unemployment rate in urban areas exceeded those in rural areas by about 50 percentage points between 2000 and 2013 (Aryeetey & Baah-Boateng, 2015). In essence, the young population is inadequately absorbed into employment compared with the older adult cohort.

On the surface, Ghana's high youth unemployment is in stark contrast to the sustained economic growth recorded in the past three decades. However, data measuring sectoral performance reveals that the growth is concentrated in non-employment-generating sectors (such as the oil sector), while there is a decline in growth of employment-generating sectors (such as agriculture and industry).

Vulnerability in the Labor Force Market

The dearth of opportunities in Ghana's formal sector pushes significant numbers of people toward vulnerable employment. Using World Bank data, Fig. 9.3 illustrates the proportion of workers in Ghana that can be classified as vulnerable. Vulnerability is measured as the sum total of the labor force population classified as own-account or self-employed and contributing family workers (those working for members within their household).

The proportion of vulnerable employment for the entire population fell from 76% in 2008 to 68% in 2017 (World Bank, 2018). However, women are still mostly engaged in vulnerable employment, 78% in 2017, compared to 58% for men (World Bank, 2018). There are two perspectives to the high level of vulnerability faced by women in the labor force. On one side

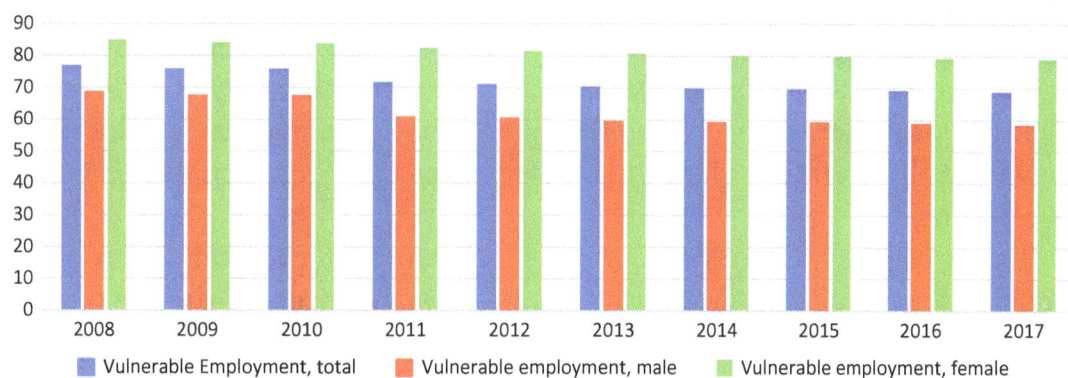

Fig. 9.3 Vulnerable employment in Ghana, 2008–2017 (Source: World Bank, 2018)

are the structural factors such as cultural practices and taboos that affect mostly women. On the other hand, the increase in labor participation of women could also play a role. As Aryeetey and Baah-Boateng (2015) observed, high labor participation of women against the backdrop of fewer employment opportunities makes them more vulnerable. The condition for young women is even more severe, as they combine job searching with motherhood.

While this result represents the entire labor force, it is possible to draw an inference regarding the circumstances of the youth. The fact that youths are dominant in the informal sector clearly suggests they will be more vulnerable (see Aryeetey & Baah-Boateng, 2015). Also, based on earnings data reported in Baah-Boateng, Ansu, and Amoak-Tuffour (2013), the least paid workers in Ghana are the contributing family and own-account workers, earning the equivalent of about $2.25 and $4.95 per day, respectively. In comparison, workers in wage employment earn $10 per day, while employers earn $20 per day. Similarly, formal sector workers (private and public) earn at least $15.35 daily, while informal sector workers earn $5.75 daily (Baah-Boateng et al., 2013). Essentially, since the majority of the youth workers are within the informal sector, where they are engaged mostly as contributing family or own-account workers, they are more likely to be poorly remunerated and therefore likely end up in vulnerable employment.

Conceptual Framework

Following the observation that youths are more exposed to vulnerability in the labor market relative to other age groups, we discuss some notable labor market theories that explain this observed pattern. Specifically, we discuss the labor market features that make youths more susceptible, over and beyond some of their individual characteristics that may contribute to their risk of vulnerability. This will help to situate the analysis of vulnerability within the context of labor market features that are amenable to policy fine-tuning.

The greater exposure of youths to labor market vulnerability is often explained using neoclassical economic theories, particularly the job search, school-to-work transition, and human capital theories (Doeringer & Piore, 1975). For instance, these theories postulate that youth unemployment is a form of frictional unemployment arising due to skill mismatch between work demand and educational setting. This observation suggests a minimal role for policy intervention. Specifically, the theories rely on market mechanism to correct the mismatch. Also, this class of theories suggests the experience of vulnerability is a stage toward greater labor market integration in adult years and therefore policies should be directed toward supply-side interventions, so far as other dimensions of discrimination are not established among the youth population.

Another category of theories emphasizes the structural factors that make youths more vulnerable in the labor market. Some observable demographic and socioeconomic factors, among other structural drivers, disproportionately make youths more vulnerable (Barret et al., 2015; Dietritch, 2012; Sparreboom & Staneva, 2014). Moreover, the effect of youth vulnerability in the labor market remains persistent for the most affected youths into adulthood (Mavromaras et al., 2013; Nilsen & Reiso, 2011).

The internal and external labor market theory formulated by Doeringer and Piore (1970) is the theory most widely adhered to. The labor market is conceptualized as a segmented framework. Particularly, the internal labor market, characterized by high wages, good working conditions, and high job stability, is often shielded from direct competition with the external labor market, characterized by low wages, poor working conditions, and casual work, where most youths find themselves. The implication is therefore the concentration of youths in the external labor market.

We discuss these theories to analyze the Ghanaian labor market and explain recurrent unemployment spells—one of the drivers of labor market vulnerability among youths—as well as examine how these may affect labor market outcomes over time, as the statistics demonstrate. In the case of Ghana's labor market, structural theories tend to explain the pattern and level of vulnerability observed in the labor market. In particular, although youth are observed to be more vulnerable than older cohorts, all demographic groups are exposed to poor labor market outcomes, signaling structural problems within the labor market. The policy relevance of recognizing and understanding these segments within the labor market is the identification of two channels for intervention. The first channel is the possibility of introducing schemes that facilitate the mobility between the informal/external and formal/internal labor market. The second is the possibility of implementing schemes that improve the quality of jobs in the informal/external labor market.

Methodology

This section details the empirical approach adopted in this study to measure vulnerability in the labor market. It also discusses the empirical strategy and dataset used in analyzing the conditions of the youth compared with older cohorts.

Measuring Vulnerability from Employment Status

According to the ILO (1993), workers can be classified under six employment status categories:

1. Wage and salaried workers: These are a class of employees who work in the formal sector, either private or public, and receive compensation in the forms of salary, wage, and commission. Workers in this setting are recognized as skilled components of the labor force and are often provided with formal contracts and better remuneration.
2. Employers: The ILO (1993) defines these workers as people working on their own account or with one or a few partners, and in this capacity, on a continuous basis (including the reference period) have engaged one or more persons to work for them in their business as employees.
3. Own-account workers: These are people that are self-employed and have not engaged any other employees to work for them. It is mostly borne out of failure to secure gainful employment within the formal sector.
4. Contributing family workers: According to the Organisation for Economic Co-Operation and Development (OECD) (2003), these are people who hold a self-employment job in a private establishment operated by a related person living in the same household, and who cannot be regarded as a partner because of the degree of his or her commitment to the operation of the establishment, in terms of the working time or standard labor contract.
5. Domestic employees: This broadly entails work performed in or for the household. This class of employee has no explicit or implicit contract.
6. Apprentice: This type of employment dominates the informal economy and mostly engages the youths. Specifically, it entails a

young apprentice learning a particular skill through observation and imitation. They receive compensation only to meet their basic living costs.

For this study, vulnerable employment is defined as workers within the last four employment statuses: own-account workers, contributing family workers, domestic employees, and apprentices. This definition builds on and extends the World Bank definition of vulnerability, which only includes own-account and contributing family workers. We add domestic employees and apprentices given the context of the labor market in Ghana. Domestic employees and apprentices are subjected to no formal contract and receive little remuneration. In many instances, they are paid in kind through foods, clothing, and other basic needs in exchange for their services. Also, apprentices often transition to own-account workers after graduation, thereby remaining within the vulnerable employment segment.

Determining Why Youths Are More Vulnerable

The theoretical and empirical evidence discussed above shows that youths are more vulnerable in the Ghanaian labor market. This raises an important question as to why and what factors predispose them to labor market vulnerability. It also raises the question of what implications current labor market vulnerability might have for future labor market participation of youth as they transition into the middle and older cohorts.

To answer these questions, we divide participants in the labor market into three groups: (1) youths aged 15 to 24 years (those just entering the labor market), (2) middle-aged adults aged 25 to 54 years (those in their prime working lives), (3) older adults aged 55 to 65 years (those passing the peak of their career and approaching retirement). We then estimate the probability of being vulnerable under different socioeconomic profiles. For instance, to what extent does being female make youth vulnerable compared to male youths and females in the older cohorts, and how does this evolve over time? Exploring the dynamics of labor market vulnerability will indicate the future possibilities for youths as they transition to adulthood. This illustrates the business-as-usual scenario in which, if there is no concerted effort from government, the vulnerability persists into adulthood and is even passed on to subsequent generations.

The probability of being vulnerable is estimated based on a multiple logistic model in which our measure of vulnerability is regressed against some selected independent variables that have been observed in the literature to be likely drivers of vulnerability. For the statistical analysis, vulnerability is measured as a binary variable, which takes the value of "1" if a worker belongs to any of the four vulnerable classes of employment (own-account workers, contributing family workers, domestic employees, and apprentices), Otherwise, it takes the value of "0" if the worker is in wage and salary employment or is an employer. We then control for the following independent variables[5]: gender, education level, industry of employment, location, and region. Any variable not significant at 10% level of significance is not reported.

Data

This study used data from the GLSS 6 by the Ghana Statistical Service (2014). Of the nationally representative sample of 18,000 households in 1200 enumeration areas, 16,772 were successfully enumerated leading to a response rate of 93.2%. The GLSS 6 had a Labor Force Module that was used to collect data on labor indicators of 71,523 individual household members.

The GLSS 6 labor module sample contains observations for all individuals, irrespective of their ages and labor market participation status. However, seeing that this study focuses on examining labor market vulnerability constraints (i.e., conditions of potential and actual labor market participants), we streamlined the sample to include only individuals aged between 15 and 65 years (which is the official labor market participation age in Ghana), and we also dropped all people in the sample who are enrolled in educational institutions. There is considerable evidence in the literature to show that the proportion of younger people participating in the labor force is generally less than that for older age groups due to schooling. Hence, removing all individuals enrolled in educational programs or schools means that the analysis can be narrowed essentially to account for the conditions of young people who are participants in the Ghanaian labor market. Given that our sample targets individuals actively engaged in the labor market, we also exclude discouraged workers, retir-

---

[5] All the independent variables are measured as a categorical variable.

ees, dependents, housewives, the disabled or sick, and redundant workers. Hence, the sample size is reduced to 33,687 individuals.

EMPIRICAL RESULTS

This section presents the result of the multiple logistic regression. The full result is presented in Table 9.6 in the Appendix. However, for ease of exposition, we extract from the full result estimated vulnerability probability by gender (Table 9.2), location (Table 9.3), education (Table 9.4), and industry of employment (Table 9.5).

An Assessment of the Vulnerability of Youths Vis-à-Vis Other Cohorts

Gender
Table 9.2 reports the vulnerability likelihood across gender. The rows show the estimated probability across age cohorts, while the columns compare vulnerability between males and females. There is about a 90% chance of being vulnerable for female youths in the labor market compared to about 85% for males. However, some interesting dynamics emerge when comparison is made across age cohorts. Vulnerability probability declines to about 79% for females in the middle age group but is elevated again to 85% for older adults. A similar pattern is observed for males and by extension across other socioeconomic profiles analyzed below. This suggests a U-shape relationship between age level and vulnerability. It also confirms the general hypothesis of this study that youths are more vulnerable and that this is due to underlying structural issues.

The observed higher vulnerability probability for women in the labor market can be explained in terms of structural factors that are not favorable to women and, therefore, hamper their effective participation in decent wage employment. For example, according to GLSS 6, Ghanaian

Table 9.2 Vulnerability probability by gender

Gender	15–24 years	25–54 years	55–65 years
Female	0.9009	0.7898	0.8452828
Male	0.8496	0.6543	0.772681

Source: Extracted from the multiple logistic regression in Table 9.6 in the Appendix

women are less likely to attend schools, relative to their male counterparts (Ghana Statistical Service, 2014). From the survey data, about 36% of females that are actively engaged in the labor force never attended school, compared to 22% of males. Another reason for the high vulnerability of females in the labor market in Ghana is the fact that women tend to face greater constraints in owning productive resources or accessing capital to expand their businesses and are therefore limited in economic and entrepreneurial opportunities (World Bank, 2016).

Location

Location has a significant influence on the probability of being in vulnerable employment in Ghana. The result in Table 9.3 indicates that vulnerability likelihood is higher for youths in rural areas compared to those in urban areas, although the difference is marginal. Focusing on regional variation in vulnerability, we found that youths in Greater Accra have the least probability of being engaged in vulnerable employment (with about 77% probability) while those in the Northern and Upper East region are the most vulnerable (with probability of about 91% and 92%, respectively).

Greater Accra is the administrative seat of Ghana and the most urbanized region in the country, with about 87.4% of its inhabitants living in urban centers (Songsore, 2009). The region has a high level of commercial and governmental activities as well as some reasonable degree of industrial ventures. Therefore, workers in Greater Accra are more likely to

Table 9.3 Vulnerability probability by location

Residence	15–24 years	25–54 years	55–65 years
Rural residence	0.8842	0.7553	0.8296
Urban residence	0.8718	0.7050	0.7864
Region			
Western	0.863	0.6755	0.7933
Central	0.8357	0.7418	0.8285
Greater Accra	0.777	0.652	0.7558
Volta	0.900	0.769	0.8538
Eastern	0.870	0.7420	0.8099
Ashanti	0.869	0.7304	0.808
Brong-Ahafo	0.898	0.751	0.823
Northern	0.917	0.794	0.862
Upper East	0.923	0.752	0.822

Source: Extracted from the multiple logistic regression in Table 9.6

engage in wage employment than other regions in Ghana—an explanation for the relatively low probability of employment vulnerability in the region.

On the other hand, the Northern region, although the largest in terms of landmass, has a drier climate with 73% of its economically active population involved in agriculture (Ghana Statistical Service, 2013). Also, the Upper East region is the least urbanized part of Ghana. The region's economy is based on agriculture—primarily cattle rearing and planting of cereals such as rice, millet, and sorghum (Government of Ghana, Department of Children and United Nations International Children's Emergency Fund [UNICEF], n.d.). Generally, workers in the region are mostly peasant farmers and are vulnerable to adverse weather and other climate-induced shocks. This may explain the higher probability of employment vulnerability in the region.

Furthermore, youths are the most vulnerable group across regions in Ghana, and this is true for both industrial and agrarian regions. Again, we found a U-shape relation between vulnerability and age cohort, such that vulnerability reduces after transition from youth to middle age but increases thereafter. Again, this illustrates that in a business-as-usual scenario, vulnerable youths in Ghanaian society will simply transition to vulnerable adults. Therefore, there is likely to be low intergeneration mobility in economic opportunities and performance, thereby creating a vicious cycle perpetuating vulnerability from parents to their offspring. In essence, there is an urgent need to address the development challenges facing the rural and agrarian areas in Ghana.

Education

The analysis of vulnerability across levels of education attainment shows that Ghanaian workers with primary education have the most vulnerable employment, while those with university education record the least vulnerability (see Table 9.4). For the entire labor market, workers with university education are also the least likely to be in vulnerable employment—75% for youths, 58% for middle age, and 63% for the older cohort.

Another noteworthy finding is the lower vulnerability probability recorded by youths with no education compared to those with primary and adult education. This could be explained by a lack of integration between lower-level education and the labor market in Ghana. For example, Ghana's Ministry of Employment and Labor Relations noted that the

Table 9.4 Vulnerability probability by education

Educational attainment	15–24 years	25–54 years	55–65 years
No formal education	0.8730	0.7618	0.8425
Primary education	0.9012	0.7377	0.8154
Secondary education	0.8386	0.6993	0.7336
Technical education	0.7667	0.6476	0.7293
Tertiary education	0.7510	0.5865	0.6328
Formal adult education	0.9076	0.7546	0.8541

Source: Extracted from the multiple logistic regression in Table 9.6

high level of youth unemployment in the country is partly due to the introduction of the Junior and Senior High School (JHS and SHS) systems without adequate planning for integrating them into trade/vocation and job placement (Baffour-Awuah, 2013). Specialized technical and vocational training for young people in Ghana, therefore, represent a viable option to reduce vulnerability and further systematically integrate the skillset acquired from schooling and labor market skill requirements.

Industry of Employment
In terms of the industry of employment, youths engaged in the agricultural (98%) and manufacturing sector (81%) are the most vulnerable (see Table 9.5). A similar pattern holds for middle-aged and older adults.

Table 9.5 Vulnerability probability by industry of employment

Industry	15–24 years	25–54 years	55–65 years
Agriculture and fishing	0.9782	0.9143	0.915
Mining	0.2269	0.2102	–
Manufacturing	0.8102	0.6622	0.736
Electricity and utilities	0.2704	0.2325	–
Construction	0.5672	0.5103	0.317
Commerce	0.787	0.7316	0.827
Transportation & communication	0.479	0.3659	0.3089
Financial, insurance, & real estate	0.129	0.2071	0.138
Public administration	–	0.0259	0.0899
Education, health & social work	0.1232	0.0910	0.2108

Note that "–" means the vulnerability probability is not reported because the coefficient is not statistically significant

Source: Extracted from the multiple logistic regression in Table 9.6

Interestingly, youths in the financial sector are the least vulnerable, even better off than the other cohorts. This may be due to the stringent entry requirements into the sector relative to other economic sectors and the preference of formal financial firms for young graduates in Ghana for entry-level positions. Similarly, those in the mining, education and health services, and electricity sectors fare well in the labor market. However, the proportion of youth in these sectors is low. The overall analysis indicates that youths are in fact better off in more formal sectors. This, therefore, suggests that a crucial pathway to reduce youth vulnerability will be through the expansion of formal sector employment and equipping youths with school-to-work transition skills to secure formal jobs.

Conclusion

This study has examined the extent and determinants of vulnerability among youths in the Ghanaian labor market. The results of the study largely support the extant literature that youths aged 15 to 24 years are more vulnerable than older cohorts, both in accessing the formal sector and in transitioning from formal to informal employment. The fact of Ghanaian youths' lack of access to standard work offered within formal employment has far-reaching and lifelong wage and income scarring effects. The study revealed that one aspect of the scarring effect is a dynamic in which for any given socioeconomic profile, vulnerability is high for workers that are young, falls for those in the middle age, and rises again as workers approach retirement. This trend reveals the likely trajectory of youths' work lives as they transition to adulthood and the persistence of vulnerability. Hence, in order to mitigate labor market vulnerability in Ghana, youths and older adults should figure high among priorities for policy intervention.

We also conclude that policies and actions aimed at enhancing the overall social mobility of young people in Ghana will be more effective if planned to fit specific contexts. For instance, establishing mechanisms to ensure mobility from work back to school could be instrumental in enabling youths to move from informal to formal sector employment. Interventions such as this combined with ongoing efforts aimed at revamping vocational education and integrating it with the school curriculum will be an important public policy.

APPENDIX

Table 9.6 Multiple logistic regression of labor market vulnerability equation for various age cohorts in Ghana (dependent variable: vulnerability)

Independent variable	15–24 years	25–54 years	55–65 years
Gender			
Female	0.9009033***	0.7898811***	0.8452828***
	(0.0035166)	(0.0031177)	(0.0067626)
Male	0.8496206***	0.6543065***	0.772681***
	(0.0047919)	(0.0042217)	(0.0089811)
Location of residence			
Rural residence	0.8842404***	0.755368***	0.8296399***
	(0.0040609)	(0.0035761)	(0.0070999)
Urban residence	0.8718873***	0.7050978***	0.7864635***
	(0.0043638)	(0.003794)	(0.0098311)
Educational attainment			
No formal education	0.8561391***	0.7461034***	0.8405594***
	(0.0107763)	(0.0053209)	(0.0093703)
Primary education	0.8973997***	0.7378416***	0.8124948***
	(0.0050702)	(0.0064008)	(0.0172303)
Secondary education	0.8450967***	0.7094158***	0.7421411***
	(0.0085607)	(0.0079946)	(0.0361786)
Technical education	0.7913415***	0.6683465***	0.7353936***
	(0.0300716)	(0.013463)	(0.0309056)
Tertiary education	0.7648842***	0.6152413***	0.6524647***
	(0.0472552)	(0.0168964)	(0.0480943)
Formal adult education	0.8771642***	0.7386784***	0.8589***
	(0.0611978)	(0.0165824)	(0.0261744)
Industry of employment			
Agriculture and fishing	0.9756471***	0.9098103***	0.9145664***
	(0.00231)	(0.0035101)	(0.006775)
Mining	0.2526738***	0.2278755***	
	(0.0469135)	(0.0275475)	
Manufacturing	0.8205489***	0.6697519***	0.7514908***
	(0.014968)	(0.0107243)	(0.0301686)
Electricity and utilities	0.2896095*	0.2411071***	
	(0.1567811)	(0.0606977)	
Construction	0.5952893***	0.5241562***	0.3393696***
	(0.0401123)	(0.0195731)	(0.0781089)
Commerce	0.8053336***	0.742422***	0.8317581***
	(0.0122775)	(0.0071915)	(0.0180033)
Transportation & communication	0.5224159***	0.3806821***	0.3108498***
	(0.0399782)	(0.0187189)	(0.0705853)

(*continued*)

Table 9.6 (continued)

Independent variable	15–24 years	25–54 years	55–65 years
Financial, insurance, & real estate	0.139791* (0.0746769)	0.2219283*** (0.0469038)	0.1507738 (0.132958)
Public administration		0.0256245 (0.0196327)	0.0901949 (0.0704513)
Education, health & social work	0.1396186*** (0.0358978)	0.0845015*** (0.0112126)	0.2013682*** (0.042313)
Region			
Western	0.8631071*** (0.0090033)	0.6755129*** (0.0077349)	0.7933918*** (0.0174239)
Central	0.8357605*** (0.01334)	0.7418513*** (0.0077793)	0.8285589*** (0.0150804)
Greater Accra	0.7773982*** (0.0149158)	0.652552*** (0.0077525)	0.7558884*** (0.0222083)
Volta	0.9000875*** (0.0087484)	0.7691318*** (0.007092)	0.8538841*** (0.0138621)
Eastern	0.8709197*** (0.0085545)	0.7420323*** (0.0071657)	0.8099771*** (0.013989)
Ashanti	0.8693569*** (0.0086308)	0.7304593*** (0.0066556)	0.8082494*** (0.0150767)
Brong-Ahafo	0.8987747*** (0.0082098)	0.7516783*** (0.0074132)	0.823182*** (0.0164098)
Northern	0.9179383*** (0.0074342)	0.7940117*** (0.0068935)	0.8620807*** (0.0144685)
Upper East	0.9235513*** (0.0054311)	0.7522132*** (0.01432)	0.8229605*** (0.02239)

Source: Authors' computation

Notes: Standard errors are given below the coefficients. The asterisks indicate significance at the following levels: ***$p < 0.01$, **$p < 0.05$, *$p < 0.1$

REFERENCES

African Union Commission. (2015). *Agenda 2063. The Africa we want: A shared strategic framework for inclusive growth and sustainable development. First ten-year implementation plan: 2014–2023.* Retrieved March 19, 2019, from http://www.un.org/en/africa/osaa/pdf/au/agenda2063-first10yearimplementation.pdf

Arnold, D., & Bongiovi, J. R. (2013). Precarious, informalizing, and flexible work: Transforming concepts and understandings. *American Behavioral Scientist, 57*(3), 289–308. https://doi.org/10.1177/0002764212466239

Aryeetey, E., & Baah-Boateng, W. (2015). *Understanding Ghana's growth success story and job creation challenges* (No. 2015/140). Helsinki, Finland: The United Nations University World Institute for Development Economics Research (UNU-WIDER).

Baah-Boateng, W., Ansu, Y., & Amoak-Tuffour, J. (2013). *Mapping of country information on employment, unemployment and policy initiatives.* Accra: African Center for Economic Transformation.

Baffour-Awuah, D. (2013). *Effectiveness of Ghana's targeted actions to promote youth employment.* Abidjan, Côte d'Ivoire: Association for the Development of Education in Africa. Retrieved January 22, 2017, from http://www.adeanet. org/min_conf_youth_skills_employment/sites/default/files/u24/Ghana%20 Country%20Report_0.pdf

Bălan, M. (2014). Youth labor market vulnerabilities: Characteristics, dimensions and costs. *Procedia Economics and Finance, 8,* 66–72.

Barret, Z., Berrios, A., He, Y., Larsen, S., Novoa, M., Twumasi-Ankrah, K., et al. (2015). *Youth employment in Ghana: Conditions and determinants.* College Station, TX: Texas A & M University, Bush School of Government & Public Service.

Bhorat, H., Lilenstein, K., Oosthuizen, M., & Thornton, A. (2016). *Vulnerability in the labor market: Jobs, livelihood strategies & poverty in South Africa.* Rondebosch: University of Cape Town, Development Policy Research Unit.

Bhorat, H., Oosthuizen, M., Sharp, M., Lilenstein, K., & Yu, D. (2016). *Modelling labor markets in low income countries with imperfect data.* Retrieved January 22, 2017, from http://conference.iza.org/conference_files/ GLMLICNetwork_2016/sharp_m24274.pdf

Calvès, A.-E., & Schoumaker, B. (2004). Deteriorating economic context and changing patterns of youth employment in urban Burkina Faso: 1980–2000. *World Development, 32*(8), 1341–1354.

Dietritch, H. (2012). *Youth unemployment in Europe: Theoretical considerations and empirical findings.* Bonn: Friedrich Ebert Stiftung.

Doeringer, P. B., & Piore, M. J. (1970). *Internal labor markets and manpower analysis.* Washington, DC: Manpower Administration (DOL), Office of Manpower Research.

Doeringer, P. B., & Piore, M. J. (1975). Unemployment and the "dual labor market". *The Public Interest, 38,* 67–79.

Ghana Statistical Service. (2013). *The 2010 population and housing census: National analytical report.* Accra: Author.

Ghana Statistical Service. (2014). *Ghana living standards survey round 6 (GLSS 6) labor force report*. Accra: Author.

Ghana Statistical Service. (2019). *Demographic database*. Retrieved January 24, 2019, from http://www.statsghana.gov.gh/nationalaccount_macros. php?Stats=MTA1NTY1NjgxLjUwNg==/webstats/s679n2sn87

Government of Ghana, Department of Children, & United Nations International Children's Emergency Fund (UNICEF). (n.d.). *Child protection baseline research: Upper East regional profile*. Retrieved January 24, 2019, from https:// www.unicef.org/ghana/P1417_unicef_ghana_UPPER_EAST_WEB.pdf

Gregg, P., & Tominey, E. (2004). *The wage scar from youth unemployment* (CMPO Working Paper Series No. 04/097). Bristol, England: Centre for Market and Public Organisation. Retrieved March 12, 2018, from http://www.bristol.ac. uk/media-library/sites/cmpo/migrated/documents/wp97.pdf

International Labour Organization. (1993). *Resolution concerning the International Classification of Status in Employment (ICSE), adopted by the Fifteenth International Conference of Labour Statisticians*. Retrieved March 12, 2018, from https://www.ilo.org/wcmsp5/groups/public/%2D%2D-dgreports/%2D%2D-stat/documents/normativeinstrument/wcms_087562.pdf

International Labour Organization (ILO). (2015). *Global employment trends for youth 2015: Scaling up investments in decent jobs for youth*. Geneva: Author.

Ismail, O. (2016). What is in a job? The social context of youth employment issues in Africa. *Journal of African Economies, 25*(suppl_1), i37–i60.

Mavromaras, K., Sloane, P., & Wei, Z. (2013). *The scarring effects of unemployment, low pay and skills under-utilisation in Australia compared*. Bonn: Institute for the Study of Labor.

Nilsen, Q., & Reiso, K. H. (2011). *Scarring effects of unemployment*. Bonn: Institute for Study of Labor.

Organisation for Economic Co-operation and Development (OECD). (2003). *Glossary of statistical terms*. Retrieved December 23, 2018, from https://stats. oecd.org/glossary/detail.asp?ID=443

Porter, G., Blaufuss, K., & Acheampong, F. O. (2007). Youth, mobility and rural livelihoods in sub-Saharan Africa: Perspectives from Ghana and Nigeria: Poverty, development and livelihoods. *Africa Insight, 37*(3), 420–431.

Saunders, R. (2003). *Defining vulnerability in the labor market*. Ottawa: Canadian Research Policy Networks. Retrieved September 23, 2018, from http://www. envision.ca/pdf/w2w/definingvulnerability.pdf

Shehu, E., & Nilsson, B. (2014). *Informal employment among youth: Evidence from 20 school-to-work transition surveys*. Geneva: International Labor Organisation (ILO). Retrieved September 23, 2018, from http://www.ilo. org/wcmsp5/groups/public/%2D%2D-dgreports/%2D%2D-dcomm/documents/publication/wcms_234911.pdf

Songsore, J. (2009). *The urban transition in Ghana: Urbanization, national development and poverty reduction*. London: International Institute for Environment and Development.

Sparreboom, T., & Staneva, A. (2014). *Is education the solution to decent work for youth in developing economies? Identifying qualifications mismatch from 28 school-to-work transition surveys*. Geneva: International Labor Organisation. Retrieved September 23, 2018, from http://www.un.org/youthenvoy/wp-content/uploads/2014/10/Work4Youth-Publication.pdf

Williams, T., & Pompa, C. (2017). *Invisible lives: Understanding youth livelihoods in Ghana and Uganda*. Toronto: The Mastercard Foundation. Retrieved March 19, 2019, from https://mastercardfdn.org/wp-content/uploads/2018/05/Report_YouthLivelihoods_Feb2017v2-Accessible-3-1-accessible.pdf

World Bank. (2016). *Harnessing youth potential in Ghana: A policy note*. Retrieved January 24, 2019, from http://documents.worldbank.org/curated/en/299731470375262940/Harnessing-youth-potential-in-Ghana-a-policy-note

World Bank. (2018). *World development indicators*. Retrieved January 24, 2019, from http://datatopics.worldbank.org/world-development-indicators/

Youth Policy Factsheets. (2014, June 11). *Factsheet: Ghana*. Retrieved January 23, 2017, from http://www.youthpolicy.org/factsheets/country/ghana/

The Role of "eTrash2Cash" in Curtailing "Almajiri" Vulnerability in Nigeria Through Waste Management Social Micro-entrepreneurship

Alh. Muhammad Salisu Abdullahi

Introduction

The northern region of Nigeria is commonly associated with the term *Almajiri*,[1] a system of religious education. In *Almajiranci*,[2] poorer families send their children away from home to seek knowledge through an Islamic education based on the Holy Qur'an, with traditional teachers known as Mallams serving as the children's guardians. These children, who are mainly between the ages of 5 and 19, are sent over long distances across the northern states, usually to specified destinations. But their Mallam guardians are proscribed by tradition from providing anything to

---

[1] The term originated from the Arabic word *Almuhajir*, which means a migrant. It was used in history to describe patriots of the holy Prophet Muhammad who migrated from Mecca to Medina during the early days of the Islamic religion.

[2] Almajiranci is the term being used to describe the system of Almajiri education.

A. M. S. Abdullahi (✉)
eTrash2Cash, eT2C Company Nigeria, Azare, Nigeria

© The Author(s) 2020
M. L. McLean (ed.), *West African Youth Challenges and Opportunity Pathways*, Gender and Cultural Studies in Africa and the Diaspora, https://doi.org/10.1007/978-3-030-21092-2_10

213

support their living. In the rare instances in which children are taken to unspecified destinations where they know no one, the children's parents or their guardians look for the established traditional schools in their final destination and settle there. Whatever the children's final destination, the expectation is that they undertake small jobs and fend for themselves by begging. In the rainy season, they are expected to help their designated Mallam with his own family's needs by doing farm work.

The National Council for the Welfare of the Destitute (NCWD) (2001) puts the current population of the Almajiri in Nigeria at about seven million. According to Abdulkadir (2010), children who comprise this population fall into two broad categories: the most vulnerable are children aged 5 to 11 and vulnerable youth are those aged 12 to 26. Most of them are from the Hausa-/Fulani-speaking ethnic groups and have little or no formal education (Abdulkadir, 2010).

Historically, between the eighteenth and nineteenth century when great centers of Islamic learning were established and flourishing, the phenomenon was a recognized and acceptable socioreligious practice. However, with a challenging economic situation in the country, many in the rural areas in Hausaland are pressured to move to the urban communities to better their livelihoods. This makes the practice of Almajiranci widespread amongst low-income rural parents, bearing further negative consequences on the welfare of innocent children entrusted to a Mallam who would take them elsewhere to impart a proper Islamic education.

The issue of Almajiranci in Nigeria as a whole, and particularly in northern Nigeria, has been an integral part of the country's social challenges for decades. Multiple attempts have been made by scholars and researchers, political leaders and other well-meaning Nigerians to conceive of and implement a lasting solution to curb the rampant increase of Almajiranci. Some have alleged that the practice is a cheap avenue for recruiting agents for violence and terrorism, but these allegations have not been supported by sound research (Ogunmade, 2013). However, the increasing prevalence of Almajiranci has been documented by researchers, who attribute the trend to parents who see it as the most expeditious avenue of enrolling their children in the informal Qur'anic schools which they find culturally acceptable and can afford (Hoechner, 2011).

The eTrash2Cash project was conceived and launched as a social enterprise to bring an immediate solution to the Almajiri social issue in Nigeria. The project provides the victims with professional training that enables them to earn money from resource recovery, waste collecting activities that simultaneously clean the local environment and boost economic growth.

This chapter is divided broadly into two parts: the first section provides a more detailed description of the current practice of Almajiranci in northern Nigeria, by exploring the author's personal experience; the perceived viability, attractiveness, challenges, and impact on child discipline; and the documented economic and social effects. The second section discusses the sustainable eTrash2Cash solution, the history of the enterprise, its youth employment and entrepreneurship program, and how the victims benefit from it and other similar programs.

Description of Almajiranci in Northern Nigeria Today

Critics of the current practice of Almajiri in northern Nigeria point to evidence that it has a completely different meaning than it did traditionally. Today, the term Almajirai (the plural form of Almajiri) is conventionally used to refer to beggars, or people who cannot provide for themselves and thus roam the streets in Nigeria's towns and cities. These critics, including the reformist Islamic scholars in Nigeria, bemoan the far-reaching negative impact on the children and youth deprived of the comfort and protection of their own homes and parents at a very tender age and also on the nation, which is deprived of the contributions of future leaders, young people who might otherwise have grown up to enter respectable vocations as judges, accountants, and engineers (Sa'id, 1992).

Because, according to the practice, the Mallam guardian is not responsible for feeding the Almajiris, the children are forced to beg for food and other basic necessities of life (Garba, 1996), roaming the hot streets, approaching passengers in cars and pedestrians for money or alms. The children are completely dependent upon strangers—and each other—for their food, shelter, and other basic needs, which often go unmet (Ibrahim, 2008). In this process, they become victims of economic hardship, child neglect, and abuse, all in the name of Qur'anic education (Salis, 1995).

As Almajiris roam the streets, motor parks, and marketplaces and go from door to door begging for food and other necessities of life, some attach themselves to sellers of Hausa daily food items such as beans cake, breads, and groundnut cakes, in hopes of attracting sympathy from customers inclined to share some portion of their food purchases (Babangida,

1993). Most Almajiris temporarily migrate to the city from rural areas to look for greener pastures (Ibrahim, 2008). Most of them travel to nearby cities, with a few of them traveling as far as Lagos or even neighboring African countries like Benin, Senegal, and Chad. The availability of Almajiris as a source of cheap labor is believed to contribute to adult unemployment in northern Nigeria's poorest communities. At a number of public places such as markets and cinema houses, disputes arise between Almajirai and non-Almajirai adults over who should be paid for looking after parked vehicles. The unprecedented influx of migrants from the neighboring African nations, such as Ghana, Mali, and Niger among others, is a compounding factor.

The children and youth receive Qur'anic religious instruction inside Almajiri schools, which are usually situated on the premises of the local mosque or *tsangaya*, an informal building meant for the Qur'anic school. Religious instruction can also take place outside of formal classroom settings, in the vicinity of the Mallam's house, under the shade of a tree, and with slates as reading materials (Ya'u, 2001). Rather than follow a standard curriculum, most of the Qur'anic schools have developed their own syllabi, methodology, school calendar, and curriculum.

The conditions under which the Almajiris are expected to learn can be challenging to their physical as well as mental health. They usually receive instruction while sitting on the bare floor, as most of the schools cannot even afford mats, and live in congested tiny classrooms, which mostly serve as both their schooling and sleeping places. The Almajiri schools are normally not coeducational; it is a very rare instance for a girl to be sent for Almajiri education away from her place of birth. Even in Almajiri schools where girls participate as day students (who study during the day and return home to sleep in their parents' houses), they are clearly separated from the boys. These informal Almajiri schools have an average population of 180 pupils, the majority or all being boys, under the control of one Mallam. Without a formal register for the students, it is very difficult for the Mallam to determine daily attendance and absenteeism of his students.

It is not uncommon for all instruction to take place in one small classroom which has a normal capacity of 50 pupils or so, certainly far less than 180 (Sule, 1994). Toilet facilities, where available, are limited and in the most unhygienic conditions. Because of the large number of these children under the care of one Mallam, himself being a low-income earner, it is not uncommon to find an Almajiri school without any toilet facility. In these situations, the Almajiri resort to the use of bushes, city outskirts, or other uncompleted buildings, if available, for any toilet needs.

Amidst the health hazards, the Almajiris of today cannot even afford the most basic health services; therefore, they receive no treatment for common ailments or injuries they may face like diarrheas, wounds, and malaria fever, which can be directly traced to their unhygienic vulnerable conditions and exposure. Some do buy medicine to treat themselves, prescribed by medical personnel such as nurses that support the system and purchased from drug stores. Even where there should be free hospitals and health services, because of their socially marginalized positions they cannot be treated (Perverz, 2005).

To supplement begging, some Almajirai take up menial job services as plate washers in restaurants and even prohibited places, such as commercial sex workers' houses, hotels that serve alcohol, and bars and clubs, which may lead to some intermingling with adults engaged in undesirable behaviors.

Almajiris are also vulnerable to exploitation by the Mallams to whom their parents entrusted them. They become part of an informal child labor system in which they are forced to earn a living by begging not only to feed themselves but also to contribute to the welfare of the Mallam's household by working on the Mallam's farm, fetching water for his domestic use, collecting fire wood, and sometimes even contributing part of what they get from begging (Sulaiman, 1996). Also, the Almajiris are prone to hearing all kinds of embarrassing words, such as curses on them and their parents who sent them on the mission, insults on their faces, verbal expressions to humiliate them, and so on, which are potentially damaging to both the psychological and physical development of a child or young person (Kabir, 2002). It has never been easy for the Almajiri child, whose life experience is influenced by growing up in an environment of disapproval and often various forms of maltreatment, open assault, and contempt for only being Almajirai (Hoechner, 2011). There is a perceived emotional instability associated with distress which results from the accumulated psychological effects of exposure to rejection; this would probably explain reported cases of suicide committed by Almajiri children for undocumented reasons.

Traditionally, and now, mostly amongst the rural populace, the system of Almajiranci is valued and regarded highly for its Qur'anic education, which implies religious devotion and is considered to be an avenue to building moral character. Because of the strict hardships associated with the Almajiranci journey, the children are forced to train themselves in virtuous characteristics like being extremely patient and humble, which are highly regarded as very valuable life skills in rural settings, as well as the core elements of the Islamic faith the Almajiri children believe in (Ware, 2014).

Recent research illustrates how deep-rooted extreme poverty and a lack of access to better alternatives fuels the Almajiri practice (Hoechner, 2015), which has gradually transcended to something that looks like major forms of child abuse. The practice is common among polygamous, poor, and uneducated families (Perverz, 2005). Hoechner (2015) has shown that the Almajiri phenomenon persists even though it no longer promises access to political power or increased social status—that is, in spite of the fact that its economic viability has been undermined and its religious merit has come under attack. Structural factors constraining the opportunities available to poor peasant households play an important role in fueling its demand. The decline of Nigeria's rural economy in response to the oil boom beginning in the mid-twentieth century, the structural adjustment program imposed by the World Bank and International Monetary Fund in the mid-1980s, along with the country's massive demographic growth—its population has more than quadrupled since 1950 (United Nations, 2008)—all combined to create distortions in what was formally viewed as a normal rite of passage for Muslim youth. The result is the perpetuation of both poverty and educational disadvantage. The poor quality of Nigeria's modern education system, particularly in rural areas, its costs (students are routinely expected to obtain their own books and other school supplies), its association in the public's memory with the Christian missionaries that first offered it during the colonial era, and its low returns in terms of employment account for low enrollment rates. The erosion of the rural economy simultaneously leads many to migrate seasonally, or permanently, to the cities. Faced with such constraints, families make sense of their decisions to send their children to live as Almajirai in the urban centers not only with reference to their high regard for Qur'anic learning, but also mindful of the educational value of a certain degree of hardship for the social and moral training of their children (Hoechner, 2015).

Personal Experience on Almajiranci

I was born and bred in Azare (Bauchi State) of middle-class religiously observant parents. My primary and secondary school education took place in day schools, while I received religious instruction through the reformist modern Islamic education classes in the evenings. Through my teenage years I saw firsthand how the typical Almajiri child was viewed negatively in the society and suffered from gross neglect from his parents. I befriended many Almajiri children and their Mallam guardians within my neighborhood, as my parents would often provide housing for the Almajiri and their Mallams. This made it possible for me to gain the young people's trust and to witness both their vulnerability and resilience in the situations they were trapped in.

Several Almajiri friends I made in this way confided life secrets that helped me to understand how a major change in circumstance—for instance, the death of a parent—compelled their family caregivers to send them on the "sacred" mission. My Almajiri friends would openly express how they wished they were in my situation, with parents who lived and worked in the city and could afford to send me to school and otherwise provide for me. I gained their trust to the extent that they entrusted me to help them set aside portions of their personal earnings to be used for special circumstances, like emergencies and to buy new clothing on festive occasions. The majority of them earned a living from pushing carts to sell water during lesson-free days.

For several years I observed how hard-working and full of hope and vision most of the Almajiri I encountered were, but I also saw how the hardship and vulnerability they faced made some of them easy recruits for unleashing violence and thuggery.

However, overall, in my own personal conviction and from experience, I believe that the majority of Almajirai, if given the chance and resources, would be better citizens and follow every norm that deviates from any ugly path of violence or civil unrest.

I recall my childhood Almajiri friend, Sallau,[3] who lived with his Mallam next door and was orphaned at the age of one. He memorized the Holy Qur'an at the age of 13, and went on to start secular education from scratch, toiling with his own hands to pay every cost of his education without the support of anyone. Today, he is a proud Almajiri who works as a

---

[3] Pseudonym used; real name withheld for privacy.

banker with a first class degree in Accounting from Bayero University, Nigeria. Another instance is Adamu Garba II, who rose from being an Almajiri to become a founder of one of the biggest software and technology companies in the country and who is making plans to run for political office. Many similar instances of individuals who grew up Almajiri, and who either persevered and overcame their circumstances or, as was more commonplace, could not overcome the odds stacked against them and remained trapped in poverty and handicapped by the physical and emotional injuries inflicted on them from a young age, inspired me into critical thinking for a sustainable solution to support Almajiri youth.

Notwithstanding the few Almajiri people who overcame poverty and are doing well to some extent, as Hoechner (2015) has opined, due to the obvious lack of political will and poor economy in northern Nigeria, the likelihood for the Almajiri people to escape poverty and have a successful and bright future is very limited. Inusa[4] and Sirajo[5] are also my Almajiri friends from childhood; neither of them have memorized all parts of the Qur'an for more than two decades now, and they have not made significant progress in studying Western knowledge. The former, a bit responsible, works as a bus conductor earning less than $25 monthly to support his one wife and six children. The latter has the worst case scenario; he is a drug addict with very little likelihood to make any meaning of his life, whose own relatives have abandoned him for years without wanting to even hear how his life goes.

From the outset I knew that a feasible solution would have to come to terms with the fact that the present-day practice of Almajiri is perceived as a viable and attractive form of education by the people who both believe in and are victimized by it.

Perceived Advantages and Impact of Almajiranci

While critics regard Almajiranci as a throwback to "backward" tradition to the poor families in northern Nigeria who practice it, it is an alternative to the so-called modern education system in which they have lost all confidence. Khalid (2013) made known during a presentation delivered at the Nigerian National Symposium on Almajiri Education that the traditional and religious Almajiri schools are the preferable choice for many traditional

---

[4] Real name withheld for privacy.
[5] Real name withheld for privacy.

Muslim Hausa/Fulani societies for several reasons. First, the flexibility in their timetable makes it suitable for rural communities that rely solely on agriculture as occupation and also allows every student to progress at his own pace. Further, the multiple entry points of the traditional Almajiri schools allow parents to enroll their children anytime they wish, scheduling their children's enrollment around seasonal agricultural activities, unlike the formal schools that have single entry points at the beginning of the academic year. Dr. Khalid also noted that the schools' egalitarian outlook and affordability (incurring zero or very few costs for school fees, uniforms, texts and notebooks, feeding and transport money, etc.) are also extremely attractive to parents, since they can barely afford such expenses. Above all, these schools do not prevent children from partaking in their traditional occupations as the formal schools would.

Apart from education, Almajiranci is also viewed as a place for instilling discipline in children and youth. It is believed that Almajiranci teaches young people to be dutiful to their parents, teachers, and the larger society. The system is also regarded as a last resort for rehabilitating the youth who are labeled as undisciplined and stubborn, or *kangararrun yara*. Some parents are of the belief that the modern "reformist" Islamic schools, *Makarantar Islamiyya*, are not of the same disciplinary level as the Almajiri school, hence a perceived advantage of the Almajiranci. Most Almajiri schools have strict disciplinary codes, and will, for instance, expel a student for stealing or fighting, and inflict heavy punishment for lying. Some schools go to the extent of using chains for beating the legs of "the stubborn ones" (M. Ibrahim, personal communication, December 16, 2017; Anas, 2017).

The preceding section of this chapter described how Almajirai functions as a source of cheap labor. In cities like Kano, youth perform menial jobs for their subsistence. The youngest children are especially inclined to accept whatever compensation they are given in return for their services rendered. The fact that so many children are floating laborers, especially in Hausaland—available and ready for work at the lowest wages—is an advantage from the point of view of families that want to engage part-time house help or "house boys." Some landlords take in these youth as unofficial "security guards" for buildings that are vacant or under construction, while others have them stay in the *zaure*, the entrance room to a house. For the youth, these practices provide shelter they would otherwise not have (Abba & Kurfi, 2012).

Older youth contribute to the large-scale production of the traditional embroidered caps, otherwise known in Hausa language as *kube*; in the Hausa/Fulani culture, wearing a *kaptan* and *kube* forms a complete formal dress code. It is typical of a Hausa/Fulani man to wear it in a professional capacity or at the office. In many instances, without the hat, it is considered an informal dress code. It is therefore not surprising that eight or nine of every ten men in Hausaland can be seen wearing the locally made caps. The demand is so large, especially in some local Hausa communities in Hausaland, that many Almajirai end up abandoning their Islamic studies and make caps as a profession.

Almajiri children have long suffered their circumstances in silence, circumstances created by adults and a failed system. Deep poverty and firmly held misinterpretations of the Quran wrongly attribute the practice to Islam, which makes it harder to reform or eliminate the practice of Almajiri. However, the twenty-first century Almajiri child could be emancipated through better alternatives designed by activists seeking to bring a sustainable solution to the suffering of children. One such solution, eTrash2Cash, uses waste management microsocial entrepreneurship support and training to give Almajiri youth economic freedom and the ability to fend for themselves, whilst pursuing Islamic knowledge.

EMERGENCE OF A LOCAL SOLUTION TO ADDRESS TWO CRISES

According to the Bauchi State Environmental Protection Agency (BASEPA) (2012), greater than 9000 metric tons of wastes is generated daily in the state. It is also estimated that about 84% of the waste contains potential reusable materials. Unfortunately, inadequate infrastructure and facilities provide the means to collect less than 10% of the total waste generated (BASEPA, 2012). Such huge amounts of uncollected waste present enormous threats to the environment, from land, air, and water pollution to deforestation, flooding, and greenhouse gas generation, especially in the face of low-income communities that live from hand to mouth. It is not uncommon to see various kinds of waste blocking the limited drainage systems within towns in the state, which causes flooding during every rainy season and also increases susceptibility to disease-causing organisms like the malarial parasite, which is most prevalent during the rainy season (BASEPA, 2012).

In 2012, the Federal Government of Nigeria unveiled YouWiN[6] through the Federal Ministry of Finance with support from the World Bank and Department for International Development (DFID) as part of its efforts to encourage youth entrepreneurship and curve youth unemployment in the country. The program supports young entrepreneurs with grants and technical assistance to launch new or support existing businesses. Based on a comprehensive feasibility analysis, undertaken by its founders with guidance from Mr. AbdulKadir Sarauta, an environmental scientist in Abubakar Tafawa Balewa University, an initiative named Haleematus-Sa'adiyya emerged as one of the pioneer beneficiaries of this program, launching in Azare (Bauchi), a northeastern state. This social enterprise was named after my youngest sister, whose name roughly translates from Arabic to English as "The Patient One." The cofounders conceived this enterprise as an emerging platform that will provide a local solution (waste management) that addresses a wide variety of social challenges (environmental impacts, Almajiri education, economic impact, etc.) in the society. Although northern Nigeria remains conservative on the issue, my personal conviction is that educating girls means educating a whole society. Along with my cofounders, I envision this social enterprise taking the path of my soon-to-be well-educated sister (and so, her name) by having an exponentially far-reaching and positive impact on the lives it touches.

The feasibility study revealed the acute need for local and sustainable waste management solutions. Surveys conducted as part of the study revealed that only 12% of community residents disposed of their waste appropriately and were aware that improper waste disposal poses risks to the environment like climate change. More than 50% could not relate the negative effects of waste burning to global warming. Less than 20% knew that the majority of their waste could be potential resources.

The major town in the state, Azare, which generates almost 4000 metric tons of waste daily, has very limited government facilities in place to collect the waste from the households and industries for proper disposal. Local people and industries are left with no option but to dispose of their waste into any unauthorized landfill or open space, which in turn causes a heavy nuisance to the people.

---

[6] Youth Enterprise with Innovation in Nigeria, an initiative of the Federal Government of Nigeria to support young entrepreneurs to reduce youth unemployment (see www.youwin. org.ng).

In early 2012, in the midst of growing unemployment rates and severe waste management challenges, Haleematus-Sa'adiyya Enterprises kicked off as a pioneer for-profit waste management company in Bauchi state that supports informal waste collectors (scavengers) who exchange specific types of plastic waste for money. This plastic waste is then recycled by the company into reusable polythene shopping bags for sale to small and medium enterprises (SMEs). From its inception up to the end of 2015, the company has diverted from the landfills more than 10,000 metric tons of waste, thus resulting in its reprocessing and recycling into a variety of reusable materials, such as polythene shopping bags made from plastic waste collected from the streets. The company further engaged more than 200 local waste pickers, who were thereafter transformed into some professionally trained and motivated waste managers. Thus, the company was able to change their lives.

Haleematus-Sa'adiyya Enterprises was founded by four young and passionate entrepreneurs: Muhammad Salisu Abdullahi (author), Chiroma Hassan, Usman Abubakar, and Ibrahim Sale. All four were born in Azare (Bauchi State) and have obtained bachelor's degrees in various disciplines related to the natural sciences and the environment. Having fully grown up in the local environment, they continue to work as a team to design sustainable solutions for the lingering problems of waste management to suit their local terrain and largely uninformed communities with limited awareness on waste management and climate change crisis.

Although none of them have been through the Almajiri informal system as described in this chapter, all of them have attended a formal Islamic system of education, which does not in any way present challenges like the informal one. Being indigents of the Azare community, it is very easy for them to distinguish between the two systems because of their own experience through a formal system and their encounters with the Almajiri children in day-to-day activities.

With the rapidly growing number of problems faced by the Almajiri children and the increase in population growth, which connotes an increase in quantities of waste generation in communities and the demand for holistic waste management solutions across the wider northern parts of Nigeria, the company sought the advice and help of stakeholders to officially launch another social enterprise project, called the eTrash2Cash, in 2016. This program is an independent social enterprise that would not only divert waste generated in vulnerable or low-income communities for sustainable environmental development but also professionally train and engage the vulnerable Almajiri youth.

Evolving as an initiative of northern Haleematus-Sa'adiyya Enterprises, eTrash2Cash enjoys partnership with another indigent non-governmental organization called the Centre for Information Technology and Development (CITAD).[7] These two organizations designed a plan to take advantage of pressing community problems, seeing them as opportunities to make a positive difference or impact in the society by focusing on a subgroup of the Almajiri children. These two organizations observed that, as in any other metropolitan and commercial state in Nigeria, more than 10,000 tons of waste are being generated daily in each of Nigeria's main cities, including Kano, Kaduna, Lagos, and Ibadan. This poses a substantial threat to the environment, causing pollution; causing flooding in communities, which often leads to loss of life and property; and contributing to deforestation and greenhouse gasses that cause climate change and global warming. More worrisome, as they carefully observed, is that less than 16% of the total waste generated in Kano State (the second largest commercial city in Nigeria with about 13 million people) is recollected and processed into reusable materials, while 84% of such waste has the potential to be reused (Hyuwa, 2010). Further, the unemployment rate is very high, with more than 100 million Nigerians earning and living on less than $1 per day. Worst of all, this is still in a region that is inflicted with the Boko Haram insurgency, where over two million people (more than 58% youth) have been displaced from their homes, necessitating rural-urban migration on already depleted resources and worn-out social amenities.

They, therefore, unveiled eTrash2Cash to leverage technology to make positive impacts on the environment and public health and to empower the low-income and economically disadvantaged groups of young men and women to earn from their waste. This is also in addition to training a group of Almajiri children to work to expand entrepreneurship and learning opportunities for them.

---

[7] CITAD, a non-governmental organization based in the northern part of Nigeria (www.citad.org).

The eTrash2Cash Initiative

eTrash2Cash registers low-income people in Kano, Nigeria, on its website as "waste providers" and helps them to earn cash incentives in exchange for their waste, be it plastics, papers, food, or metals. eTrash2Cash sorts this waste and makes reusable materials from them at its material and resources recovery facility (MRF) in Dakata Industrial Area in Kano State. For example, plastic floor tiles and polythene shopping bags are made from plastic wastes, tissue papers are made from paper waste, and organic fertilizer is made from food waste.

Registered households are encouraged to use their earned incentives toward supporting education for girls. Young people registered are supported in special entrepreneurship training programs to build their capacities and skills in safe waste collection, sorting, and recycling waste into reusable materials, as well as business planning, financial management, and locating funding opportunities available to them. Therefore, they earn more from their waste or become self-reliant by establishing similar or related social enterprises along the waste management value chain.

Although this initiative is owned by a for-profit venture that aims to make some profit from the waste collected and recycled to be sold to end users, its impacts are big and bold in these key areas:

- *Environmental Impact*: It helps to collect, evacuate, dispose, and recycle all major types of waste, which is very detrimental to air, land, and water, therefore reducing pollution from all angles, reducing flooding (preventing waste from blocking drainage systems), mitigating the harsh effects of climate change, and reducing deforestation by providing substitutes for timber from trees.
- *Training Support, Social, and Job Creation Impact*: It helps to train marginalized low-income youth registered as "waste providers" on waste management and entrepreneurship. Also, through its activities in waste collection, sorting, and recycling, it creates many jobs, directly and otherwise.
- *Awareness and Sensitization*: With our proactive online web presence and social and traditional (radio, television, newspaper) media presence using local native languages, the community is rapidly sensitized on key environmental issues and encouraged to participate.

- *Local Economy*: It makes reusable products from waste exchanged for cash and also provides raw materials to support local industries and recycled end products, building up the economy.
- *Educational Support*: Households registered as "waste providers" are highly encouraged to use cash incentives paid to them for their waste to support education for girls in their respective homes.

So far, eTrash2Cash has 923 people registered as "waste providers" through 19 social micro-entrepreneurs in Kano, Nigeria, out of which 47% (434) are Almajiri young people, who are among the most active participants in providing all kinds of waste. The rest are low-income households and individuals. Without eTrash2Cash, the Almajiris would still be in the custody of their Mallams, studying Islamic education, because that is the primary reason they left their parents. eTrash2Cash supports them in earning a living and provides them with concrete financial support. From collecting waste and depositing it at collection hubs, they earn money based on quantities in kilogram units and the quality of the waste they provide. Through eTrash2Cash, they no longer need to engage in begging or menial jobs; the system helps them earn the minimum Nigerian wage each month.

As a payback, empowerment strategy, and of course, a social responsibility, eTrash2Cash is giving special attention and focus to this group of economically disadvantaged and most vulnerable and marginalized young people, Almajiri children, boys and girls between the ages of 9 and 14. Through eTrash2Cash, they arc empowered with relevant new knowledge and skills that can help them earn more from their waste, if they so wish, or even set up similar or related ventures on their own, all through Youth Entrepreneurship Training. To make our work easier, we work with several informal schools that have a large enrollment of Almajiri children. There has been no resistance so far from the parents, because they are not in sight, or from the Mallams, perhaps because they benefit in some way when the Almajiri children benefit, as some of them have a sharing formula on every Almajiri earning.

eTrash2Cash faced some early phase challenges in its work. They include limited literacy and numerical knowledge of vulnerable Almajiri children, which limited their comprehension and business mentoring capabilities. Another challenge is limited funding to enroll them in basic fast-track literacy and numeracy classes to enhance our impact and limited capacity as well as handle the large numbers of vulnerable children interested in our training programs and waste-to-wealth social micro-entrepreneurship.

A special thanks must be given to advocates and other community-based supporters like the Modern Almajiri Creative School (MACS),[8] which strives to shine a spotlight on the plight of the vulnerable Almajiri children, and the Mandela Washington Fellowship experience at Rutgers University in New Jersey as part of President Barack Obama's Young African Leadership Initiative program, which helped provide further research on the various sustainable methods to recover waste resources from primary sources and sustainably make bio-friendly products from them. This is especially useful during our scale-up, as large quantities and types of waste are expected to be recovered from empowered Almajiri turned micro-entrepreneurs, whose sustainability lies in the project's ability to make revenue-generating and marketable products for reuse in the communities.

Local Partners that Complement the Work of eTrash2Cash

One sister initiative to be highlighted is the Modern Almajiri Creative School (MACS) in Gombe State, located in the northeastern part of the country. MACS works hard to reduce vulnerability and expand youth learning and opportunity pathways in Nigeria, especially in the acquisition of vocational skills to help them earn income for the sustenance of their lives. MACS is a non-governmental organization, which seeks to empower every Almajiri youth with a modern formal education, in addition to the Islamic knowledge they are pursuing, while at the same time enrolling them into vocational centers to learn self-employment skills like carpentry, blacksmithing, and tailoring. MACS uses technology and collaborates with state governments, parents, and Mallams to streamline the whole process, from registration to vocational skills assignments, modern education enrollment, and progress tracking. So far, it has registered more than 1000 Almajiri young people, enrolled them in primary and secondary schools, and provided them access to a variety of vocational centers or workshops, where they apprentice to learn the skills and become self-employed in those services.

[8] Modern Almajiri Creative School is a non-governmental organization that supports Almajiri people through formal school and vocational training.

Another sister initiative worth mentioning here is the A'ishatu Bint Abubakar School located in Azare (Bauchi State), a nonprofit school that primarily targets the most vulnerable and Almajiri children in the society to acquire literacy and numeracy skills training through a formal setting under a scholarship. This formal school has supported MACS through providing scholarships to its registered Almajiri children and is continuing to advocate for formalizing the Almajiri schools to include basic literacy and numeracy knowledge.

It is imperative to note that both eTrash2Cash and MACS target the same Almajiri youth in Nigeria; while eTrash2Cash focuses specifically on supporting them through waste management microsocial entrepreneurship, MACS enrolls them into diverse entrepreneurial self-employment activities. Although there is no formal collaboration presently between the two, one of our long-term goals is to establish a working relationship, in which Almajiri youth would be registered in both programs, collecting waste to earn a living while undergoing formal school training.

Conclusion

The activities of eTrash2Cash in providing entrepreneurship training, although limited in capacity, in the waste management value chain specifically to the set of vulnerable and young people called Almajiri youth are clear strategies in expanding youth learning and opportunity pathways, but this is only the tip of the iceberg. More of such interventions in a variety of forms are needed in larger quantities and capacities, especially in the northern part of Nigeria, to accommodate the large numbers of not only the Almajiri groups, but the low-income, vulnerable, and economically disadvantaged youth in general that number in the tens of millions across the country (Daily Trust, 2011) and West Africa.

Nevertheless, for the Almajiri young people, some of the most economically disadvantaged and vulnerable groups in northern Nigeria, interventions like Youth Entrepreneurship Training programs or any vocational skills training through waste management models and other social enterprises could be replicated easily, since many cities in Africa battle with the same waste management challenges and the same Almajiri scenario. Variations of this social problem exist in so many countries in Africa, like Senegal, Ghana, Niger, Chad, and Burkina Faso. These programs would have a far-reaching impact in helping them become self-reliant and responsible young people in the society, aside from creating jobs for other people;

positively impacting community health, education, and the local economy; and ensuring environmental sustainability in Africa and the world at large.

REFERENCES

Abba, I. A., & Kurfi, H. M. (2012). An assessment of Kano state Almajiri pilot feeding program 2003-2007. *Bayero Sociologist, A Journal of Sociological Studies, 1*(2), 46–49.

Abdulkadir, I. (2010). Child street begging, A gruesome future of neglected child: The Almajiri perspective. *Al-ilm Magazine, 10*(7), 14–15.

Anas, L. (2017). *An assessment of the Almajiranci phenomenon in Kaduna Metropolis from 1976–2006.* Unpublished B.A. project, Kaduna State University, Kaduna State, Nigeria.

Babangida, I. (1993). *Comparative studies between traditional Quranic schools and modern Quranic schools in Katsina State.* Unpublished thesis, Ahmadu Bello University, Zaria.

Bauchi State Environmental Protection Agency (BASEPA). (2012). The role of Bauchi State Environmental Protection Agency (BASEPA) in solid waste management in Bauchi Metropolis. *Maiduguri Journal of Arts and Social Sciences, 6*(3), 23–26.

Daily Trust. (2011, August 9). Minister: 68m Nigerian youths out of job. *Daily Trust.* p. 3.

Garba, I. (1996). *Qur'anic schools and their roles in U.P.E scheme in Gumel, Jigawa State.* Unpublished thesis, Ahmadu Bello University, Zaria, Nigeria.

Hoechner, H. (2011). Striving for knowledge and dignity: How qur'anic students in Kano, Nigeria, learn to live with rejection and educational disadvantage. *European Journal of Development Research, 23*(5), 712–728.

Hoechner, H. (2015). Porridge, piety and patience: Young Qur'anic students' experience of poverty in Nigeria. *Africa, 85*(2), 269–288. https://doi.org/10.1017/S0001972015000029

Hyuwa, B. A. (2010, June). *Solid waste management in Nigeria: An outline.* Paper presented at The Maiden Annual National Conference on Environmental Challenges: Local Action Plans, Nigerian Environmental Society, Kaduna State University, Kaduna State, Nigeria.

Ibrahim, S. (2008). Menace of street begging in Kano State. *National Dailies.* Retrieved July 3, 2008, from http://www.nationaldalies.org

Kabir, G. (2002). *Almajiri school system* (4th ed.). Ibadan: Hills Publication Limited.

Khalid, S. (2013, June). *The Almajiranci phenomenon in northern Nigerian religious, social, economic, political, and security dimension.* Paper presented at the

National Symposium on Almajiri Education in Nigeria: The Journey So Far, Sokoto, Nigeria.

National Council for the Welfare of the Destitute. (2001). *Almajir and Qur'anic education*. Kaduna: Author.

Ogunmade, O. (2013, May 23). Terrorism: Mark seeks Almajiri system's ban. *The Nation Online*. Retrieved September 25, 2013, from http://thenationonlineng.net/terrorism-mark-seeks-almajiri-systems-ban/

Perverz, T. (2005). *Situational analysis of street children in Pakistan*. Retrieved July 8, 2008, from http://www.NCLPA.org

Sa'id, I. (1992). *Menace of Almajiris in Kano municipal*. Paper presented at Faculty of Education, Ahmadu Bello University, Zaria, Nigeria.

Salis, T. (1995). *Impact of Islamic education in Kano metropolitan nursery school on Muslim children*. Unpublished thesis, Ahmadu Bello University, Zaria.

Sulaiman, J. (1996). Health impact of street beggars. *Journal of Medicinal Food, 10*(4), 70–87.

Sule, M. (1994). Situation of Almajiri in Nigeria. *Research Journal of Education, 4*(10), 23–30.

United Nations. (2008). *World population prospects: The 2008 revision*. New York, NY: United Nations, Population Division of the Department of Economic and Social Affairs of the United Nations Secretariat.

Ware, R. (2014). The walking Qur'an. In *Islamic education, embodied knowledge, and history in West Africa*. Chapel Hill, NC: University of North Carolina University Press.

Ya'u, K. (2001). *Almajiri school system in Northern Nigeria*. Paper presented at conference organized by the Qur'anic Education Review committee, Katsina, Nigeria.

CHAPTER 11

Burden, Drivers, and Impacts of Poor Mental Health in Young People of West and Central Africa: Implications for Research and Programming

Kenneth Juma, Frederick Murunga Wekesah,
Caroline W. Kabiru, and Chimaraoke O. Izugbara

K. Juma (✉)
African Population and Health Research Center, Nairobi, Kenya
e-mail: kjuma@aphrc.org

F. M. Wekesah
African Population and Health Research Center, Nairobi, Kenya

Julius Center for Health Sciences and Primary Care,
University Medical Center Utrecht, Utrecht University, Utrecht, The Netherlands
e-mail: fwekesah@aphrc.org

C. W. Kabiru
Population Council, Nairobi, Kenya
e-mail: ckabiru@popcouncil.org

C. O. Izugbara
International Center for Research on Women, Washington, DC, USA
e-mail: cizugbara@icrw.org

233

INTRODUCTION

Mental disorders are a leading cause of disability in young people globally (Charlson et al., 2014; Mokdad et al., 2016). As many as 20% of the world's young people (aged between 10 and 24 years) suffer a neuropsychiatric condition (Belfer, 2008), including common disorders like depression and anxiety, or severe forms like psychosis, schizophrenia, and bipolar disorder, as well as alcohol and substance dependence (Remschmidt & Belfer, 2005). Individuals suffering from these disorders have higher mortality risks than the general population (Chesney, Goodwin, & Fazel, 2014). While the onset of most mental disorders occurs during youth (age 12 to 24 years), few disorders are diagnosed or treated in this period (Remschmidt & Belfer, 2005). These conditions often persist for a long time, severely disrupting young people's access to livelihoods, health care, and education, and exposing them to stigma, isolation, discrimination, and human rights abuses (Sartorius, 2007; Tarter, 2002; Tims et al., 2002). While mental disorders are commonly known for their impact on health and well-being, they are also associated with severe economic losses due to high cost of treatment and impaired ability to work, especially among young people (Esan, Kola, & Gureje, 2012). Inadequate documentation and characterization of young people's mental health problems hampers planning and appropriate provision of services in most low- and middle-income countries (LMICs) (Jacob et al., 2007).

West and Central Africa (WCA) is one of the youngest subregions of the world (Izugbara et al., 2017). Young people make up more than one-third of the population of the subregion. WCA is also the only subregion of the world where the population of young people is projected to continue growing over the next decade (Ngom, 2017). Key risk factors for mental illness—such as civil conflicts and political instability, poverty, underemployment and unemployment, substance abuse, and human immunodeficiency virus (HIV)/AIDS—are prevalent in the subregion (Betancourt, McBain, Newnham, & Brennan, 2013; Pacione, Measham, & Rousseau, 2013; Sharma, Fine, Brennan, & Betancourt, 2017; United Nations International Children's Emergency Fund [UNICEF] and Overseas Development Institute [ODI], 2009). Nevertheless, data on young people's mental and substance use disorders in WCA are limited. A few studies conducted using small, nonrepresentative samples suggest a high burden of child and adolescent mental, neurological, and substance use disorders across several countries in the subregion (Abiodun, 1992; Asare & Danquah, 2016; Cortina, Sodha, Fazel, & Ramchandani, 2012; Ngasa et al., 2017; Nwagu, 2016; Tunde-Ayinmode, Adegunloye,

Ayinmode, & Abiodun, 2012; World Health Organization [WHO], 2011; Yoder, Tol, Reis, & de Jong, 2016). Compared to Africa's other subregions, WCA is projected to experience some of the largest increases in burden of mental and substance use disorders (i.e., Central Africa [196%] and West Africa [129%] compared to Southern Africa [28%] and East Africa [139%]) by 2050 (Charlson, Diminic, Lund, Degenhardt, & Whiteford, 2014), with a significant proportion occurring among young individuals (Cortina et al., 2012). There are, therefore, increasing calls for WCA governments to prioritize the provision of accessible and quality mental health services to their citizens (Abdulmalik et al., 2014; Daar et al., 2014; Kleintjes, Lund, & Flisher, 2010; Semrau et al., 2015).

Arguably, the majority of WCA countries share similar mental health profiles (Abdulmalik et al., 2014). Most of these countries have low policy priority for mental health, with acute funding gaps and inadequate human resources for mental health, widespread misconception about mental health issues, stigmatization, and human rights abuses (Gureje, Lasebikan, Ephraim-Oluwanuga, Olley, & Kola, 2005; Oshodi et al., 2014; Read, Adiibokah, & Nyame, 2009; Saraceno et al., 2007). Therefore, a large "treatment gap" for mental illness exists—over 90% of people with mental illness in LMICs, including in the WCA, are untreated compared to between 44% and 70% in high-income countries (HICs) (Wang et al., 2007). For instance, a review of community-based psychiatric epidemiology studies showed that only 5.9% of young adult Jews in Israel with schizophrenia remained untreated, while the rate in New Zealand in a population of 21-year-olds was 61.5% (Kohn, Saxena, Levav, & Saraceno, 2004). Ironically, this huge gap exists despite considerable evidence that, even within resource-limited countries, cost-effective strategies, such as medications and psychosocial interventions, are available and effective for most mental illnesses (Barry, Clarke, Jenkins, & Patel, 2013; Gureje, Chisholm, Kola, Lasebikan, & Saxena, 2007).

Whereas in HICs there is increasing recognition of mental health problems in young people and their associated impairments and comorbidities, in WCA, the mental health concerns of young people remain neglected, misunderstood, and under-researched (Atilola, Ayinde, Emedoh, & Oladimeji, 2014; Kleintjes et al., 2010). Consequently, there is limited understanding of the burden, drivers, and impact of adolescent mental health in the WCA subregion and of the gaps in research and program implementation. This chapter summarizes existing knowledge on mental health among young people in the subregion. It highlights the burden, drivers, and impact of poor mental health among the subregion's young people. We also discuss available interventions aimed at improving mental health among these young people and draw attention to gaps in knowledge and programming as well as challenges that get in the way of promoting mental health in WCA. Findings of this study can inform policy-making as well as the design and delivery of programs related to young people's mental health and well-being.

This chapter draws on insights from relevant peer-reviewed and gray literature on mental and substance abuse disorders among young people in WCA. Mental disorders were defined according to the Diagnostic and Statistical Manual of Mental Disorders (DSM) (American Psychiatric Association [APA], 2000) and the International Classification of Diseases (ICD) (World Health Organization, 1992). We utilized the World Health Organization Assessment Instrument for Mental Health Systems (WHO-AIMS) (only available for Benin, Ghana, and Nigeria) as well as reports from the Ministries of Health to describe the mental health systems available for young people. WHO-AIMS reports on the status of mental health systems in LMICs based on six domains: policy and legislative framework, mental health services, mental health in primary care, human resources, public information and links with other sectors, and monitoring and research. This chapter focuses on the mental health services domain only.

BURDEN OF MENTAL AND SUBSTANCE USE DISORDERS IN YOUNG PEOPLE OF WCA

Sources of Data for Mental Disorders Among Young People in WCA

There is very limited coverage of representative prevalence data on mental disorders in children and adolescents in WCA. Coverage refers to the proportion of the target population (aged 10 to 24 years) represented by the available data. Virtually no country in sub-Saharan Africa (SSA), including the WCA subregion, has more than 2% coverage for any disorder (Erskine et al., 2017). So far, only Nigeria has conducted a WHO survey of Mental Health and Well-Being to assess the lifetime and 12-month prevalence of mental disorders (Gureje, Lasebikan, Kola, & Makanjuola, 2018). In the absence of large-scale epidemiological surveys on mental disorders, most prevalence data are a product of cross-sectional community-based or clinic-based surveys, which have quality challenges arising from the use of different mental health assessment tools (e.g., screening questionnaires and clinical diagnostic instruments). Other key sources of reliable data include the WHO 2015 country estimates for prevalence and burden of depression and anxiety disorders (not reported by age groups), and a systematic review of the Global Burden of Disease (GBD) Study 2013 (Ferrari et al., 2013) and 2016 (Charlson, Baxter, et al., 2014).

Burden of Mental Disorders Among Young People in WCA

Some of the most common child and adolescent psychiatric disorders worldwide include anxiety disorders, depressive disorders, conduct disorders and delinquency, learning disabilities, and mental retardation (Cortina et al., 2012). In the context of WCA, a systematic review by Cortina et al. (2012) found that between 12% and 30% of children and young people aged 5 to 24 years had mental health problems. Community-based epidemiological studies in various WCA countries have estimated varied degrees of prevalence for different types of mental disorders as shown in Table 11.1. In addition, variations exist across gender. For instance, anxiety and mood disorders are known to affect boys and girls more or less equally, but adolescent girls are much more vulnerable to depression than boys (Bradley, 2001).

Mental disorders are also known to be highly disabling. In the WCA subregion, depressive disorders are among the largest contributors to years lived with disability (YLDs) for both sexes of young people aged 15 to 24 years, even though these disorders affect females more than males in all age groups (Mokdad et al., 2016), and vary by region and country (Institute for Health Metrics and Evaluation, 2017). Among young people, early onset of depressive and anxiety disorders predicts other indirect consequences such as low educational attainment, and consequently lower income, poverty, and noncommunicable diseases (NCDs), such as cardiovascular diseases. A study in Nigeria, for example, showed that child psychiatric disorders are associated with various impairments, reduced functionality, physical illness, premature mortality, and increased inequality in access to economic opportunity (Tunde-Ayinmode et al., 2012).

Poor mental health increases health expenditures and rates of health care utilization, (Charlson, Diminic, et al., 2014), which may in turn act as a barrier to mental health service uptake, as was observed in Nigeria (Jack-Ide & Uys, 2013). Additional highlights from a Nigerian study indicate that the cost of antipsychotic medicines alone accounts for more than

Table 11.1 Prevalence of mental and substance use disorders among young people in WCA

Country, tool used	Psychiatric disorder	Substance abuse	Anxiety disorders	Depressive disorders	ADHD/ conduct disorders	Learning disabilities	Reference
Nigeria, DISC-IV BDI	10%–18.6%	23%–40% Alcohol 12%–32% Illicit drugs 18%	10%–31.4%	6.9%–28.4%	8.8%–23%	3.3%–19%	Tunde-Ayinmode et al., 2012; Adewuya et al., 2007; Adewuya, 2005; Akpan, Ojinnaka, & Ekanem, 2010
DR Congo, DSM-IV	12%	–	–	–	6%–10%	–	Cortina et al., 2012; Kashala, Elgen, Sommerfelt, & Tylleskar, 2005
Sierra Leone	–	–	–	80%	20.2%	–	Yoder et al., 2016
Ghana, CES-D10	17.0%	Marijuana 16.2% Alcohol 12%–25%	–	11.9%–39%	3%–12.8%	10%	Oppong, Meyer-Weitz, & Petersen, 2014
Cameroon Burkina Faso CES-DC	– PTSD, 17.8%	–	2.4%	31% 15%	–	–	Ngasa et al., 2017; Ismayilova, Gaveras, Blum, Tô-Camier, & Nanema, 2016
Gambia	12%	Cannabis misuse 16%	5.2%	3.4%	–	–	Kretzschmar, Nyan, Mendy, & Janneh, 2012
Equatorial Guinea	–	–	–	–	–	–	–

Table created by the co-authors

ADHD, attention-deficit/hyperactivity disorder; *DISC-IV*, Diagnostic Interview Schedule for Children Version IV; *BDI*, Beck Depression Inventory; *CES*, Centre for Epidemiological Studies Short Depression Scale; *PTSD*, posttraumatic stress disorder; *CES-DC*, Center for Epidemiological Studies Depression Scale for Children; *DSM-IV*, Diagnostic and Statistical Manual of Mental Disorders

50% of the cost of treating schizophrenia (Suleiman, Ohaeri, Lawal, Haruna, & Orija, 1997). Also, out-of-pocket expenditures for child mental health services are 71.4% in African countries compared to 12.5% in Europe (Belfer, 2008). A study by the World Economic Forum and the Harvard School of Public Health predicted that over the next two decades, mental illness will account for the largest proportion (35%) of global economic losses from NCDs; in absolute terms, this means that the economic toll of mental illness will be over $16 trillion globally and $7.3 trillion in LMICs by 2030 (Bloom et al., 2011).

Substance Use Disorders Among Young People in WCA

The types and prevalence rates of substances used vary remarkably according to context and geographical location (e.g., youths in HICs usually use injecting drugs and other substances not commonly used by adolescents from LMICs) (Embleton, Mwangi, Vreeman, Ayuku, & Braitstein, 2013). Igwe, Ngozi, Ejiofor, Emechebe, and Ibe (2009) reported that 33.7% of 860 senior secondary school adolescents in Enugu (Nigeria) were involved in psychoactive substance abuse, while 32% and 4.1% of these adolescents had abused alcohol and used cannabis, respectively (Igwe et al., 2009). Similarly, Kayembe et al. (2008) found that 82% of street children in the Democratic Republic of Congo used marijuana, 63.5% used alcohol, and 3.8% used cocaine (Kayembe et al., 2008). Across the WCA subregion, similar or higher prevalence levels of substance abuse among senior secondary school adolescents have been reported, including in Ghana (Addo, Mainoo, Dapaah, & Babayara, 2016; Peltzer & Pengpid, 2018).

The use of illicit drugs and psychoactive substance abuse among young people is associated with severe outcomes. For instance, studies in Nigeria (among students) and in Ghana (among homeless youth) found that alcohol and substance use is associated with an increased likelihood of risky sexual behavior, with accompanied increased risk for sexually transmitted infections including HIV (Nwagu, 2016; Oppong et al., 2014). While circumstances on the street may render children and youth vulnerable to various kinds of psychological problems and health risks (Burns, Daileader, & Finger, 2004), street children using drugs and psychoactive substances are more likely to engage in crime and interpersonal violence and are also more likely to suffer traffic accidents (Doran, Luczak, Bekman, Koutsenok, & Brown, 2012).

DRIVERS OF MENTAL AND SUBSTANCE USE DISORDERS IN YOUNG PEOPLE OF WCA

Adversities in early life are associated with increased risk of mental and substance use disorders (Kabiru, Beguy, Crichton, & Ezeh, 2010). Household and family conditions and quality of parenting also have a significant impact on risk of mental and physical health (Omigbodun, 2004). Notably, key contributors to poor mental health are broadly grouped under biological factors (e.g., age and sex), social factors (e.g., relationships with caregivers during childhood), and structural factors (e.g., poverty, urbanization, change, conflict, and natural disasters) (Allen, Balfour, Bell, & Marmot, 2014). While it is challenging to identify specific elements responsible for the onset and continuity of mental health problems, a complex interrelationship of risk factors and co-occurrence of factors exist.

In WCA, poverty is rife, as are other risk factors for mental disorders including unemployment, low incomes, poor housing, food insecurity, and low education status (Lund et al., 2010). In Nigeria, Omigbodun (2004) found that more than 50% of children at a psychiatric clinic suffering from various psychosocial stressors had experienced problems with primary support, such as separation from parents, disruption of the family, abandonment by their mother, psychiatric illness in a parent, and sexual/physical abuse in the year preceding the study. Likewise, civil conflicts, warfare, and disease have all been identified as vulnerabilities and risk factors to child and adolescent mental health in the WCA subregion (Gupta & Zimmer, 2018; Lokuge et al., 2013). Other common events during armed conflicts include sexual violence (sexual assault and rape), and the most common disorder in such settings is posttraumatic stress disorder (PTSD).

In recent years, the WCA subregion has experienced increased internal and regional displacement of people. According to UNICEF (2017b), over seven million children are on the move in West and Central Africa each year, mainly because of violence, poverty, and climate change and drought in countries such as the Central African Republic, Côte d'Ivoire, Liberia, Mali, Chad, Nigeria, and Sierra Leone. Unaccompanied migrant children are common among refugee populations, and these young children are often at increased risk of abuse, exploitation, or trafficking (UNICEF, 2017a). Studies have found that challenges of adjustment after migration in an often hostile context, history of family separation after migration, discriminatory experiences, as well as other postmigration adaptation issues (e.g., unemployment) are independently associated with depression and posttraumatic stress among migrants, who suffer from a significant burden of mental distress (Thela, Tomita, Maharaj, Mhlongo, & Burns, 2017).

A study in the Democratic Republic of Congo reported that children exposed to armed conflict presented with anxiety-related complaints (including symptoms such as stress, worry, and fear), as well as mood-related, behavior-related, and somatization problems (Lokuge et al., 2013). Moreover, in Sierra Leone, which experienced years of civil conflict, more than 7000 children were recruited as child soldiers and participated as spies, sex slaves, porters, and frontline soldiers, among other roles (Coalition to Stop the Use of Child Soldiers, 2008). Child soldiers were not only involved in the perpetration of violence but they were also often subjected to repeated physical, sexual, and emotional violence (Betancourt, Newnham, McBain, & Brennan, 2018). Betancourt et al. (2010) conducted a two-year study that followed up with former child soldiers and found increased hostility in these individuals. Similarly, youths who survived rape experienced higher levels of anxiety and aggressive behaviors but also demonstrated greater confidence and prosocial attitudes at follow-up (Betancourt et al., 2010). Children in WCA who experienced other war-related atrocities have been shown to have elevated levels of emotional distress and traumatic stress symptoms, as well as persistent bad dreams, nightmares, and intense arousal symptoms (Yoder et al., 2016). Other drivers of early mental health problems include high demands of academic performance on school children (Asare & Danquah, 2016), rapid social change and migration, social isolation, unemployment and poverty, increasing social pressures to perform well, peer pressure, individual and family crises, changes in traditional values, and conflict with parents (Burns, 2012).

Many countries in WCA have a generalized human immunodeficiency virus (HIV) epidemic (i.e., overall prevalence is 2.2% [6.1 million], with wide variation between countries, ranging from 0.5% in Niger and Senegal to 4.9% in Equatorial Guinea). The epidemic also left many children orphaned or infected in the subregion. More than 25% of children aged 0–14 years living with HIV worldwide are in the WCA subregion (Joint United Nations Programme on HIV/AIDS [UNAIDS] and UNICEF, 2016). A study in Ghana showed that orphaned or HIV-infected children suffer poor physical and mental functioning and sometimes live in isolation.

Consequently, these children may develop neuropsychological dysfunction, including dementia, depression, and other disorders, which go largely untreated and lead to increased morbidity (Doku, 2016). While risk factors for mental problems in infancy and early childhood have not been widely studied, this period is the time for maximum brain growth and of formation of emotional regulatory patterns that affect later mental health outcomes (Klitzing, Döhnert, Kroll, & Grube, 2015).

IMPACTS OF MENTAL AND SUBSTANCE USE DISORDERS IN YOUNG PEOPLE OF WCA

In the absence of any psychosocial or pharmacologic intervention to prevent or treat mental disorders, benign mental health problems among young people in Ghana and Nigeria have been shown to degenerate into grave and costly conditions, as well as social problems such as school failure, delinquency, and substance misuse (Igwe et al., 2009; Nwagu, 2016; Oppong et al., 2014; Warner & White, 2003). Poor mental health has also been associated with teenage pregnancy, HIV/AIDS, other sexually transmitted infections, interpersonal violence, child abuse, motor vehicle crashes, crime, homicide, and suicide (Doku, 2016; Doran et al., 2012; Nwagu, 2016). In addition, mental disorders are known to perpetuate a negative cycle of poverty, social exclusion, and reduced productivity, impacting the victim's family and the broader community (Lund et al., 2010, 2011). Even with limited documentation of the impact of mental health disorders in young people of WCA, the few existing studies provide insights on trajectories for a range of mental disorders that young people experience. For instance, a recent GBD report showed that of the top ten causes of death and disability in young people, suicide and self-harm (a likely presentation of mental health problems) are leading causes of mortality among females and males aged 10 to 24 years (Mars, Burrows, Hjelmeland, & Gunnell, 2014), and 75% of global suicide deaths are in LMICs (McKinnon, Gariepy, Sentenac, & Elgar, 2016), while at the same time alcohol and drug use (also associated with mental disorders) are leading risk factors for disability-adjusted life years (DALYS) (Mokdad et al., 2016).

In the Democratic Republic of Congo, researchers concluded that mental disorders impaired school-going children's social and educational capacities thereby affecting their school performance (Kashala et al.,

2005), while in Nigeria, adolescents with higher levels of depressive symptoms have been found to experience elevated rates of school absenteeism and dropout, cultism, social violence, and engagement in other social ills (Tunde-Ayinmode, 2010). Some scholars have argued that depression may be both a catalyst and a consequence of these academic challenges (Verboom, Sijtsema, Verhulst, Penninx, & Ormel, 2014). Moreover, behavioral and emotional deviance, most common among young people with mental disorders, can lead to severe stigma and exclusion from family and communities, as found in a study in Sierra Leone (Gupta & Zimmer, 2018). Mental disorders are also linked to risky sexual behaviors, thus predisposing individuals to increased risk of HIV infections, morbidity, and mortality (Nwagu, 2016). A study in Ghana among homeless youth found that alcohol consumption was associated with four indices of risky sexual behavior (ever had sex, non-condom use, multiple sexual partners, and survival sex) (Oppong et al., 2014). In addition, heavy alcohol and substance use is associated with elevated risk of impaired brain development, brain functioning, and neuropsychological performance and long-term dependence (Adu-Gyamfi & Brenya, 2015).

MENTAL HEALTH SYSTEMS AND INTERVENTIONS

Mental Health Systems Services for Young People in WCA

While variations exist in the availability of mental health policies, strategies, and resources across countries in WCA, mental health services are generally delivered within: (a) mental hospitals and specialist clinics, (b) psychiatric services in general hospitals, (c) mental health services through primary health care (PHC) units or integrated mental health service, and (d) community mental health services. The majority of WCA countries have limited documentation of the extent to which mental health services are available specifically for young people (either to promote positive mental health or to treat mental disorders). This is partly because many countries in the subregion (such as Liberia, Sierra Leone, and Congo) are recovering from political instabilities and protracted civil wars that degraded health systems (Jacob et al., 2007; Semrau et al., 2015). Our reviews of the WHO-AIMS survey reports available for few WCA countries (i.e., Benin [WHO-AIMS, 2007], Nigeria [WHO-AIMS, 2006], and Ghana [WHO-AIMS, 2011]), as well as Ministry of Health and WHO Atlas reports for Sierra Leone (Sierra Leone Ministry of Health, 2009) and the Democratic Republic of Congo (WHO, 2011) suggest that mental health care services targeted to young people are largely unavailable (see Table 11.2).

Available outpatient, inpatient, and community-based inpatient psychiatry services in the WCA subregion do not reflect prioritization of young people's mental health needs. For instance, there are often no dedicated beds for adolescents and children in inpatient units and no community outreaches designed to target young people in neighborhoods and schools where young individuals typically spend most of their time. Most of the mental hospitals and mental health care staff in WCA are located in cities. Rural areas (where approximately 70% of the population resides) often lack essential mental health services. Regionally, patient-to-psychiatrist ratios are high, and in Sierra Leone, for example, there are just 0.02 specialist psychiatrists per 1000 people (Alemu et al., 2012). Importantly, within the WCA subregion, where access to professional psychiatric care is limited for most mental health patients, traditional and spiritual healers play a significant role in providing mental health services to individuals (Patel, 2011).

Mental Health Interventions Available to Young People in WCA

Several mental health interventions targeting young people have been implemented in the WCA subregion, including those that are provider-led, community-based, peer-led, and home/family/culture-based. Several local and international nongovernmental organizations (NGOs) support mental health services in the subregion by training traditional healers and non-medical personnel (e.g., in Sierra Leone), expanding access to mental health services (e.g., in Ghana) (Hushie, 2016), and providing medicines to supplement government allocations (Roberts, Mogan, & Asare, 2014). In post-conflict Liberia and Sierra Leone, local and external NGOs also partnered with governments and other international organizations such as the WHO to "Build Back Better" mental health systems (McDaid, Knapp, & Raja, 2008). Other mental health interventions have utilized a variety of platforms (i.e., schools, churches, health care facilities, and digital platforms) to tackle multiple mental issues including self-esteem, life skills, self-efficacy, resilience, and coping skills. Some interventions are population-wide, including legislation (i.e., laws to control alcohol demand and restrict its access). For example, a survey to estimate alcohol policy restrictiveness reported that Equatorial Guinea and Liberia have implemented a

Table 11.2 Mental health care services in select WCA countries

Services	[a]Nigeria (WHO-AIMS, 2006)	[a]Ghana (WHO-AIMS, 2011)	[a]Benin (WHO-AIMS, 2007)	[b]Sierra Leone (Sierra Leone Ministry of Health, 2009)	[b]DRC (Okitapoy On'okoko et al., 2010; WHO, 2011)
Outpatient services	Outpatient clinics available No follow-up care in community, and no mobile mental health teams *No services exclusively for children and adolescents* (2% of all treated in outpatient clinics are children/ adolescents)	123 Outpatient units *No services exclusively for children and adolescents* (14% of all treated are children/ adolescents)	No ambulatory structures of mental health.	District and regional/national hospitals	1 Outpatient facility *No services exclusively for children and adolescents*
Day-treatment services	1 day-treatment facility in the surveyed areas (and possibly in the country), and it is available to all age groups	1 day-treatment service (Damien House in Western Region) *No services exclusively for children and adolescents*	No day-treatment facilities in the country		1 day-treatment facility

(continued)

Table 11.2 (continued)

Services	[a]Nigeria (WHO-AIMS, 2006)	[a]Ghana (WHO-AIMS, 2011)	[a]Benin (WHO-AIMS, 2007)	[b]Sierra Leone (Sierra Leone Ministry of Health, 2009)	[b]DRC (Okitapoy On'okoko et al., 2010; WHO, 2011)
Inpatient services Bed capacity (beds/100,000 population)[a]	7 Mental hospitals in the surveyed areas 1.99 per 100,000[a] *No beds specifically reserved for children and adolescents*	3 Mental hospitals 5.42 per 100,000[a] *No beds specifically reserved for children/ adolescents*	4 Mental hospitals (1 public and 3 private) 0.44 per 100,000[a] *No beds reserved for children and adolescents*	1 Mental hospital (psychiatric hospital in Freetown)	6 Mental hospitals 0.009 per 100,000[a] *No beds specifically reserved for children/ adolescents*
	Inpatient services at general community hospitals or pediatric hospitals *None of which have beds for children and adolescents*	7 Inpatient units (in general hospitals and clinics) 0.49 per 100,000[a]	12 Community-based inpatient units (2 in the public sector and 10 denominational/ private)		
	1 Community residential facility available in surveyed areas (10 beds) *No beds specifically reserved for children/ adolescents*	4 Community residential units 0.45 per 100,000[a]	No community residential structures		No community residential structures
	5 Community-based psychiatric inpatient units 0.45 per 100,000[a] *No beds specifically reserved for children/ adolescents*		No community-based psychiatric inpatient units	Community-based psychosocial care services Community health posts	

(continued)

Table 11.2 (continued)

Services	[a]Nigeria (WHO-AIMS, 2006)	[a]Ghana (WHO-AIMS, 2011)	[a]Benin (WHO-AIMS, 2007)	[b]Sierra Leone (Sierra Leone Ministry of Health, 2009)	[b]DRC (Okitapoy Om'okoko et al., 2016; WHO, 2011)
Women and children	Wards are separated by sex in psychiatry hospital in Calabar	Mental health care wards segregated by sex *15 beds reserved solely for children*	–	–	–
Integration into primary health care (PHC)	No integration of mental health within PHC	No integration within PHC	No integration within PHC	No systematic integration; PHC staff trained to offer basic mental health care	
Informal primary health care	Faith-based organizations and traditional healers	10 Faith-based and 10 traditional practitioners	Faith-based organizations available	Faith-based organizations and traditional healers	Traditional healers, herbal healers, and Christian pastors available

Table created by the co-authors

WCA, West and Central Africa

[a]Data based on WHO-AIMS Report on Mental Health Systems

[b]Data based on WHO atlas report

mix of alcohol control policies (Ferreira-Borges, Esser, Dias, Babor, & Parry, 2015). Other existing population-level interventions include policies, strategies, and regulations that are meant to establish a legal framework for mental health care services, as well as limit vulnerabilities associated with mental health problems. For example, Liberia has an official mental health policy that was reviewed in 2009 (Ministry of Health and Social Welfare, 2010). Community-wide interventions implemented in collaboration with individuals within schools, families, refugee camps, and churches also exist (Das et al., 2016).

While rigorous evidence on the effectiveness of these interventions is limited, a few studies in the subregion show a wide range of beneficial effects of mental health intervention on children, families, and communities, beyond just mental health. In the Democratic Republic of Congo, for example, brief trauma-focused therapy and counseling provided by community lay counselors to children with anxiety-related complaints led to observable behavior change, symptom reduction, and improved functioning of victims (Lokuge et al., 2013). In Ghana, a national mass media and community-level stigma-reduction program using religious leaders led to increased knowledge of HIV, reduced stigma, and improved attitudes toward people living with HIV or AIDS (Boulay, Tweedie, & Fiagbey, 2008). There is increasing interest in using schools as an opportunity to develop the foundations for positive mental health and prevent mental health problems among young people (Fazel, Patel, Thomas, & Tol, 2014).

Notably, school-based mental health interventions have been shown to create resilience, providing young people with resources to thrive and, in adverse conditions, to cope by buffering negative stressors (Oduguwa, Adedokun, & Omigbodun, 2017; Tolulope, Ani, Ajuwon, & Omigbodun, 2016). In addition, school-based interventions for mental health problems have been associated with improved social functioning, academic and work performance, and general health behaviors. Key informants in one study in Nigeria acknowledged the need for school mental health programs and identified strengths, barriers, and the core components of a successful school-based program (Ibeziako, Omigbodun, & Bella-Awusah, 2008). School-based mental health interventions can act along the entire continuum of mental health promotion and prevention and mental disorder screening/diagnosis and treatment. For example, Oduguwa et al. (2017) reported that the use of mixed-method training sessions for school children in Nigeria facilitated by the study researchers produced a positive and sustained change in knowledge and attitude toward mental illness.

Likewise, Bella-Awusah et al. (2016) demonstrated that using a school-based cognitive behavioral therapy program (CBT) reduced depression symptoms among adolescents in Nigeria. The same strategy was effective among multi-symptomatic war-affected youth (aged 15 to 24 years) in Sierra Leone (Betancourt et al., 2014).

CHALLENGES OF PROMOTING MENTAL HEALTH FOR YOUNG PEOPLE IN WCA

Several challenges related to legislation and policy, finances and resources, organization and planning, and availability of appropriately adapted evidence-based interventions and training affect mental health promotion among young people in the WCA subregion. Underlying these factors are specific issues such as lack of data on the burden of mental disorders, unavailability of mental health services, as well as lack of trained mental health professionals and scarcity of resources (Abdulmalik et al., 2014). Data on the burden of mental disorders in young people and risk and protective factors are important to inform appropriate resource allocation and to support policies that address mental health needs. Unfortunately, data are rarely available, largely due to lack of services, absence of a national focal point for mental health services targeting young people, fragmentation in services, and lack of data collection systems. Consequently, large data gaps exist due to the asymmetrical balance between the mental disorders burden and the resources available to deal with it (Prince et al., 2007).

The high costs of mental health care also hinder the provision of quality mental health services for young people in most LMICs. Mental disorders are some of the most expensive health conditions to treat, and in most SSA countries, treatment facilities are limited and often inaccessible to much of the population (Sosso & Philippe, 2016). In settings of poverty, unemployment, and lack of medical insurance or social security, most young people experience mental disorders with very limited support. Further, whereas the WHO (through the Mental Health Gap Action Program) has recommended a range of psychosocial and pharmacological interventions for LMICs, many commonly used drugs are still not available in most WCA countries (Keynejad, Dua, Barbui, & Thornicroft, 2017).

While studies in Nigeria and Ghana have reported that mental health literacy is abysmally low among adolescents, worse are the societal and community stereotypes and prejudices resulting from misconceptions about mental illness. These misunderstandings of mental disorders have led to severe stigma in these settings (Gureje et al., 2005; Kleintjes et al., 2010). Detailed descriptions from a Togolese prayer camp, set up as a makeshift psychiatric ward, demonstrate how negative connotations and false assumptions about mental illness, as well as utter lack of any formal psychiatry services, cause individuals with schizophrenia to be locked in dark rooms and bound in chains for long unending days. Thought of as a consequence of evil spirit infestation, and most often due to an individual's own actions, mental disorder victims suffer from societal stigma, which significantly limits opportunities for proper health care and delays their seeking of treatment services (Ronzoni, Dogra, Omigbodun, Bella, & Atitola, 2010).

GAPS IN RESEARCH AND PROGRAMMING

Despite the WHO's Mental Health Gap Action Plan that sought to increase the profile of young people's mental health, virtually all WCA countries lack clearly defined policies and programs targeting young people. For instance, Nigeria lacks a child and adolescent mental health (CAMH) strategy, and CAMH issues have remained obscure to the country's policy-makers (Atilola et al., 2014). Low prioritization of young people's mental health by policy-makers is explained in part by the fact that mental illness has historically not been well understood (i.e., it is considered a taboo and is thought to be self-inflicted and incurable). Mental illness victims experience marked stigmatization. For a long time, traditional healers and religious actors were the source of care for mentally ill patients. These attitudes and practices are still deeply rooted in WCA populations (Aina, 2004), including among policy-makers. Consequently, this has led to negative impacts on service availability, coordination and delivery, resource allocation, and accountability (Kieling et al., 2011).

Data on the prevalence and burden of mental disorders in young people of WCA are based on small, nonrepresentative surveys. There is a need to improve surveillance and generate data (including estimates of prevalence rates and documentation of risk factors, protective factors, assessed needs, and tested interventions), to help guide areas of preventive interventions and programmatic focus to enhance mental health and well-being in the WCA countries (Jacob et al., 2007).

Efforts to improve awareness and knowledge, while reducing stigma associated with mental disorders, are critically needed, since they affect treatment-seeking behavior, symptom detection, and disclosure for early treatment. There is increasing interest in population and community-wide strategies such as social-marketing campaigns using mass media channels, social media, and social contact events to destigmatize mental disorders and reduce substance dependence (Andreason, 2004; Sampogna et al., 2017; Scheier & Grenard, 2010). These approaches could potentially reduce stigma and elicit positive attitudes among young people with regard to mental health problems. Also, there is a need for research to gain a deeper understanding of the variations in gender with regard to the burden and drivers of poor mental health, as well as the applicable gendered interventions. More evaluation research is needed to decipher important dimensions of public mental health interventions, such as their reach, effectiveness, adoption, implementation, and maintenance over time. While several interventions have been reported to have positive effects in the WCA subregion, very little is known about the extent to which these findings are appropriate to other settings.

Implications for Research and Programming on Mental Health of Young People

With limited existing data and in the absence of needs assessments to identify gaps and areas of action to enhance access, quality, and availability of mental health care for young people in the subregion, mental health care remains a relatively low priority. Improving the available unmet needs data would create a basis for investment in young people's mental health and monitoring and evaluation of these investments. Awareness of mental health is dismally low across the population (including among health care workers and policy-makers), further reflecting the low attention accorded to mental health. Employing wide population-based education and awareness strategies with a broader reach, such as social-marketing approaches employed via social media channels, mass media, and mobile phones, could reach large numbers of people simultaneously and could potentially reduce stigma associated with mental health and improve awareness.

Research is also needed on how to scale up existing mental health services targeting young people, especially the vulnerable individuals in remote settings, with limited access to services. Potential approaches to scale up these services include availing services for young people within the current mental health facilities (e.g., by increasing bed capacities reserved for children/adolescents within inpatient care units); supporting capacity building of the professional staff (e.g., nurses and doctors) and informal staff (e.g., lay workers, community health volunteers, and non-specialists); and incorporating ideas such as task-shifting and task-sharing to address large numbers of patients (whose mental health problems are not severe). With respect to task-shifting, research is needed on the possible use of non-specialist health care providers to screen and refer young people to physicians. Further research is also needed on the development of tools for screening and diagnosis, as well as protocols for treatment, low-cost treatments and therapies, and the integration of mental health care packages within primary health care (PHC) services, to take advantage of already existing service delivery platforms and leverage their resources (such as staff, data collection systems, and referral pathways).

CONCLUSION

In this study, we sought to understand the burden of mental and substance use disorders, their drivers, and their impacts among young people in WCA. Our review of the literature showed that the prevalence of mental disorders among young people ranged between 12% and 30% in the WCA subregion, with conduct, anxiety, and depressive disorders being the most common disorders. In line with previous studies (Bradley, 2001), we found gendered differences in the epidemiology of poor mental health, with adolescent girls being more vulnerable to depression than boys. A significant number of young people in primary and secondary schools were reported to use substances such as marijuana and cocaine, with a majority involved in alcohol abuse. There was a significant variation in the prevalence of mental disorders among young people across the WCA subregion. These differences may be explained by the heterogeneity in the methodologies used to diagnose mental health problems and varying degrees of exposures to risk factors and protective factors.

Multiple factors drive poor mental health and substance use disorders in young people in WCA. More worrying is the co-occurrence of risk factors for mental health problems, including social factors (such as poor family relations) and structural factors (e.g., poverty, high unemployment, urbanization, rapid social and economic change, conflict, and natural disasters) in these settings (Allen et al., 2014). The co-occurrence of these risk factors increases exposure to the stressors that precipitate the onset and continuity of mental health problems. Untreated mental disorders may result in severe negative consequences, the most serious of which is suicide. For instance, depression has been found to be the strongest single risk factor for attempted or completed suicides (Beautrais, Joyce, & Mulder, 1996). Apart from worsening the livelihoods of young people, poor mental health may predispose young people to infectious diseases (such as HIV) or worsen outcomes for diseases (such as TB) because of increased propensity to engage in risky sexual behavior and poor adherence to treatment among those with mental health and substance disorders (Nwagu, 2016; Oppong et al., 2014).

Despite the burden and impact of mental disorders among young people in WCA, programming for these key populations remains insufficient, and lack of policy, limited resources, stigma, discrimination, and socioeconomic barriers may prevent many people from accessing mental health care. Several psychosocial and pharmacological interventions (along the continuum of primary, secondary, and tertiary prevention) for mental and substance use disorders have been described in many LMICs, including WCA (Barry et al., 2013). However, data on the effectiveness of these interventions is weak or lacking, yet such evidence is critical to inform scale-up of interventions. Systematic reviews of school-based interventions from HICs (and few from WCA) show they have great potential to facilitate early detection and management of mental disorders in young people, with positive effects not only on mental health, but also on academic and work performance and general health behaviors (Fazel et al., 2014). Increasing school enrollment rates could place schools as an optimum entry point for most early mental health interventions for young people (UNICEF, 2014). Early identification and treatment of mental and substance disorders are essential. Studies in the United States and Brazil have shown that early initiation of treatment leads to decreased morbidity and mortality, including the reduction in suicidal thoughts and behaviors (March et al., 2009). Schooling also improves self-esteem, problem-solving and social skills, positive thinking, good physical health, educational opportunities, positive parenting, and availability of social support systems, which can positively modify individual response to psychosocial stress (Opler, Sodhi, Zaveri, & Madhusoodanan, 2010).

Further research is required to improve evidence on the burden and impact of mental health problems among young people in the WCA subregion. In particular, research is needed to identify young people who may be especially vulnerable to poor mental health including those in conflict and post-conflict settings, those living with chronic illness, sexual minorities, and homeless youth. Studies investigating the utilization of mental health services by young people and effective and scalable mental health interventions are also needed. With respect to the latter, our findings underscore the need for programmatic investment toward training of primary health care workers on mental health care and community-based mental health care services for young people.

In conclusion, the lack of data on the burden, drivers, and impact of mental disorders, as well as the utilization of mental services by young people in the WCA subregion, acutely hampers any action to improve mental health care for young people. A fair amount of evidence exists on mental health interventions amenable for scale-up for young people in the subregion; however, further research is required to elucidate other dimensions of these interventions such as cost effectiveness. There is a need for programmatic focus by WCA governments, donors, and other stakeholders on training of mental health care providers and the provision of quality of mental health services to young people. An integrated approach to the delivery of mental health services that includes a focus on schools, communities, households, and other settings where youth participate actively would be key to reaching the most vulnerable young people with much needed care and services.

REFERENCES

Abdulmalik, J., Fadahunsi, W., Kola, L., Nwefoh, E., Minas, H., Eaton, J., et al. (2014). The Mental Health Leadership and Advocacy Program (mhLAP): A pioneering response to the neglect of mental health in Anglophone West Africa. *International Journal of Mental Health Systems, 8*(1), 5. https://doi.org/10.1186/1752-4458-8-5

Abiodun, O. A. (1992). Emotional illness in a paediatric population in Nigeria. *East African Medical Journal, 69*(10), 557–559.

Addo, B., Mainoo, G. O., Dapaah, J. M., & Babayara, M. N. K. (2016). Prevalence of substance use in a sample of Ghanaian adolescents experiencing parental divorce. *Journal of Child & Adolescent Substance Abuse, 25*(5), 428–437. https://doi.org/10.1080/1067828X.2015.1056867

Adewuya, A. O. (2005). Validation of the alcohol use disorders identification test (audit) as a screening tool for alcohol-related problems among Nigerian university students. *Alcohol and Alcoholism, 40*(6), 575–577.

Adewuya, A. O., Afolabi, M. O., Ola, B. A., Ogundele, O. A., Ajibare, A. O., & Oladipo, B. F. (2007). Psychiatric disorders among the HIV-positive population in Nigeria: A control study. *Journal of Psychosomatic Research, 63*(2), 203–206.

Adu-Gyamfi, S., & Brenya, E. (2015). The marijuana factor in a university in Ghana: A survey. *Humanities & Social Sciences, 8*(11), 2162–2182. https://doi.org/10.17516/1997-1370-2015-8-11-2162-2182

Aina, O. F. (2004). Mental illness and cultural issues in West African films: Implications for orthodox psychiatric practice. *Medical Humanities, 30*(1), 23–26. https://doi.org/10.1136/jmh.2003.000152

Akpan, M. U., Ojinnaka, N. C., & Ekanem, E. (2010). Behavioural problems among schoolchildren in Nigeria. *South African Journal of Psychiatry, 16*(2), 50–55.

Alemu, W., Funk, M., Gakurah, T., Bash-Taqi, D., Bruni, A., Sinclair, J., et al. (2012). *WHO profile on mental health in development (WHO proMIND): Sierra Leone.* Retrieved March 8, 2018, from http://www.who.int/mental_health/policy/country/sierra_leone_country_summary_2012.pdf

Allen, J., Balfour, R., Bell, R., & Marmot, M. (2014). Social determinants of mental health. *International Review of Psychiatry, 26*(4), 392–407. https://doi.org/10.3109/09540261.2014.928270

American Psychiatric Association (APA). (2000). *Diagnostic and statistical manual of mental disorders* (4th ed.). Washington, DC: American Psychiatric Association.

Andreason, A. R. (2004). A social marketing approach to changing mental health practices directed at youth and adolescents. *Health Marketing Quarterly, 21*(4), 51–75. https://doi.org/10.1300/J026v21n04_04

Asare, M., & Danquah, S. (2016). Observation report from clinical practice in Ghana: Children and adolescent depression. *Journal of Child and Adolescent Behavior, 4*(2), 286. https://doi.org/10.4172/2375-4494.1000286

Atilola, O., Ayinde, O., Emedoh, C. T., & Oladimeji, O. (2014). State of the Nigerian child – Neglect of child and adolescent mental health: A review. *Paediatrics and International Child Health, 35*(2), 135–143. https://doi.org/10.1179/2046905514Y.0000000137

Barry, M. M., Clarke, A. M., Jenkins, R., & Patel, V. (2013). A systematic review of the effectiveness of mental health promotion interventions for young people in low and middle income countries. *BMC Public Health, 13*, 835. https://doi.org/10.1186/1471-2458-13-835

Beautrais, A. L., Joyce, P. R., & Mulder, R. T. (1996). Risk factors for serious suicide attempts among youths aged 13 through 24 years. *Journal of the American Academy of Child and Adolescent Psychiatry, 35*(9), 1174–1182. https://doi.org/10.1097/00004583-199609000-00015

Belfer, M. L. (2008). Child and adolescent mental disorders: The magnitude of the problem across the globe. *Journal of Child Psychology and Psychiatry and Allied Disciplines, 49*(3), 226–236. https://doi.org/10.1111/j.1469-7610.2007.01855.x

Bella-Awusah, T., Ani, C., Ajuwon, A., & Omigbodun, O. (2016). Effectiveness of brief school-based, group cognitive behavioural therapy for depressed adolescents in south west Nigeria. *Child and Adolescent Mental Health, 21*(1), 44–50. https://doi.org/10.1111/camh.12104

Betancourt, T., Borisova, I. I., Williams, T. P., Brennan, R. T., Whitfield, T. H., de la Soudiere, M., et al. (2010). Sierra Leone's former child soldiers: A follow-up study of psychosocial adjustment and community reintegration. *Child Development, 81*(4), 1077–1095. https://doi.org/10.1111/j.1467-8624.2010.01455.x

Betancourt, T., McBain, R., Newnham, E., & Brennan, R. (2013). Context matters: Community characteristics and mental health among war-affected youth in Sierra Leone. *Journal of Child Psychology and Psychiatry and Allied Disciplines, 55*(3), 217–226. https://doi.org/10.1111/jcpp.12131

Betancourt, T., McBain, R., Newnham, E. A., Akinsulure-Smith, A. M., Brennan, R. T., Weisz, J. R., et al. (2014). A behavioral intervention for war-affected youth in Sierra Leone: A randomized controlled trial. *Journal of the American Academy of Child and Adolescent Psychiatry, 53*(12), 1288–1297. https://doi.org/10.1016/j.jaac.2014.09.011

Betancourt, T., Newnham, E. A., McBain, R., & Brennan, R. T. (2018). Post-traumatic stress symptoms among former child soldiers in Sierra Leone: Follow-up study. *British Journal of Psychiatry, 203*(3), 196–202. https://doi.org/10.1192/bjp.bp.112.113514

Bloom, D. E., Cafiero, E. T., Jané-Llopis, E., Abrahams-Gessel, S., Bloom, L. R., Fathima, S., et al. (2011). *The global economic burden of non-communicable diseases.* Retrieved March 11, 2018, from http://www.weforum.org/docs/WEF_Harvard_HE_GlobalEconomicBurdenNonCommunicableDiseases_2011.pdf

Boulay, M., Tweedie, I., & Fiagbey, E. (2008). The effectiveness of a national communication campaign using religious leaders to reduce HIV-related stigma in Ghana. *African Journal of AIDS Research, 7*(1), 133–141. https://doi.org/10.2989/AJAR.2008.7.1.13.441

Bradley, S. J. (2001). Anxiety and mood disorders in children and adolescents: A practice update. *Paediatrics & Child Health, 6*(7), 459–463.

Burns, A., Daileader, C., & Finger, W. (2004). *Reaching out-of-school youth with reproductive health and HIV/AIDS information and services* (YouthNet Issues Paper 4). Arlington, VA: Family Health International, YouthNet Program.

Burns, J. K. (2012). The social determinants of schizophrenia: An African journey in social epidemiology. *Public Health Reviews, 34*(2), 1–18. https://doi.org/10.1007/bf03391676

Charlson, F., Baxter, A. J., Dua, T., Degenhardt, L., Whiteford, H. A., & Vos, T. (2014). Excess mortality from mental, neurological, and substance use disorders in the global burden of disease study 2010. *Epidemiology and Psychiatric Sciences, 24*(2), 121–140. https://doi.org/10.1017/S2045796014000687

Charlson, F., Diminic, S., Lund, C., Degenhardt, L., & Whiteford, H. A. (2014). Mental and substance use disorders in sub-Saharan Africa: Predictions of epidemiological changes and mental health workforce requirements for the next 40 years. *PLoS One, 9*(10), e110208. https://doi.org/10.1371/journal.pone.0110208

Chesney, E., Goodwin, G. M., & Fazel, S. (2014). Risks of all-cause and suicide mortality in mental disorders: A meta-review. *World Psychiatry, 13*(2), 153–160. https://doi.org/10.1002/wps.20128

Coalition to Stop the Use of Child Soldiers. (2008). *Child soldiers: Global report 2008.* London: Author.

Cortina, M. A., Sodha, A., Fazel, M., & Ramchandani, P. G. (2012). Prevalence of child mental health problems in sub-Saharan Africa: A systematic review. *Archives of Pediatrics and Adolescent Medicine, 166*(3), 276–281. https://doi.org/10.1001/archpediatrics.2011.592

Daar, A. S., Jacobs, M., Wall, S., Groenewald, J., Eaton, J., Patel, V., et al. (2014). Declaration on mental health in Africa: moving to implementation. *Global Health Action, 7*(1), 24589. https://doi.org/10.3402/gha.v7.24589

Das, J. K., Salam, R. A., Lassi, Z. S., Khan, M. N., Mahmood, W., Patel, V., et al. (2016). Interventions for adolescent mental health: An overview of systematic reviews. *Journal of Adolescent Health, 59*(4, Suppl), S49–S60. https://doi.org/10.1016/j.jadohealth.2016.06.020

Doku, P. (2016). Depression, delinquency and peer problems among children and adolescents affected by HIV/AIDS in Ghana: The mediating role of child labour. *Journal of Depression & Anxiety, 05*(2), 221. https://doi.org/10.4172/2167-1044.1000221

Doran, N., Luczak, S. E., Bekman, N., Koutsenok, I., & Brown, S. A. (2012). Adolescent substance use and aggression: A review. *Criminal Justice and Behavior, 39*(6), 748–769. https://doi.org/10.1177/0093854812437022

Embleton, L., Mwangi, A., Vreeman, R., Ayuku, D., & Braitstein, P. (2013). The epidemiology of substance use among street children in resource-constrained settings: A systematic review and meta-analysis. *Addiction, 108*(10), 1722–1733. https://doi.org/10.1111/add.12252

Erskine, H. E., Baxter, A. J., Patton, G., Moffitt, T. E., Patel, V., Whiteford, H. A., et al. (2017). The global coverage of prevalence data for mental disorders in children and adolescents. *Epidemiology and Psychiatric Sciences, 26*(4), 395–402. https://doi.org/10.1017/s2045796015001158

Esan, O. B., Kola, L., & Gureje, O. (2012). Mental disorders and earnings: Results from the Nigerian National Survey of Mental Health and Well-Being (NSMHW). *The Journal of Mental Health Policy and Economics, 15*(2), 77–82.

Fazel, M., Patel, V., Thomas, S., & Tol, W. (2014). Mental health interventions in schools in low-income and middle-income countries. *The Lancet Psychiatry, 1*(5), 388–398. https://doi.org/10.1016/S2215-0366(14)70357-8

Ferrari, A. J., Charlson, F. J., Norman, R. E., Patten, S. B., Freedman, G., Murray, C. J. L., et al. (2013). Burden of depressive disorders by country, sex, age, and year: Findings from the global burden of disease study 2010. *PLoS Medicine, 10*(11), e1001547. https://doi.org/10.1371/journal.pmed.1001547

Ferreira-Borges, C., Esser, M. B., Dias, S., Babor, T., & Parry, C. D. H. (2015). Alcohol control policies in 46 African countries: Opportunities for improvement. *Alcohol and Alcoholism, 50*(4), 470–476. https://doi.org/10.1093/alcalc/agv036

Gupta, L., & Zimmer, C. (2018). Psychosocial intervention for war-affected children in Sierra Leone. *British Journal of Psychiatry, 192*(3), 212–216. https://doi.org/10.1192/bjp.bp.107.038182

Gureje, O., Chisholm, D., Kola, L., Lasebikan, V., & Saxena, S. (2007). Cost-effectiveness of an essential mental health intervention package in Nigeria. *World Psychiatry, 6*(1), 42–48.

Gureje, O., Lasebikan, V. O., Ephraim-Oluwanuga, O., Olley, B. O., & Kola, L. (2005). Community study of knowledge of and attitude to mental illness in Nigeria. *British Journal of Psychiatry, 186*, 436–441. https://doi.org/10.1192/bjp.186.5.436

Gureje, O., Lasebikan, V. O., Kola, L., & Makanjuola, V. A. (2018). Lifetime and 12-month prevalence of mental disorders in the Nigerian survey of mental health and well-being. *British Journal of Psychiatry, 188*(5), 465–471. https://doi.org/10.1192/bjp.188.5.465

Hushie, M. (2016). Public-non-governmental organisation partnerships for health: An exploratory study with case studies from recent Ghanaian experience. *BMC Public Health, 16*(1), 963. https://doi.org/10.1186/s12889-016-3636-2

Ibeziako, P., Omigbodun, O., & Bella-Awusah, T. (2008). Assessment of need for a school-based mental health programme in Nigeria: Perspectives of school administrators. *International Review of Psychiatry, 20*(3), 271–280. https://doi.org/10.1080/09540260802000354

Igwe, W., Ngozi, O., Ejiofor, S. O., Emechebe, G. O., & Ibe, B. C. (2009). Socio-demographic correlates of psychoactive substance abuse among secondary school students in Enugu, Nigeria. *European Journal of Social Sciences, 12*(2), 277–283.

Institute for Health Metrics and Evaluation. (2017). *GBD compare | Viz hub.* Retrieved March 12, 2018, from https://vizhub.healthdata.org/gbd-compare/

Ismayilova, L., Gaveras, E., Blum, A., Tô-Camier, A., & Nanema, R. (2016). Maltreatment and mental health outcomes among ultra-poor children in Burkina Faso: A latent class analysis. *PLoS One, 11*(10), e0164790.

Izugbara, C., Wekesah, F., Kabiru, C., Amo-Adjei, J., Tsala Dimbuene, Z., & Emina, J. (2017). *Young people in West and Central Africa: Health, demographic, education and socioeconomic indicators.* Nairobi: African Population and Health Research Center.

Jack-Ide, I. O., & Uys, L. (2013). Barriers to mental health services utilization in the Niger Delta region of Nigeria: Service users' perspectives. *The Pan African Medical Journal, 14*, 159. https://doi.org/10.11604/pamj.2013.14.159.1970

Jacob, K. S., Sharan, P., Mirza, I., Garrido-Cumbrera, M., Seedat, S., Mari, J. J., et al. (2007). Mental health systems in countries: Where are we now? *Lancet, 370*(9592), 1061–1077. https://doi.org/10.1016/s0140-6736(07)61241-0

Joint United Nations Programme on HIV/AIDS (UNAIDS), & United Nations International Children's Emergency Fund (UNICEF). (2016). *Step up the pace: Towards an AIDS-free generation in West and Central Africa.* Dakar: UNICEF.

Kabiru, C. W., Beguy, D., Crichton, J., & Ezeh, A. C. (2010). Self-reported drunkenness among adolescents in four sub-Saharan African countries: Associations with adverse childhood experiences. *Child and Adolescent Psychiatry and Mental Health, 4*(1), 17. https://doi.org/10.1186/1753-2000-4-17

Kashala, E., Elgen, I., Sommerfelt, K., & Tylleskar, T. (2005). Teacher ratings of mental health among school children in Kinshasa, Democratic Republic of Congo. *European Child and Adolescent Psychiatry, 14*(4), 208–215. https://doi.org/10.1007/s00787-005-0446-y

Kayembe, P. K., Mapatano, M. A., Fatuma, A. B., Nyandwe, J. K., Mayala, G. M., Kokolomami, J. I., et al. (2008). Knowledge of HIV, sexual behavior and correlates of risky sex among street children in Kinshasa, Democratic Republic of Congo. *East African Journal of Public Health, 5*(3), 186–192.

Keynejad, R. C., Dua, T., Barbui, C., & Thornicroft, G. (2017). WHO Mental Health Gap Action Programme (mhGAP) intervention guide: A systematic review of evidence from low and middle-income countries. *Evidence Based Mental Health, 21*(1), 30–34.

Kieling, C., Baker-Henningham, H., Belfer, M., Conti, G., Ertem, I., Omigbodun, O., et al. (2011). Child and adolescent mental health worldwide: Evidence for action. *Lancet, 378*(9801), 1515–1525. https://doi.org/10.1016/s0140-6736(11)60827-1

Kleintjes, S., Lund, C., & Flisher, A. J. (2010). A situational analysis of child and adolescent mental health services in Ghana, Uganda, South Africa and Zambia. *African Journal of Psychiatry, 13*(2), 132–139.

Klitzing, K., Döhnert, M., Kroll, M., & Grube, M. (2015). Mental disorders in early childhood. *Deutsches Ärzteblatt International, 112*(21–22), 375–386. https://doi.org/10.3238/arztebl.2015.0375

Kohn, R., Saxena, S., Levav, I., & Saraceno, B. (2004). The treatment gap in mental health care. *Bulletin of the World Health Organization, 82*(11), 858–866. https://doi.org/10.1590/S0042-96862004001100011

Kretzschmar, I., Nyan, O., Mendy, A., & Janneh, B. (2012). Mental health in the Republic of The Gambia. *International Psychiatry, 9*(2), 38–40.

Lokuge, K., Shah, T., Pintaldi, G., Thurber, K., Martínez-Viciana, C., Cristobal, M., et al. (2013). Mental health services for children exposed to armed conflict: Médecins Sans Frontières' experience in the Democratic Republic of Congo, Iraq and the occupied Palestinian territory. *Paediatrics and International Child Health, 33*(4), 259–272. https://doi.org/10.1179/2046905513Y.0000000098

Lund, C., Breen, A., Flisher, A. J., Kakuma, R., Corrigall, J., Joska, J. A., et al. (2010). Poverty and common mental disorders in low and middle income countries: A systematic review. *Social Science & Medicine, 71*(3), 517–528. https://doi.org/10.1016/j.socscimed.2010.04.027

Lund, C., De Silva, M., Plagerson, S., Cooper, S., Chisholm, D., Das, J., et al. (2011). Poverty and mental disorders: Breaking the cycle in low-income and middle-income countries. *The Lancet, 378*(9801), 1502–1514. https://doi.org/10.1016/S0140-6736(11)60754-X

March, J., Silva, S., Curry, J., Wells, K., Fairbank, J., Burns, B., et al. (2009). The Treatment for adolescents with depression study (TADS): Outcomes over 1 year of naturalistic follow-up. *American Journal of Psychiatry, 166*(10), 1141–1149. https://doi.org/10.1176/appi.ajp.2009.08111620

Mars, B., Burrows, S., Hjelmeland, H., & Gunnell, D. (2014). Suicidal behaviour across the African continent: A review of the literature. *BMC Public Health, 14*(1), 606. https://doi.org/10.1186/1471-2458-14-606

McDaid, D., Knapp, M., & Raja, S. (2008). Barriers in the mind: Promoting an economic case for mental health in low- and middlc-income countries. *World Psychiatry, 7*(2), 79–86.

McKinnon, B., Gariepy, G., Sentenac, M., & Elgar, F. J. (2016). Adolescent suicidal behaviours in 32 low- and middle-income countries. *Bulletin of the World Health Organization, 94*(5), 340–350f. https://doi.org/10.2471/blt.15.163295

Ministry of Health and Social Welfare. (2010). *Liberia national mental health policy.* Retrieved March 15, 2018, from http://apps.who.int/medicinedocs/documents/s18362en/s18362en.pdf

Mokdad, A. H., Forouzanfar, M. H., Daoud, F., Mokdad, A. A., El Bcheraoui, C., Moradi-Lakeh, M., et al. (2016). Global burden of diseases, injuries, and risk factors for young people's health during 1990–2013: A systematic analysis for the global burden of disease study 2013. *The Lancet, 387*(10036), 2383–2401. https://doi.org/10.1016/S0140-6736(16)00648-6

Ngasa, S. N., Sama, C. B., Dzekem, B. S., Nforchu, K. N., Tindong, M., Aroke, D., et al. (2017). Prevalence and factors associated with depression among medical students in Cameroon: A cross-sectional study. *BMC Psychiatry, 17*(1), 216. https://doi.org/10.1186/s12888-017-1382-3

Ngom, M. (2017). *UNFPA Regional Office for West and Central Africa - Annual Report 2016: Working together to put young people and women first.* Retrieved March 17, 2018, from https://reliefweb.int/report/world/unfpa-regional-office-west-and-central-africa-annual-report-2016-working-together-put

Nwagu, E. N. (2016). Alcohol and drug usage; and adolescents' sexual behaviour in Nigeria. *Health Promotion International, 31*(2), 405–413. https://doi.org/10.1093/heapro/dav001

Oduguwa, A. O., Adedokun, B., & Omigbodun, O. O. (2017). Effect of a mental health training programme on Nigerian school pupils' perceptions of mental illness. *Child and Adolescent Psychiatry and Mental Health, 11*(1), 19. https://doi.org/10.1186/s13034-017-0157-4

Okitapoy On'okoko, M., Jenkins, R., Mampunza Ma Miezi, S., Okitundu, D., Andjafono, L. E., & Muteba Mushidi, I. (2010). Mental health in the Democratic Republic of Congo: A post-crisis country challenge. *International Psychiatry, 7*(2), 41–42. https://doi.org/10.1192/S1749367600005737

Omigbodun, O. (2004). Psychosocial issues in a child and adolescent psychiatric clinic population in Nigeria. *Social Psychiatry and Psychiatric Epidemiology, 39*(8), 667–672. https://doi.org/10.1007/s00127-004-0793-x

Opler, M., Sodhi, D., Zaveri, D., & Madhusoodanan, S. (2010). Primary psychiatric prevention in children and adolescents. *Annals of Clinical Psychiatry, 22*(4), 220–234.

Oppong, K., Meyer-Weitz, A., & Petersen, I. (2014). Substance use and risky sexual behaviours among street connected children and youth in Accra, Ghana. *Substance Abuse Treatment, Prevention, and Policy, 9*, 45. https://doi.org/10.1186/1747-597X-9-45

Oshodi, Y. O., Abdulmalik, J., Ola, B., James, B. O., Bonetto, C., Cristofalo, D., et al. (2014). Pattern of experienced and anticipated discrimination among people with depression in Nigeria: A cross-sectional study. *Social Psychiatry and Psychiatric Epidemiology, 49*(2), 259–266. https://doi.org/10.1007/s00127-013-0737-4

Pacione, L., Measham, T., & Rousseau, C. (2013). Refugee children: Mental health and effective interventions. *Current Psychiatry Reports, 15*(2), 341. https://doi.org/10.1007/s11920-012-0341-4

Patel, V. (2011). Traditional healers for mental health care in Africa. *Global Health Action, 4*, 7956. https://doi.org/10.3402/gha.v4i0.7956

Peltzer, K., & Pengpid, S. (2018). Cannabis and amphetamine use and associated factors among school-going adolescents in nine African countries. *Journal of Child & Adolescent Substance Abuse, 27*(2), 112–118. https://doi.org/10.1080/1067828X.2017.1420512

Prince, M., Patel, V., Saxena, S., Maj, M., Maselko, J., Phillips, M. R., et al. (2007). No health without mental health. *Lancet, 370*(9590), 859–877. https://doi.org/10.1016/s0140-6736(07)61238-0

Read, U. M., Adiibokah, E., & Nyame, S. (2009). Local suffering and the global discourse of mental health and human rights: An ethnographic study of responses to mental illness in rural Ghana. *Globalization and Health, 5*, 13. https://doi.org/10.1186/1744-8603-5-13

Remschmidt, H., & Belfer, M. (2005). Mental health care for children and adolescents worldwide: A review. *World Psychiatry, 4*(3), 147–153.

Roberts, M., Mogan, C., & Asare, J. B. (2014). An overview of Ghana's mental health system: Results from an assessment using the World Health Organization's Assessment Instrument for Mental Health Systems (WHO-AIMS). *International Journal of Mental Health Systems, 8*, 16. https://doi.org/10.1186/1752-4458-8-16

Ronzoni, P., Dogra, N., Omigbodun, O., Bella, T., & Atitola, O. (2010). Stigmatization of mental illness among Nigerian schoolchildren. *International Journal of Social Psychiatry, 56*(5), 507–514. https://doi.org/10.1177/0020764009341230

Sampogna, G., Bakolis, I., Evans-Lacko, S., Robinson, E., Thornicroft, G., & Henderson, C. (2017). The impact of social marketing campaigns on reducing mental health stigma: Results from the 2009–2014 Time to Change programme. *European Psychiatry, 40*, 116–122. https://doi.org/10.1016/j.eurpsy.2016.08.008

Saraceno, B., van Ommeren, M., Batniji, R., Cohen, A., Gureje, O., Mahoney, J., et al. (2007). Barriers to improvement of mental health services in low-income and middle-income countries. *Lancet, 370*(9593), 1164–1174. https://doi.org/10.1016/s0140-6736(07)61263-x

Sartorius, N. (2007). Stigma and mental health. *The Lancet, 370*(9590), 810–811. https://doi.org/10.1016/S0140-6736(07)61245-8

Scheier, L. M., & Grenard, J. L. (2010). Influence of a nationwide social marketing campaign on adolescent drug use. *Journal of Health Communication, 15*(3), 240–271. https://doi.org/10.1080/10810731003686580

Semrau, M., Evans-Lacko, S., Alem, A., Ayuso-Mateos, J. L., Chisholm, D., Gureje, O., et al. (2015). Strengthening mental health systems in low- and middle-income countries: The emerald programme. *BMC Medicine, 13*(1), 79. https://doi.org/10.1186/s12916-015-0309-4

Sharma, M., Fine, S. L., Brennan, R. T., & Betancourt, T. S. (2017). Coping and mental health outcomes among Sierra Leonean war-affected youth: Results from a longitudinal study. *Development and Psychopathology, 29*(1), 11–23. https://doi.org/10.1017/s0954579416001073

Sierra Leone Ministry of Health. (2009). *Ministry of health and sanitation (MOHS)*. Retrieved March 21, 2018, from http://health.gov.sl/

Sosso, F., & Philippe, K. (2016). The African burden of mental health. *Journal of Mental Disorders and Treatment, 2*(2), 122–126. https://doi.org/10.4172/2471-271X.1000122

Suleiman, T. G., Ohaeri, J. U., Lawal, R. A., Haruna, A. Y., & Orija, O. B. (1997). Financial cost of treating out-patients with schizophrenia in Nigeria. *British Journal of Psychiatry, 171*(4), 364–368.

Tarter, R. E. (2002). Etiology of adolescent substance abuse: A developmental perspective. *American Journal on Addictions, 11*(3), 171–191. https://doi.org/10.1080/10550490290087965

Thela, L., Tomita, A., Maharaj, V., Mhlongo, M., & Burns, J. K. (2017). Counting the cost of Afrophobia: Post-migration adaptation and mental health challenges of African refugees in South Africa. *Transcultural Psychiatry, 54*(5–6), 715–732. https://doi.org/10.1177/1363461517745472

Tims, F. M., Dennis, M. L., Hamilton, N., Buchan, J. B., Diamond, G., Funk, R., et al. (2002). Characteristics and problems of 600 adolescent cannabis abusers in outpatient treatment. *Addiction, 97*(S1), 46–57.

Tunde-Ayinmode, M. (2010). Audit of child and adolescent psychiatry in a teaching hospital in Nigeria: Prevalence, pattern and implication for improved services. *South African Journal of Psychiatry, 16*(1), 20–26. https://doi.org/10.4102/sajpsychiatry.v16i1.209

Tunde-Ayinmode, M., Adegunloye, O., Ayinmode, B., & Abiodun, O. (2012). Psychiatric disorders in children attending a Nigerian primary care unit: Functional impairment and risk factors. *Child and Adolescent Psychiatry and Mental Health, 6*(1), 28. https://doi.org/10.1186/1753-2000-6-28

United Nations International Children's Emergency Fund (UNICEF). (2014). *Achieving universal primary education and eliminating gender disparity in education; West and Central Africa.* Retrieved May 11, 2018, from https://www.unicef.org/wcaro/overview_1898.html

United Nations International Children's Emergency Fund (UNICEF). (2017a). *A deadly journey for children: The central Mediterranean migration route.* Retrieved April 2, 2018, from https://www.unicef.org/publications/files/EN_UNICEF_Central_Mediterranean_Migration.pdf

United Nations International Children's Emergency Fund (UNICEF). (2017b). *Over 7 million children are on the move in West and Central Africa each year* [Press release]. Retrieved April 19, 2018, from https://www.unicef.org/media/media_96585.html

United Nations International Children's Emergency Fund (UNICEF), & Overseas Development Institute (ODI). (2009). *Strengthening social protection for children: West and Central Africa.* Retrieved April 23, 2018, from https://www.odi.org/publications/3478-strengthening-social-protection-children-west-and-central-africa

Verboom, C. E., Sijtsema, J. J., Verhulst, F. C., Penninx, B. W., & Ormel, J. (2014). Longitudinal associations between depressive problems, academic performance, and social functioning in adolescent boys and girls. *Developmental Psychology, 50*(1), 247–257. https://doi.org/10.1037/a0032547

Wang, P. S., Aguilar-Gaxiola, S., Alonso, J., Angermeyer, M. C., Borges, G., Bromet, E. J., et al. (2007). Use of mental health services for anxiety, mood, and substance disorders in 17 countries in the WHO world mental health surveys. *Lancet, 370*(9590), 841–850. https://doi.org/10.1016/s0140-6736(07)61414-7

Warner, L. A., & White, H. R. (2003). Longitudinal effects of age at onset and first drinking situations on problem drinking. *Substance Use and Misuse, 38*(14), 1983–2016.

World Health Organization (WHO). (1992). *The ICD-10 classification of mental and behavioural disorders: Clinical descriptions and diagnostic guidelines.* Retrieved March 2, 2018, from http://www.who.int/iris/handle/10665/37958

World Health Organization (WHO). (2011). *Mental health atlas Democratic Republic of Congo.* Retrieved March 15, 2018, from https://www.who.int/mental_health/evidence/atlas/profiles/cod_mh_profile.pdf?ua=1

World Health Organization Assessment Instrument for Mental Health Systems (WHO-AIMS). (2006). *WHO-AIMS Report on mental health system in Nigeria.* Retrieved March 16, 2018, from https://www.who.int/mental_health/evidence/nigeria_who_aims_report.pdf?ua=1

World Health Organization Assessment Instrument for Mental Health Systems (WHO-AIMS). (2007). *WHO-AIMS report on mental health system in the Republic of Benin.* Retrieved March 16, 2018, from https://www.who.int/mental_health/WHO AIMS_benin_English.pdf

World Health Organization Assessment Instrument for Mental Health Systems (WHO-AIMS). (2011). *WHO-AIMS Report on mental health system in Ghana.* Retrieved March 18, 2018, from https://www.who.int/mental_health/who_aims_country_reports/ghana_who_aims_report.pdf

Yoder, H. N. C., Tol, W. A., Reis, R., & de Jong, J. T. V. M. (2016). Child mental health in Sierra Leone: A survey and exploratory qualitative study. *International Journal of Mental Health Systems, 10*(1), 48.

INDEX[1]

A

Access, 5, 7, 8, 11, 15, 17, 27–32, 35–36, 40, 44, 47, 55, 58, 60, 64, 68, 82, 91, 95, 96, 119, 135, 137, 144, 151, 175, 179, 188, 203, 206, 218, 228, 234, 237, 244, 251, 253

Accra, v, 33, 42, 43, 46, 157, 162, 163, 165, 178

Achievement, 10, 12, 14, 15, 89, 95, 98, 103–108, 113–116, 122, 123, 165, 167, 172–174, 176–178, 180, 182

Achievement-oriented identities, 175, 177, 178, 181

Admission requirements, 30

Adolescents, 8, 18, 97, 112, 234–237, 239, 240, 243, 244, 249, 250, 252

Adult, 3, 10, 29, 30, 42, 89, 94, 136, 139–153, 158, 165, 167, 175, 188, 189, 196, 198, 200, 202, 204–206, 216, 217, 222, 235

African immigration, 81, 83–88, 91, 96

African studies, 4, 89–97, 133n1

Age, 6, 15–17, 27, 28, 32, 36, 37, 39, 41, 55, 63, 64, 106, 122, 123, 134, 136, 138, 140, 140n3, 142, 144–146, 148, 151, 157, 158, 160, 164, 166, 178, 189–191, 193, 194, 197, 201, 202, 204, 206, 215, 219, 220, 234, 237, 240

Age at immigration, 36–37

Almajiri, 8, 16, 213–230

Apprentice, 139, 142, 143, 145, 160, 188, 199–201, 228

Apprenticeship, 140, 141, 143–147

Aspirations, 7, 9, 11–15, 67, 103–106, 108, 109, 112, 124

---

[1] Note: Page numbers followed by 'n' refer to notes.

267

M. L. McLean (ed.), *West African Youth Challenges and Opportunity Pathways*, Gender and Cultural Studies in Africa and the Diaspora, https://doi.org/10.1007/978-3-030-21092-2

www.ingramcontent.com/pod-product-compliance
Lightning Source LLC
Chambersburg PA
CBHW081431270326
41932CB00019B/3164